The
SAN ANTONIO
Report

The SAN ANTONIO Report

Your Will be Done
Mission in Christ's Way

Edited by Frederick R. Wilson

WCC PUBLICATIONS, GENEVA

Cover design: Rob Lucas

ISBN 2-8254-0974-X

© 1990 WCC Publications, World Council of Churches,
150 route de Ferney, 1211 Geneva 2, Switzerland

Printed in Switzerland

Contents

Introduction

Frederick R. Wilson

The conference on world mission and evangelism held by the World Council of Churches on the campus of Trinity University, San Antonio, Texas, in May 1989 took place under a constitutional mandate. The language of the constitution of the conference (dating from the integration of the International Missionary Council and the World Council of Churches in 1961) is direct:

> There shall be a conference on world mission and evangelism of the World Council of Churches. Its aim is to assist the Christian community in the proclamation of the gospel of Jesus Christ by word and deed, to the whole world to the end that all may believe in him and be saved. The main task of the conference is to provide opportunities for church, mission agencies, groups and national and regional councils concerned with Christian mission to meet together for reflection and consultation leading to common witness. The conference shall normally meet once between assemblies of the World Council of Churches.

The mandate is indeed clear. No constitutional provision, however, could determine the content, the form or the style of the gathering. These were decisions to be made with freedom and grace. Transparently. And with many persons involved. So many, in fact, and in such lively fashion that by the end of the conference some discerning critics described this as a "populist event". If a populist is rightly defined as "a believer in or advocate of the rights, wisdom or virtues of the common people" then those primarily responsible for planning the conference accept that description.

● Frederick Wilson was conference administrator.

The history

The historical precedents which influenced this conference and with which it may be compared reach back over a century. There is no proof that William Carey's call for decennial missionary conferences in 1810 actually gave impetus to the Edinburgh conference a century later, but a succession of somewhat similar conferences did take place. These occurred in New York and London in 1854, in Liverpool in 1860, in London in 1878 and 1888, all together leading up to a major ecumenical assembly in New York in 1900.

In an era of slow, laborious international travel these global events were exceptional, and participation was limited to the privileged senior leadership of the churches and organizations invited to attend. Much has changed in the evolution of the nine world mission conferences held since Edinburgh 1910, not only by way ·of greater inclusiveness in the participation but in the nature, function and preparation of these conferences.

The Edinburgh conference was overwhelmingly Anglo-American (and male) in its composition with no participation from the Orthodox or Roman Catholic churches which had not been invited. Very few of the participants came from Asia and Africa. The conference provided a forum to discuss global mission strategy and the prevailing theological consensus which undergirded it. It was not convened with an explicit institutional agenda even though the synergism of minds and spirits at Edinburgh was sufficient to lead to the subsequent birth of three major streams of ecumenical witness (International Missionary Council, 1921; Life and Work, 1925; Faith and Order, 1927).

In contrast, the Jerusalem conference in 1928 was constituted as a regular meeting of the International Missionary Council (IMC) with both administrative and deliberative aspects to its agenda. The preparation for the forum-dimension of the conference was formidable. Seven preparatory volumes were published including topics wider in scope than at Edinburgh: education, racial conflict, rural and industrial problems, secularism, etc. Participation was also more representative, with nearly 25 percent coming from Asia, Africa and Latin America.

The Tambaram conference in 1938 accelerated this evolution towards a more truly inclusive gathering. Slightly more than half of the participants came from Asia, Africa and Latin America. Among the preparatory publications widely circulated in advance two volumes became classics in their own right. The most vigorously debated was *The Christian Message in a Non-Christian World* by Hendrik Kraemer. The other preparatory volume of great significance was *The Economic and Social Environment of the Younger Churches* edited by J. Merle Davis.

Although the International Missionary Council had been conceived in 1921 as an instrument "to help coordinate the activities of the national missionary organizations of the different countries and to unite Christian forces of the world in seeking justice in international and inter-racial relations", it became a unique global forum for an ecumenical exploration of theologies of mission. The need for both functions was especially evident after the second world war at the Whitby (Canada) meeting in 1947. This gathering of the IMC was notable for critical and complex efforts to coordinate global mission activities in the course of intense and often emotional debate on basic church-mission relationships. It was necessary for representatives of the "sending" and the "receiving" churches to meet separately to discuss the acute problems arising from the rapidly changing circumstances of the post-war, post-colonial era. The findings of the two groups showed such remarkable agreement that the conference was able to adopt a common statement on partnership in obedience to the gospel imperative.

With the inauguration of the World Council of Churches in 1948 the role of the International Missionary Council began to change significantly. The IMC meeting in Willingen (Germany) in 1952 focused its attention on the missionary obligation of the church. The vigorous debate over the uniqueness of the church as an instrument in God's hands for mission had direct bearing on the discussion of the future role and function of the IMC in its relationship to the World Council of Churches.

Five years later debate regarding the continuing autonomy of the International Missionary Council was renewed at a momentous meeting of the IMC in Ghana. This gathering made the watershed decision to commit the IMC to integration with the World Council of Churches in order for it to function within this ecumenical community as the Commission on World Mission and Evangelism (CWME). This integration was achieved at the next assembly of the World Council of Churches which met in New Delhi in 1961.

The first meeting of the new CWME was in Mexico City in 1963. In this gathering it became clear that the deliberative role of the former conferences of the International Missionary Council would grow as a result of the steady diminution of the earlier need for an administrative role after integration within the World Council of Churches. Although often remembered for the phrase to which it gave wide currency, "mission in six continents", this meeting carried forward from Tambaram 1938 the discussions on the locus of mission. The Tambaram conference had placed the Christian mission firmly in a churchly context. Willingen had struggled to broaden the vision of God's options for instrumentalities for mission. The Mexico City meeting is appropriately remembered as the one which conceived the missionary task to be always in the context of what God is doing on the contemporary secular scene.

The Bangkok meeting in 1973 grew directly out of the tumultuous decade which separated it from Mexico City. Remembered for the term "moratorium" as a call for a temporary cessation of North Atlantic missionaries going into the third world, the conference strongly affirmed the right of every Christian and every church to formulate its own response to God's calling in a theology, a liturgy, a praxis, a form of community rooted in its own culture.

By the time plans were made for the conference on world mission and evangelism in Melbourne in 1980, the deliberative nature of these gatherings had become firmly established. Preparations no longer took the form of the publication in English of a small library of bound texts written by scholars years in advance essentially for study by professionals in the field. Rather, preparatory Bible studies and issue papers were produced in English, French, Spanish and German (with translations in several languages in Asia and Africa) in paperback editions intended for a broadly-based constituency. A poster contest and a variety of local and regional consultations were also held to enlist participation among persons who were keenly interested in the work of the conference even though they would not have an opportunity to travel to Australia.

The substance of the deliberations in Melbourne confirmed the validity of this perspective by illustrating in multiple ways the manner in which Jesus throughout his ministry consistently moved to the periphery of his society in search of the common people and those who were marginalized. Under the theme "Your Kingdom Come", the declarations from Melbourne were unambiguous: The kingdom of God is good news to the poor.

The theme
With such a history of widening participation it was not surprising that early in 1985 when CWME sent out a general letter inviting responses, over 150 persons and organizations offered proposals for a theme for the next conference on world mission and evangelism. From this remarkably diverse list of proposals four major categories were established: unity and mission; newness in Christ; power/powerlessness; and faithfulness/obedience.

In June 1985 a globally diverse group joined the CWME executive committee and staff at Bossey for an intensive discussion of the theme for the next conference. Early on, a strong consensus emerged: the purpose of this conference would not be to polish prose to define once again the meaning of mission and evangelism. The 1982 "Ecumenical Affirmation" had done this admirably. The perceived need was rather for active response to what faithfulness quite obviously required. All the while the group was very mindful of the theme of the Melbourne conference, "Your Kingdom Come".

Concern for continuity, together with this clear focus upon active obedience, resulted in the choice:

YOUR WILL BE DONE
MISSION IN CHRIST'S WAY

This was conceived as a single theme, not two. Each phrase defines and interprets the other. Neither was judged to be adequate by itself. To pray "Your will be done" is to be propelled into mission, for such is the nature of God. Equally so, mission in Christ's way is carried out not according to human choices but as God wills. It is the same Jesus who prayed in Gethsemane who had earlier said to his disciples: "Even as the Father has sent me, so I send you." Mission in Christ's way begins with the prayer that God's will be done in and through the one who prays.

Under this theme slowly emerged four sub-themes:
— turning to the living God;
— participating in suffering and struggle;
— the earth is the Lord's;
— towards renewed communities in mission.
But these sub-themes were not formulated until a series of other decisions had been made.

The form and style

Several decisions were to prove to be as significant to the outcome as the choice of the theme. These began to emerge in January 1986 when another globally diverse group of persons met for several days with the CWME executive committee and staff to give basic direction to the shaping of the conference. In its report to the WCC Executive Committee this consultation said in part:

> Jesus identified himself with the men and women of his day and place, many of whom were poor, hungry and dispossessed, crushed by the religious

and political powers. The kingdom of God made itself known to them through him, and empowered by the Holy Spirit their lives were dramatically transformed in the most surprising ways as they entrusted themselves to God.

In continuity with the prayer and acclamation "Your Kingdom Come" (Melbourne 1989) we are called to follow Jesus and to discern in our own day the working of God's will for the furtherance of the kingdom. Slowly and with much pain we are learning how surprising is the will of God, and how it challenges us in and from the most unexpected places, in unforeseen ways, often through the people whose voices and actions are ignored or silenced by the powers of this world. Mission in Christ's way must enable their voices to be heard.

But how? What style of meeting will enable these voices to be heard in the conference? It was agreed to make vigorous efforts along three lines:

1) by *recruitment* to assure that people who can authentically voice such concerns are present;
2) by as much *visitation* as possible before, during and after the conference to allow persons to make comparative assessments of their own circumstances;
3) by a *programme design* which would allow conference participants to have maximum opportunity to listen and to speak to one another.

1. *Recruitment:* The composition of the official membership of the conference is defined in the constitution. Not less than 50 percent of the delegates were to be appointed by CWME-affiliated councils and the rest by the WCC Central Committee from nominations presented by WCC member churches.

Working within the overall norms set by the World Council in its continuing efforts to assure inclusive and broadly representative gatherings, the CWME established specific quotas for the following categories of participants:

	Goal	Result
Women	50%	44%
Youth	15%	14%
Orthodox	20%	19%
Asia, Africa, Latin America, Caribbean, Middle East, Pacific and Eastern Europe	70%	65%

Neither the WCC norms nor the CWME application of them with specific quotas was universally supported by the councils and WCC member churches. Given the intensity of resistance by some, the level of cooperation achieved is notable.

Many councils and churches did resist the impulse to send their experienced church officials and instead recruited women as well as men whose current ministries require direct engagement with people in need. One result was that 80 percent of the 275 official delegates (as well as many of the resource persons) had never before attended a major ecumenical gathering. Most of the participants under thirty years of age were in this category. Not all the affiliated councils and member churches concerned were willing to include in their delegations the requested 15 percent of youth.

Nonetheless, approximately 80 persons thirty years old or younger, were able to gather four days before the conference for a youth preparatory meeting designed to orient and equip them for maximum participation in the full conference. The theme for this three-day event was "Risking Obedience". The delegates and stewards gathered to listen to one another. Quickly they discovered that the context in which God had placed them by birth and family choice (in the North or in the South) strongly influenced what issues most acutely challenged their capacity to be obedient to the gospel as well as the nature of the particular risks their obedience would entail. Through intense encounter and debate they prepared a report to the conference which was first presented in a plenary session before the sections began their most intensive work. The written report of the youth conference, distributed later, is included here.

Among the 374 participants at the conference who were not official delegates there were 27 Orthodox (making a total of 80), and 51 Roman Catholics including an official Vatican delegation of 21 led by Archbishop Flores of San Antonio. A group of ten special guests included Bishop Lesslie Newbigin, the first director of CWME, and seven persons constituting the first delegation from the China Christian Council to attend an ecumenical gathering in forty years. Among the many consultants were ten representing conservative evangelical mission agencies and seven persons from other living faith traditions.

Altogether 649 persons from 106 countries participated, observed in all their activities by 123 representatives of the press.

2. *Visitation:* The vision set forth in the January 1986 consultation was that the conference would not be an end in itself but would be a part of a larger process. The total plan was to include an exchange of visits of many types. Three varieties of international team visits did occur:

Section leadership teams comprising a total of 65 persons made 11 visits which were designed to permit intensive examination of a few exceptional situations where the opportunity for witness and service by local Christian communities was being seized with courage and creativity. Not only did these visits allow team members to see their own context of life and work in a broader perspective, but in the process of making the visit the section leaders began the process of working together.

Section leadership teams made the following visits: Section I: China; Section II: Fiji, New Caledonia, Palestine/West Bank; Section III: Brazil, German Democratic Republic, the Netherlands, Zimbabwe, Swaziland, India; Section IV: Ghana.

Ecumenical teams of participants visited 77 communities and congregations in 28 states as well as in Canada and Puerto Rico. Over 200 persons were involved as they travelled to and from San Antonio. An open invitation had been issued to all who registered, and all who had so indicated by late March were enabled to make a team visit. With few exceptions the hosting congregations had committed themselves not only to receive the team of ecumenical visitors but also to study the conference preparatory material and to send at least one delegate to Encuentro, the parallel educational event being prepared at San Antonio. Altogether the combined experiences provided these 77 hosting communities an exceptional exposure to mission within a genuinely global perspective.

Weekend visits were made during the conference (27-28 May). Approximately 400 of the participants were enabled to visit congregations throughout Texas. Over 150 communities and congregations received teams of two or three participants as weekend guests, sharing with them the life of their communities as well as the hospitality of their homes and parishes. Effort was made to assure that most of the teams included persons from confessions and traditions different from those of their hosts in order that the experience might yield further ecumenical learning. The overwhelming majority of reports from both visitors and hosts have been enthusiastically affirmative, but not all who participated welcomed this stretching of their ecumenical horizons.

3. *Programme design:* The January 1986 consultation which gave the basic shape to the conference design was persuaded that the will of God often confronts us through the people whose voices and actions are ignored or silenced by the powers of this world. To pray "Your will be done" requires that we listen to how others discern God's will, and that we receive their witness with respect and openness.

Such listening presupposes opportunity for each to speak within a context where one may be heard. An early, basic decision was made to limit the number of formal platform presentations in order to give maximum opportunity for participants to receive one another's witness within smaller groups. There were only five addresses during the ten days, four of these in the first 24 hours and one in the closing session.

A second deliberate decision was to assure that the worship was fully participatory with ample opportunity to speak and to listen. Obviously the dialogue into which one is most often drawn in worship is with the Spirit rather than with one's neighbour. A third decision was to engage in a process of inductive Bible studies in forty small groups rather than to hold a series of lectures in a plenary mode.

For those prepared to listen as well as to speak there were many opportunities. The many diverse voices did not constitute a babel, however, for there was structure to the programme design.

1. *The worship:* It was here that the conference most tangibly became a community. From the final moments of the opening service of the conference when 2000 persons continued to sing as they poured out into the vast parking lot of the Trinity Southern Baptist Church in a joyous refusal to surrender the spirit of the convocation, it was evident that a rare benediction was being given. Precisely this gift was the subject of intercessions being offered in an ecumenical prayer vigil which began on Sunday afternoon and continued from 8 in the morning to 9 at night throughout the ten days of the conference. Fifty-two San Antonio congregations representing more than a dozen communions sent teams to pray in this continuing intercession on behalf of each participant by name.

The quality of the music and liturgy which had so stirred the congregation at the opening was to continue to feed and energize those attending the early morning worship. Each day the attendance grew as more and more recognized this was no ordinary opportunity to sing and to pray. Continuity was assured through the use of evocative symbols of seeds being planted, nurtured with light and water, plants patiently pruned and finally fruit-harvested — all metaphors of the miracle of God's loving care for us together with all creation.

No homilies were given. Many languages were used in the readings, the prayers and the singing. In the finest tradition of ecumenical worship as it is evolving in World Council of Churches events, these worship experiences were such that every participant was at times an alien. No tradition, no rite, no style was allowed to dominate and thus permit its advocate to feel totally at home. Without requiring compromising verbalizations of any sort each worshipper was invited to stretch his/her perspective of how one might most appropriately respond to the uncalculating love of the Creator. The standing-room-only attendance at the closing worship service bore eloquent witness that this experience, however disturbing, was welcome.

The pattern of daily worship was broken on Thursday when the conference participants together with those attending Encuentro were invited to join in walking the way of the cross. Small clusters of persons began this meditative journey at six in the morning and hundreds continued to follow.

The course of the walk led each worshipper through eight stations on this evocative itineration about the campus, culminating in a breakfast of tortillas and water shared in awareness of the millions of God's people who would not have even this to eat. Each station provided graphic reminders of the events surrounding the crucifixion at Golgatha. Murals on the side of a large building focused the meditation on certain events in the life of Christ. An appropriate rocky garden was marked with reminders in many languages of the agony of Gethsemane. Another location elicited sombre meditation on the current judgment halls where innocents are condemned. This led on to where a heavy wooden cross was waiting to be carried with the help of other pilgrims.

Beyond was a place ringing with the haunting sounds of hammers beating upon large iron nails. Each person was invited to write a personal or corporate sin to be eradicated and to drive a nail through the note into the cross.

The bitterness of being forsaken was evoked by drinking from a small cup of vinegar and water and then, blindfolded, each was led into the chapel for a season of meditation at the cross. From here the journey led into a quiet garden with many reminders of the joyful discovery that the tomb was empty. And then the walk led back towards the breaking of bread along a path peopled with familiar strangers as was the road to Emmaus. Many will never forget this experience.

The eucharist was celebrated at 6.30 in the morning on seven days of the conference. Each service was hosted by a different San Antonio congregation representing a particular confession or tradition. Access to the table was determined by the host. These celebrations were held in the University Presbyterian Church which also provided hospitality for the day-long prayer vigils maintained throughout the conference.

2. *The Bible studies:* It was here that the conference was nurtured within the forty groups which faithfully reflected the tremendous diversity that marked the meeting. Forty persons had been requested to facilitate the work of these groups in an inductive exploration of selected passages from Luke's Gospel. They were guided in their difficult tasks by an

ecumenical team of three: a Lutheran pastor from Brazil, a Roman Catholic nun from Samoa, and an Orthodox professor of theology from Greece.

Predictably the experiences of the forty leaders and the 700-plus participants who attended these groups were most uneven. For some the Bible study encounters became the very heart of the conference. For others the experience was one of frustration and disappointment when communication, both linguistically and theologically, was blocked. For a great majority it was a vital daily link between the emotionally evocative experience of the early morning worship and the vigorous intellectual challenges of the section debates that followed.

In a summary commentary the Rev. Milton Schwantes, moderator of the ecumenical leadership team, said to the conference plenary:

> This conference opted to promote the highest level of participation possible. Many people were involved as animators of the Bible studies. Participation is a very creative key for opening the Bible. It helps us to appropriate its contents. Participation helps us drink from that marvellous well. The words of a single interpreter can never quite say what the choir of a community is able to express.

Commenting upon the five passages chosen for study in the groups, Schwantes said:

> They are like five windows in a house. Each window enables you to look in and gain an impression of the interior as a whole, although it is also true that in each the whole is viewed from a different perspective, a different angle.
>
> We were invited to begin with the Magnificat (Luke 1:39-55). It is the high point of the Gospel, summing up the whole. It is, as it were, its heart.
>
> The Beatitudes continue the theme of the Magnificat (Luke 6:17-26). The poor are the centre of attention. Jesus' words and deeds come through them and not through the rich and well-fed. The important ones are those who are weak.
>
> At the beginning of the parable of the great banquet (Luke 14:12-24) we are reminded that we are still in the company of the Magnificat: the humble are to be lifted up. Now the suffering people become participants. It is their feast. That is the great news of the reign inaugurated by Jesus. This parable does not question rich people but it does show that their large estates are embedded in their souls. That is why the gospel of liberation is lived out so differently by the rich and the poor. The problem of the first is their fields and oxen. The problem of the latter is their suffering. Mission and evangelism need to express and live out these differences — otherwise everything becomes very confused.

The scene of Gethsemane (Luke 22:39-46) sharpens the question: if the marginalized are blessed (Luke 6) and if they are the invited guests of honour at the banquet (Luke 14) how will the Mighty One and God's strong arm (Luke 1) be revealed? Resistance continues to be affirmed. Not giving in to the violence of the oppressor is part of God's will. Mission and evangelism that do not prepare for resistance against the oppressors or for martyrdom for justice are no longer "in Christ's way".

A new perspective is opened to us with the narrative of the disciples on the road to the village of Emmaus (Luke 24:13-35.) The presence of the Risen One takes place at the table. In the breaking and sharing of the bread, in this eucharistic, communitarian practice, we have the clearest presence of the Messiah.

In our mission and evangelism today we are the heirs of a tradition, a culture, and a faith expression of the impoverished. We are part of the discipleship of women who do not receive much credit, of a handmaid who was surprised at being chosen, of the poor, the marginalized, the blind and lame who went to the banquet. Luke points to this, our heritage. This is not an additional perspective. It is not an appendix to the faith in God the Creator, Redeemer and Consoler. The defence of the little ones, the lifting up of the meek and the poor, to use the words of Mary, burst from God's heart. They are in the sweat that falls like drops of blood on the ground (Luke 22:44). That is why Luke underlines that it is prayer that most adequately perceives and most deeply distinguishes this special love, this regarding by God of the servant Israel, of Sarah and Abraham in their struggle for the land, of women, outcasts, marginalized, the poor, the blind, and the lame.

3. *The sections:* It was here that the conference set itself to work intensively on nine occasions during the eight full working days of the conference. Participants were divided into four sections of approximately comparable size. Each person had indicated preference for a particular section at registration and most found their first choice honoured.

The sections dealt with the four sub-themes. These had earlier been established as the channels through which the conference would move to explore in a global variety of circumstances the contemporary application of "Your Will Be Done: Mission in Christ's Way".

Prior to the conference a 10-page briefing paper had been sent to each participant pertaining to the section within which he/she would be working. These briefing papers defined the sub-themes in general terms and described briefly the global context within which the issues would be discussed. In addition, reports from the leadership team visits were sent together with the basic document on which the work of all the sections rested: "Mission and Evangelism: an Ecumenical Affirmation". One special publication, "Mission from Three Perspectives", had been prepared to assure wider reading of the findings of the three major consultations that had taken place earlier: URM (Manila 1986), evangelism (Stuttgart, 1987), and an Orthodox meeting (Neapolis, 1988). As the sections convened in San Antonio, reports and findings from various other workshops and consultations were also shared.

Deliberately omitted from the preparation was an annotated agenda for each section to direct and control the discussions with an anticipation of the conclusions to be reached or resolutions to be adopted. This decision was made in the confidence that those coming to the conference would be willing and able to define those aspects of the agenda which are most urgent for their lives and specific circumstances. If they were to risk speaking plainly they would need to be confident they would be heard. Until they had been heard the agenda for the section could not be firmly set.

Permeating this planning was the conviction that as surely as there is no global expert competent to interpret mission in Christ's way in authoritative terms, just as surely there are many women and men who could bear relevant witness out of the authority of their own vulnerable but faithful discipleship.

4. *The unplanned interventions:* Along with the carefully planned efforts to enable many and diverse voices to be heard through recruitment, visitation and programme design, there were numerous occasions when participants in the conference took creative initiatives not planned in advance. On two evenings a 10 p.m. plenary was convened to enable first the Rev. Dr Allan Boesak and later Bishop Lesslie Newbigin to speak. Time had been scheduled on the first full day of the conference for a women's gathering. Meeting by regions at this initial session the decision was made to gather according to the sections in which each woman was working. A third meeting was a conference-wide celebration of women in mission. A panel of women shared with the whole conference in a plenary some of the reflections exchanged in these gatherings of women participants. Regional meetings were scheduled on two occasions. The Africa regional participants used the occasion to draft a message to the whole conference. Throughout the conference there were meetings of groups of concerned persons on the basis of theological, confessional or national interests, to discuss issues of particular importance to them which had been raised or they felt needed to be raised at the conference. In some of these gatherings specific messages to the conference were drafted and subsequently read or shared as documents.

The site

While decisions were being debated and made about the theme, the content and the form and style of the conference, a parallel discussion was going on concerning the site. From one important perspective planning could and did proceed without reference to where in the world the conference was to be held. Influencing the selection of a site was the determination that the conference should simultaneously make a significant and redemptive impact upon the community within which it took place but still evolve with integrity without having been unduly influenced by the context.

A variety of possibilities were explored, each being tested against certain criteria:

— Is the local Christian community (including member churches of the WCC) issuing the invitation?
— Is there evidence of readiness to become actively involved in preparations to receive the conference and to facilitate its access to the wider community?
— Are facilities other than luxury hotels available for conference housing and meetings?
— Are air travel schedules reasonable?
— Is the national frontier open for all conference participants to travel freely?

The CWME executive committee began discussing possible locations for the conference in January 1985. In addition to the above criteria, consideration was given to where the nine previous world mission and evangelism conferences had been held. After exploration of possibilities in Brazil, Cyprus, and China the choice was narrowed down to Freetown, Sierra Leone, Birmingham, England, and San Antonio, Texas, USA. The choice of the members of the CWME was San Antonio.

Several factors influenced this judgment:

— Only one of the previous nine conferences had been held in North America — in Whitby, Canada, in 1947.
— The United States in general and Texas in particular represented all that is commonly perceived to be powerful. What better place to explore mission in Christ's way with its provocative models of how God's power is manifest?
— The economic policies of the United States directly and often negatively influence the quality of life in many parts of the world.
  What better place for a global ecumenical community to have opportunity to bear witness to these painful realities?

— San Antonio as a community enjoys an exceptionally open ecumenical climate. This was fully demonstrated when the regional planning
committee was chaired by the ecumenical officer of the San Antonio
Roman Catholic Archdiocese and the opening worship service of the
conference was held in a Southern Baptist Church.

— Trinity University (a private, church-related college) offered full
access to its exceptional dormitory and meeting room facilities at very
nominal rates.

When the decision to go to San Antonio was made by CWME those
who had issued the invitation in the United States set to work in lively
coordination with those planning the conference in Geneva to see that
there would be a mutually productive encounter between the conference
community and those hosting it.

The most visible and structured encounter was labelled precisely that:
Encuentro. It had to be assumed that thousands of North American
Christians would plan to visit this exceptional gathering of a global
Christian community. There was no doubt that a visit to the conference
would greatly benefit the visitors. It was equally certain that if a host of
visitors arrived, possibly outnumbering the conference participants
themselves, the work of the conference could be impeded. The solution
was modelled on the design which worked well at Bellingham,
Washington, in 1983 when a parallel educational event was held during
the first seven days of the sixth assembly of the World Council of
Churches.

For five days (four of which coincided with the first four days of the
conference) 499 women and men, largely but not exclusively from the
United States, shared freely in the campus life of the conference as well
as in six plenary sessions. In addition there were many Encuentro
workshops and seminars resourced by conference participants. Thus
both formally and informally there were multiple opportunities for those
who could not be enrolled as official participants to interact for four
days with those who were privileged to participate fully in the world
conference.

More numerous and far less structured encounters occurred within the
team visits which took place before, during and after the conference.
Tens of thousands of Christians in communities throughout Texas as
well as in many other parts of the United States, Canada and the
Caribbean welcomed the conference participants as fellow pilgrims in
order to exchange with them experiences in undertaking mission in
Christ's way.

The product

Seeds of hope and faith have been widely sown. The harvest is for the future. Of more immediate measure is the immediate product of the conference itself. This took three different forms.

1. The message captures the essence of the conference. The process of its preparation was routine. After a first reading followed by discussion, it was revised and adopted in the final plenary session.

2. The constitutional amendments to be proposed for WCC Central Committee action required action within the only business session of the conference. This plenary session was scheduled specifically to consider amending the constitution to bring it in line with the practice which had evolved since Mexico City. One change eliminated all references to the earlier administrative and coordinative functions of the conference, thus clearly confirming the deliberative function of the conference. Another change will make it possible for WCC member churches to nominate a larger proportion of the delegates to the next world conference on mission and evangelism.

3. The Acts in Faithfulness grew out of the conviction that to pray "Your will be done" calls for more than words. We must be prepared to act. In their experimental formulation the Acts were intended to differ from traditional conference resolutions and declarations, to be innovations in both form and function. They were to address crucial issues in the spirit of the gospel, approaching them as Jesus would. They were to be do-able, attain-able (on this earth and in this life), measurable, and clear as to whom the call was addressed, beginning but not ending with ourselves.

The Acts in Faithfulness which are presented here at the conclusion of each of the section reports only partially fulfill these criteria. Several resemble the form of many other conference resolutions. None received as full and free discussion in the plenary as its originators would have wished. This was partly because of the concern to provide maximum time for group work and the consequent decision to focus plenary discussion upon the Acts rather than upon the full section reports from which they derived. This did not allow time for the whole conference to "own" the total work of the sections.

Instead, the reports of the sections were each read and received by the conference plenary and then each section presented to the conference a limited number of Acts in Faithfulness. Lacking time for debate, amendment, revision and a second reading, the moderator asked the voting delegates a simple, novel question: "Does this Act in Faithfulness speak for you?" With some voting "no" and some abstaining, an overwhelming majority of the official delegates affirmed eleven Acts in Faithfulness presented by the four sections (these appear in italicized form within the section reports).

The direct, personal nature of the inquiry may serve the long-term purposes of the conference very well. For those delegates (and for the non-voting participants surrounding them in the Trinity University gymnasium) the question was sharply focused: "Does this section speak for you in making this commitment to this Act in Faithfulness?" Those who replied in the affirmative took the first step in the process of making a personal commitment. Only time will reveal the extent to which this is translated into a contagious, living witness received by a particular parish, community or mission organization.

Because the study and discussion which produced these Acts essentially took place within four different sections, the question arises: Was the San Antonio conference on world mission and evangelism one event or four?

For those who found the heart of the conference to be the daily worship, this was indeed an integrated, coherent experience. For those who found that the Bible studies were the essence of the conference this was equally so.

However, for those who found the greatest significance of the conference to be in the work of one particular section and then realized that some of their sisters and brothers in other sections were responding the same way, the experience resembled parallel streams never quite reaching a point of full confluence. From this perspective the work of the sections — and therefore of the conference — remains unfinished.

Working within the common gospel context provided by the worship and Bible study, each section sought diligently to discern what faithfulness required of those seeking God's will in bearing witness, in struggling for justice, in honouring creation, and in building community. This work of the conference stands. But it is possible even now for the Commission on World Mission and Evangelism to move the work of the conference towards greater coherence. The insights offered by the sections may now be focused into a whole through a disciplined submission of each to the judgments reflected in the other three.

Despite the disappointment of those who expected more explicit, directive, legislative action from the conference I believe the conversations in the sections were interrupted at a healthy point. They are demonstrably unfinished. The discussion has only begun for many of us.

The goal of the conference was never to craft a definitive word to describe mission in Christ's way as it reflects the fullness of the will of the One who sent him.

Rather, the intention expressed in multiple ways by deliberate choices made in all the planning, was to contribute to the clarity of the paradigm provided us in the life and ministry of Jesus of Nazareth. I believe this has happened. The contributions have come from many voices heretofore only heard by a few. Many persons whose lives continue to demonstrate in difficult situations inside and outside the institutional church a discernment of Christ's way of mission were enabled to engage one another together with those who carry major administrative responsibilities for mission. Both the listening and the articulation have been partial. This conversation holds so much redemptive potential that those who began it will not allow it to stop.

But what of the reader of these pages who was not present in San Antonio?

One premise of the conference was that no person or group of persons holds a monopoly on discerning what it means to pray that God's will be implemented as one engages in mission in Christ's way. The 772 persons (including the press) privileged to attend the San Antonio conference did not thereby become an exception. This report in your hands is an invitation to you to make this discussion your own: to ponder the addresses as they interpret the historical and theological context in which the conference discussion occurred; to read and reread the Gospel narrative provided by Luke; and then to reflect with others in your church and community on the work of the sections through their reports and to challenge the way each calls for commitments to particular Acts in Faithfulness.

I believe that the gradual evolution in the composition of these conferences on world mission and evangelism from Edinburgh to San Antonio and the accompanying shift in expectation as to how the results will be formulated have brought us to a critical juncture. If it is true that living illustrations of mission in Christ's way are visible, accessible paradigms to be found among all manner of folk in all parts of the world, then it is arguable that the discernment of these models is far too vital a task to be left to professionals. Rather, this is a task open to and expected of all of us.

Our hope is that the surprising discovery made by the disciples on the Emmaus road will recur again and again: that as each of us hears familiar words in unfamiliar accents we will be moved by the warmth of our hearts to recognize that in the form of strangers on the road we have again encountered the living Christ. Through the witness and encouragement of this steadily expanding global community of sisters and brothers we will grow to be more fruitful instruments of mission in God's hands.

Message of the Conference

In the name of the Triune God,
    Creator of heaven and earth,
    Saviour and Comforter,
people gathered from all parts of the world
    in San Antonio, Texas, USA,
as a Conference on World Mission and Evangelism
    of the World Council of Churches,
under the theme: YOUR WILL BE DONE — MISSION IN CHRIST'S
    WAY.

The two most significant trends of this Conference were
the spirit of universality (catholicity) of the gathering,
and its concern for the fullness of the gospel, namely:
    to hold in creative tension
        spiritual and material needs,
        prayer and action,
        evangelism and social responsibility,
        dialogue and witness,
        power and vulnerability,
        local and universal.

Mirror of that diversity,
San Antonio is a multicultural city
where many strands meet, clash and intermingle:
    Hispanic, Anglo-Saxon, black, indigenous peoples, others.

In this context, the gathered people looked ahead to 1992,
the five hundredth anniversary of the conquest of the Americas,

a time when the gospel message was brought to these lands
    under the auspices of colonial powers,
which often distorted Christian love with violence and oppression.
The heirs and survivors of the indigenous people recall this date
    with bitterness.
This past cannot be undone, but
reparation must be done to redeem the future,
and the hands of all people must join
    to weave a new world community.

* * *

Concerned with the discernment of the will of God in today's world,
the representatives of the churches gathered in San Antonio,
and spoke about shared signs of hope and renewal.
They celebrated the new opportunity
    for religious expression in many socialist countries.
They realized that the Holy Spirit,
    Spirit of truth, freedom, communion and justice,
is at work today in different parts of the world.

Communities, and even entire nations, in unexpected ways,
are involved in self-examination, repentance, renewal
    and struggle for justice,
turning to the Living God,
stressing the infinite value of human dignity,
and turning to one another to make peace.
For all this,
we rejoice in the Spirit;
we thank the Living God,
and in these signs we hear a new call to faith
    and see a new challenge for mission and evangelism.

* * *

At the same time,
Christ is still suffering in many parts of the world,
and is waiting for our concrete response:
    solidarity and action.

We have heard many voices of anguish and pain:
  voices of poor and oppressed peoples,
  voices of women who suffer discrimination,
  voices of youth challenging injustice in church and society,
  voices of children who suffer innocently in body, mind and spirit,
  voices of victims of foreign intervention and militarism,
  voices of those who are discriminated against and violated because of
      race,
  voices of those who are being destroyed by nuclear abuse,
  voices of peoples suffocating under the burden of external debt,
  voices of indigenous peoples yearning for self-determination,
  voices of refugees and displaced persons,
  voices of hunger for food and for meaning in life,
  voices of anger at blatant violation of human rights,
  voices of longing for liberation and justice,
  voices of solidarity in the quest for a new human community.

We also heard of the voiceless suffering of religious communities
  whose right to exist is denied constitutionally, as is the case in
  Albania.

In the study of Holy Scripture,
  in worship and prayer,
  in self-examination and penitence,
we have sensed anew
  the urgent voice of God calling us to love mercy,
      to act justly
      and to walk humbly with our God.

This is a time for repentance,
  to make reparation,
   to turn to the Living God.
Judgment begins in the household of God.
In faithfulness to God's will,
it is time for a new commitment to a Mission in Christ's Way,
and prayer, witness and action,
  in the power of the Holy Spirit.

God calls us, Christians everywhere, to join in:
  proclaiming the Good News of God's redeeming love in Jesus Christ;

acting in solidarity with those who suffer and struggle for justice
  and human dignity;
sharing justly the earth's resources;
bearing witness to the gospel through renewed communities
  in mission.

*   *   *

To those who hear or experience a twisted or partial gospel,
    or no gospel at all:
  Mission in Christ's Way calls us by deed and word
  to share the wholeness of the gospel,
    the love of God revealed in the incarnate Word, Jesus Christ.

To churches and nations where divisions, barriers and enmities prevail:
  Mission in Christ's Way calls us to strive
    for unity with justice as a basis for effective mission.

To peoples of wonderfully diverse cultures across the earth:
  Mission in Christ's Way calls us to extend understanding and respect,
    relating the gospel of Christ to these cultures with sensitivity.

To persons of other religious faiths of the world:
Mission in Christ's Way calls us to listen to and respect their beliefs,
    witness our faith to them in word and deed,
    seek with them for peace and justice.

To young people and all those resisting injustice and war,
    facing repression and death:
  Mission in Christ's Way calls us to solidarity in the struggle for life,
    turning hopelessness into strength.

To those whose land and livelihood are taken away, despoiled or polluted:
  Mission in Christ's Way calls us to resist all that violates human
    rights, that basic justice may extend to all.

To those who suffer and whose life is threatened, exploited, shattered
    or oppressed:
  Mission in Christ's Way calls us to commit all in our power
    to defend life in all its fullness

and self-determination for every human being, community and
nation.

Proclamation of the kingdom,
 of hope for the whole creation,
 of a Mission in Christ's Way,
is not just an affirmation,
but a way of life.
We are called to concrete acts of faithfulness,
 a living expression of the prayer that Christ taught us:

"YOUR WILL BE DONE."

Reports of the Sections

Section I: Turning to the Living God

I. Mission in the name of the living God

1. At the very heart of the church's vocation in the world is the proclamation of the kingdom of God inaugurated in Jesus the Lord, crucified and risen (ME 6[1]) **and made present among us by the Holy Spirit.**

The Triune God, Father, Son and Holy Spirit, is a God in mission, the source and sustainer of the church's mission (John 20:21; Acts 2). The church's mission cannot but flow from God's care for the whole creation, unconditional love for all people and concern for unity and fellowship with and among all human beings.

2. As we reflected on the section theme within the context of the overall conference theme we were made conscious of the fact that we are enabled to turn to the living God and become involved in God's mission only because the living God has created us for life in communion, has first turned to us in grace and love, and has done so supremely in Jesus Christ, our Lord and Saviour. Our ministry of witness therefore primarily flows from gratitude, not just from an obligation laid upon us.

3. God's people know God's will because the holy and Triune God in diverse ways has revealed himself. The prophets of the old covenant proclaim the will of God in new ways in ever-changing circumstances. Finally and uniquely, God's will is made known in Jesus Christ (Heb. 1:1-4). Testimony to this is given throughout the New Testament. We have to confess that, as sinful people, we recognize the will of God for ourselves only partially and provisionally. At the same time we are

---

[1] Details of references are given on page 37.

confident that the Holy Spirit enlightens us, teaches us to understand the will of God for ourselves and our time, and also enables us to do the will of God. The unity of the divine and human will in the person of Jesus Christ is the source of and model for our mission according to God's will.

4. "The mission of the church has cosmic dimensions" (Orthodox, p.33). "The biblical promise of a new earth and a new heaven where love, peace and justice will prevail... invites our action as Christians in history" (ME preface). Since our mission serves the coming of the reign of God, it is concerned with bringing the future into the present, serving the cause of God's reign: the new creation.

5. These tremendous affirmations have, however, to be viewed in light of the present moment in history. In some parts of the world people face a total system of death, of monstrous false gods, of exploitative economic systems, of violence, of the disintegration of the fundamental bonds of society, of the destruction of human life, of helplessness of persons in the face of impersonal forces. We are called to exercise our mission in this context of human struggle, and challenged to keep the earth alive and to promote human dignity, since the living God is both creator of heaven and earth and protector of the cause of the widow, the orphan, the poor and the stranger. To respond to all this is part of our mission, just as inviting people to put their trust in God is part of that mission. The "material gospel" and the "spiritual gospel" have to be *one*, as was true of the ministry of Jesus (ME 33). Frequently the world's poor are also those who have not yet heard the good news of the gospel; to withhold from them justice as well as the good news of life in Christ is to commit a "double injustice" (ME 32). There is no evangelism without solidarity; there is no Christian solidarity that does not involve sharing the message of God's coming reign (ME 33).

6. Mission in the name of the living God of necessity leads to repentance on the part of those who are involved in this mission. Any call to conversion and to service for the reign of God "should begin with the repentance of those who do the calling, who issue the invitation" (ME 13). "'Your Will Be Done': this prayer of Christ to the Father is a continuous reminder of the need for repentance and forgiveness of sins. It is a call to reexamine our lives in the light of Christ's life. It is a call addressed personally to each of us for metanoia and conversion, a call to literally 'turn around' our lives and recommit ourselves to Christ" (Orthodox, p.42). We have to repent of our arrogance and insensitivity, but also of our failure of nerve and inertia. "The crucified and risen Christ is a judge of shallow life-styles and invites the churches to repentance and

new life. In many situations today, renewed life-styles will be the most authentic and unambiguous way to proclaim and live out the Gospel" (Melbourne, p.190). A call to repentance is, however, not a call to drop important work, but to do it differently. In repentance, the fountains of life are cleansed. True repentance does not paralyze: it invigorates; after repentance one gets up and walks — in a new way.

7. We have been made aware of a new and widespread interest in evangelism in communities linked with the ecumenical movement in the north as well as the south. The love of God for the world is the source of our missionary motivation. This love creates an urgency to share the gospel invitingly in our time (even if we recognize with deep regret that some of our missionary endeavours may be attributed to impure motivations — concerns about declining church membership, subtle political agendas, and the like). Christians desire to "confess the life and work of Jesus Christ as unique, decisive, and universally significant" (Tambaram II); we therefore invite our churches to subscribe to the CWME aim, as endorsed by the Nairobi assembly of the WCC (1975), that the Christian community should be assisted to proclaim "the gospel of Jesus Christ, by word and deed, to the whole world to the end that all may believe in him and be saved".

II. The living God calls us to unity in mission

8. The present ecumenical movement came into being out of the conviction that the division of Christians is a scandal and an impediment to the witness of the church. There is a growing awareness among the churches today of the inextricable relationship between Christian unity and missionary calling, between ecumenism and evangelization (ME 1).

"The impulse for common witness comes from the depth of our faith. Its urgency is underlined when we realize the seriousness of the human predicament." (ME 24).

9. In a special way the theme "Mission in Christ's way" sets unity and mission in an inseparable relation. The risen Christ who sends us is our peace, who breaks down the dividing wall of hostility, reconciling us in one body through the cross (Eph. 2:14-15). The churches are called to give a common witness to this reconciling ministry in the power of the Spirit.

10. Christian mission is the humble involvement of the one body of Christ in liberating and suffering love, the witness of God's saving acts in Christ, and the practice of God's incarnational love for all humankind.

This mission is expressed through the communion of love and justice which embodies the church's self-giving solidarity with the human family.

11. When churches and missions really go *the way of Christ* instead of their own ways, they will necessarily join their actions wherever possible. Our divisions weaken our efforts at living in solidarity with the poor, the hungry and the oppressed. To be called to unity in mission involves becoming a community that transcends in its life the barriers and brokenness in the world, and living as a sign of at-one-ment under the cross. The search for visible unity "in one faith and in one eucharistic fellowship" (Vancouver, pp.43ff.) and the struggle to overcome injustice and alienation in the human family are one single response to the gospel. Unity-in-mission and advocacy of justice are therefore not differing phases of the ecumenical movement, as though we could separate between the church's being and doing, between faith and action, between theology and involvement. Consequently, unity is vital to the missional health of the church and the future of humankind. The church is called again and again to be a prophetic sign and foretaste of the unity and renewal of the human family as envisioned in God's promised reign.

12. In spite of our many failures in the area of unity in mission, we also have reason to celebrate the manifestations of such unity which have come to our attention. We were told stories of joint projects in mission in many places, and we rejoice in these. In fact, our very coming together as an ecumenical fellowship here in San Antonio is a manifestation and celebration of unity in mission and we affirm joyfully that "the churches of the WCC are on a pilgrimage towards unity under the missionary vision of John 17:21" (ME 1). We have noted with gratitude the coming into existence of united churches in many parts of the world as well as church union negotiations still in process, and we pray that the churches renewed in unity may also be renewed in mission. Yet even apart from these few scattered examples of unity-in-practice, we confess that we are already one in mission because of what the living God has done to and for us. Our unity is a reality we cannot undo, even if we wished: we are given to one another as sisters and brothers in the one household of God.

13. Mission in unity requires Christians to work for the authenticity of the apostolic faith. Doctrinal divisions, especially those that prevent the sharing of the eucharist and the full participation of women in the church, keep Christians from making a common witness. The eucharist, which is

the most central sacrament of our faith, also is the place where our divisions become most painfully apparent. The one faith we share and the one cup and one bread we are given should be vital actions for mission, particularly if "the eucharist is bread for a missionary people" (ME 21). At the same time, in light of the fact that many people around us do not even know the name of the Triune God except in blasphemy, we call into question the endless debates and time-consuming preoccupations demanding an "open" eucharist.

14. One of the most sensitive areas in our discussions on unity in mission concerned the issue of *proselytism*. The aim of our evangelism should be the building up of the body of Christ, service in the world, and the glory of God. Instead, evangelism sometimes turns into programmes for denominational aggrandizement. We believe that any evangelism that does not promote good relationships with other Christians in the community must inevitably be called into question (Stuttgart, p.27). Our witness may deteriorate into counterwitness, thereby in effect denying the authenticity of the faith experience of other Christians. All unhealthy competition in mission work should be avoided as constituting a distorted form of mission (Orthodox, p.39). At the same time we realize that faith communities may become ingrown and stagnant, lose their vision, and become unable or perhaps not even interested in getting involved in evangelism and pastoral renewal in their environment (Stuttgart, p.27). In such situations other Christians, rather than ignoring the presence and integrity of the traditional faith communities, may perhaps be privileged to play a catalytic role in renewal for mission. They will, however, only be able to do so if they identify with the local faith community and treat it with sensitivity, respect and integrity.

III. Witness in a secular society

15. **Everywhere the churches are in missionary situations. Even in countries where the churches have been active for centuries we see life organized today without reference to Christian values, a growth of secularism understood as the absence of any final meaning. The churches have lost vital contact with the workers and the youth and many others. The situation is so urgent that it demands priority attention of the ecumenical movement.** (ME 37).

16. Many would see "secularization" partly as a fruit of the gospel, releasing humankind from ancient powers and emancipating people to make mature choices and take responsibility for their destiny. "Secular-

ism", on the other hand, refers to a closed system, a context in which people live and act without reference to God. Today, many who have experienced secularization in recent decades have however given up faith in its value: a post-secular era announces itself.

17. There may be a variety of manifestations of secularism; the situation in North Atlantic countries differs from that in the socialist world, or in Latin America, or in Asia and the South Pacific. Each context calls for an appropriate response.

18. Secularism has not diminished people's desire to relate to some "ultimate reality". The shrine does not remain empty. "Secular" religion may find expression in the worship of the modern idols of consumerism, or of economic, political and military power, in which individual and collective selfishness reigns supreme. The religious quest of humankind may also find expression in the search for meaning and coherence articulated in the ideologies of our time; at other times it expresses itself in a bewildering plurality of religious sects, some of an exotic nature.

19. Our church communities are part of society and exposed to the same seemingly irresistible advance of the forces of secularism in the world. Secularism is not just something "out there": it has infiltrated and profoundly influenced our churches. Not only have some churches often adopted the same secularist ideologies that operate in society at large (pragmatism, functionalism, etc.), they have also themselves contributed to the spread of secularism. Some results of this have been the compartmentalization of life into "public" and "private" spheres and the relegation of "religion" to the latter, as well as the rise of individualism leading to breakdown in community. Specifically in our witness we have often absorbed the dichotomy between spiritual and social, and word and action, resulting in a distortion of the biblical concern for witness to persons in the totality of their need.

20. The advance of secularism and the collapse of traditional religious frames of reference also have a positive influence on our churches' practice. Stripped of their power base, they are called — in a new and challenging way — to become servants in society. In some parts of the world this means that our churches, for the first time in many centuries, have the opportunity to become what they always should have been: powerless and vulnerable witnesses to the faith they proclaim and by which they live.

21. Our churches should at all times resist the temptation both to succumb to the spirit of the age and to withdraw into a ghetto existence. One way of articulating this resistance is to reclaim for ourselves cardinal

elements of the spirit and practice of the ascetic tradition: a simple life in which sharing and solidarity have priority over possession and individualism, the boldness to refuse to conform to the pattern of this world (cf. Rom. 12:2), and the resilience to persist on the road of faith and service.

22. The fountainhead of our practice of resistance to the dominant ethos and of our witness to secular society ought to be the local worshipping community: believers gathered — sometimes in small house groups — around the word and the sacraments, empowered by the continual renewal of their faith, emboldened to become relevant to what is happening in secular society. From this base, believers go forth to meet people and witness to them, realizing that their witness depends more on who they are than on what they do or say; no matter how eloquent our verbal testimony, people will always believe their eyes first. Nevertheless, what Christians say matters and should be relevant to people's actual ways of speaking about their fears and hopes. The whole people of God — clergy and laity, women and men, mothers and fathers, single people, children and youth — are involved in this witness of life. We were greatly encouraged by stories of such witness to faith in Christ, even by small children acting as partners with the local church, often in contexts saturated with secularism and atheism.

23. For the sake of their survival — no, for the sake of the gospel itself and of the cause of Christ — the Christian churches will have to conduct ongoing and penetrating studies of the issues of secularization and secularism and of ways of responding to this challenge faithfully, sensitively, and with integrity.

IV. Witness among people of other living faiths

24. **True witness follows Jesus Christ in respecting and affirming the uniqueness and freedom of others.... Such an attitude springs from the assurance that God is the creator of the whole universe and that he has not left himself without a witness at any time or any place. The Spirit of God is constantly at work in ways that pass human understanding. In entering into a relationship of dialogue with others, Christians seek to discern the unsearchable riches of God and the way he deals with humanity** (ME 41,43).

The proclamation of the gospel includes an invitation to recognize and accept in a personal decision the saving lordship of Christ. It is the announcement of a personal encounter, mediated by the Holy Spirit, with the living Christ, receiving his forgiveness and making a

personal acceptance of the call to discipleship and a life of service
(ME 10).

**Christians owe the message of God's salvation in Jesus Christ to
every person and to every people.... The wonder of [Jesus'] ministry of love persuades Christians to testify to people of every religious
and non-religious persuasion of this decisive presence of God in
Christ. In him is our salvation** (ME 41,42).

25. In reaffirming the "evangelistic mandate" of the ecumenical movement, we would like to emphasize that we may never claim to have a full
understanding of God's truth: we are only the recipients of God's grace.
Our ministry of witness among people of other faiths presupposes our
presence with them, *sensitivity* to their deepest faith commitments and
experiences, *willingness* to be their servants for Christ's sake, *affirmation*
of what God has done and is doing among them, and *love* for them. Since
God's mystery in Christ surpasses our understanding and since our
knowledge of God's saving power is imperfect, we Christians are called
to be *witnesses* to others, not judges of them. We also affirm that it is
possible to be non-aggressive and missionary at the same time — that it
is, in fact, the only way of being truly missionary.

26. We cannot point to any other way of salvation than Jesus Christ; at
the same time we cannot set limits to the saving power of God. At times
the debate about salvation focuses itself only on the fate of the individual's soul in the hereafter, whereas the will of God is life in its fullness
even here and now. We therefore state: (a) that our witness to others
concerning salvation in Christ springs from the fact that we have encountered him as our Lord and Saviour and are hence urged to share this with
others; and (b) that in calling people to faith in Christ, we are not only
offering personal salvation but also calling them to follow Jesus in the
service of God's reign.

27. We have paid attention to the complex debate about the relationship
between *witness* and *dialogue*. We recognize that both witness and
dialogue presuppose two-way relationships. We affirm that witness does
not preclude dialogue but invites it, and that dialogue does not preclude
witness but extends and deepens it.

28. Dialogue has its own place and integrity and is neither opposed to
nor incompatible with witness or proclamation. We do not water down
our own commitment if we engage in dialogue; as a matter of fact,
dialogue between people of different faiths is spurious unless it proceeds
from the acceptance and expression of faith commitment. Indeed, life
with people of other faiths and ideologies is by its very nature an

encounter of commitments (ME 45). In dialogue we are invited to listen in openness to the possibility that the God we know in Jesus Christ may encounter us also in the lives of our neighbours of other faiths. On the other hand, we also see that the mutual sharing with people of other faiths in the efforts for justice, peace and service to the environment engages us in dialogue — the dialogue of life. We wish to commend that, in recognition that all humankind is responsible before God and the human family.

29. In affirming the dialogical nature of our witness, we are constrained by grace to affirm that "salvation is offered to the whole creation through Jesus Christ" (Tambaram II). "Our mission to witness to Jesus Christ can never be given up" (Melbourne, p.188). We are well aware that these convictions and the ministry of witness stand in tension with what we have affirmed about God being present in and at work in people of other faiths; we appreciate this tension, and do not attempt to resolve it.

30. We affirm our unequivocal endorsement of the principle and practice of religious freedom. We are aware that many people are discriminated against, harassed and even persecuted for their faith, often when they have converted from one faith to another; we deplore this and every manifestation of religious or ideological fanaticism. We commend to our Christian communities all those who suffer for their faith, whatever their religious persuasion may be.

V. Communicating the gospel today

31. **To receive the message of the kingdom of God is to be incorporated into the body of Christ, the church, the author and sustainer of which is the Holy Spirit. The churches are to be a sign for the world. They are to intercede as he did, to serve as he did. Thus Christian mission is the action of the body of Christ in the history of humankind — a continuation of Pentecost** (ME 20).

Churches are free to choose the ways they consider best to announce the gospel to different people in different circumstances. But these options are never neutral. Every methodology illustrates or betrays the gospel we announce. In all communications of the gospel, power must be subordinated to love (ME 28).

32. The Vancouver assembly of the WCC (1983) recommended that "the church must relate to the media in a manner which is pastoral, evangelical and prophetic" (Vancouver, p.107). In communicating the gospel to people, we acknowledge the ambivalence of the media at our

disposal. We recognize that the media not only *reflect* reality, but also shape, distort, and hide it. In its use of the media the church must be critical of these characteristics of the modern media and at the same time guard against becoming guilty of similar abuses. The way we use the media should be in harmony with the gospel we seek to proclaim. In communicating the gospel, both message and response are shaped by the authenticity of the communicator. The gospel proclaims a personal, interactive relationship among and between God and human persons; therefore, our means of communication must not only reflect but demonstrate the image we wish to transmit.

33. The faith evoked through the communication of the gospel needs nurture within the body of Christ. This nurture includes prayer and the study of God's word in a language and cultural form which communicates without alienation and which facilitates the discernment of the contours of God's reign in all realms of life. We can and may never determine in advance the way the gospel will come alive in the life, context and culture of a community. We affirm true Christian communication to be an act of worship, a praise of God through the shared word and action of persons-in-community, reflecting the life of the Holy Trinity. Christ's mission to the world manifests the outpouring of God's love through the Son and the Spirit. The ground of unity of the church, the body of Christ, is the love and unity eternally manifested in the life of the Triune God. The church as God's chosen instrument for proclaiming the good news of the reign of God is meant to embody and communicate values of oneness, reconciliation, equality, justice, freedom, harmony, peace and love. In the image of the Trinity, we must hold together this witness of the worshipping and serving community united in love, with that of its evangelistic task of sending forth persons to proclaim the word to those who have not yet heard or realized its fulfilling and saving grace.

34. As we seek to communicate God's image to others, we realize that our own lives and stories, as well as non-discursive ways of communicating through hymn or song, icon or symbol, movement or silence, may be more effective personal and experiential ways of sharing the faith than some forms of mass media. The church is also challenged to proclaim the gospel today in new languages, in both written and oral forms, and in the idioms and symbols of the cultures in which it is carried. Many millions have not heard the story of Jesus, even in cultures where historically the gospel was common knowledge.

35. Christian communication does not end with the proclamation of the message, but continues in an unending process directed to the education

and formation of persons in the Christian life, helping them to grasp more deeply and to enter more fully into the Christian story. The development of one's spirituality involves the capacity to communicate with God through prayer, and to apprehend how Christ enters into and claims all of life, guiding one's priorities and actions in every aspect of life.

36. "The vicarious work of Christ demands the presence of a vicarious people" (ME 25). We stand in awe in the awareness of the belief that God has committed to our faltering faith communities the message of God's love and reign. We witness to the humble power and servant lordship of the Crucified and Risen, seeking to be faithful to him who called us into discipleship and into the ministry of witnessing to the living God.

ACTS IN FAITHFULNESS[2]

1. Unity in mission/mission in unity

37. We express joy for the growing unity among Christians and, at the same time, we have once again been made aware of the pain caused by our divisions. We have affirmed the inseparable character of mission and unity. Therefore:

a) *We commit ourselves anew to common witness, by word and deed, to the whole gospel.*

b) *We enlist our member churches and the bodies represented at the conference to build meaningful relations for more effective mission at the local level, through joint prayer, Bible study, worship and actions.*

c) *We challenge ourselves and the churches we represent to make* Mission and Evangelism — an Ecumenical Affirmation *our own and give expression to the holistic understanding of mission reflected in it.*

d) *We ask CWME and all churches and bodies represented in San Antonio to work for a joint world mission conference in the future, as we take note of the fact that separate world mission conferences — in San Antonio and Manila — are being held in 1989.*

---

[2] The Acts in Faithfulness printed in italics indicate those that received an affirmative indication from the great majority of the conference voting delegates in response to the moderator's question: "Does this speak for you?" The other Acts in Faithfulness were received by the conference plenary as part of the section reports.

2. Witnessing to Jesus Christ today

a) Witnessing in a secular society

38. We realize anew that degrees of secularism are present in our societies and that our churches are faced with many challenges as well as new opportunities for Christian witness. We have been encouraged by reports of a joint pilot consultation on "Missionary Congregations in a Secularized Europe" held earlier this year, sponsored by WCC/CWME together with the Conference of European Churches. Therefore:

a) *We recommend that the project be continued and that similar projects be launched for other parts of the world.*

b) *We suggest the broadening of such projects so as to pay special attention to children and youth.*

c) *We commend the report of section I to the WCC member churches, stressing the importance of cooperation between clergy and laity at the local level.*

d) *We call the WCC member churches to study the Christian ascetic tradition, so that they may discover the importance of a lifestyle characterized by sharing as a means of witnessing to the gospel in the context of the secular society.*

b) Witnessing among people of other faiths

39. We have again listened to the WCC affirmations that "the proclamation of the gospel includes an invitation to recognize and accept in personal decision the saving lordship of Christ" (ME 10), that "Christians owe the message of God's salvation in Jesus Christ to every person and every people" (ME 41), and that "true witness follows Jesus Christ in respecting and affirming the uniqueness and freedom of others" (ME 41). Therefore:

a) *we commit ourselves and challenge our churches to cooperate in witnessing to the millions of people who have not yet had an opportunity to respond to the gospel.*

b) *We affirm that witness does not preclude dialogue with people of other living faiths, but that dialogue extends and deepens our witness.*

c) *We commit ourselves and challenge our churches to engage in dialogue with people of other faiths wherever possible, and to work together with them for justice, peace and the integrity of creation.*

c) Witnessing among young people

40. We have been made aware that the churches have at their disposal an amazing variety of means for proclaiming and communicating the gospel. We have been particularly sensitized by the efforts made by youth, who often interpret their values through music. Noting that the World Association for Christian Communication document, "Christian Principles of Communication" (May 1986), provides inspiration, we commit ourselves to assist and enable the WCC to:

a) develop and evaluate one significant music ministry project for youth from each continent to communicate the gospel message and values;

b) provide an opportunity for cross-cultural exchange with another such music ministry project.

41. Finally, we request that each of the above Acts in Faithfulness be monitored and assessed, and that reports be submitted to the Canberra assembly of the WCC, 1991.

REFERENCES

ME: *Mission and Evangelism — an Ecumenical Affirmation*. Geneva: WCC, 1982.

Melbourne: *Your Kingdom Come — Mission Perspectives, Report on the World Conference on Mission and Evangelism, Melbourne, 1980*. Geneva: WCC, 1981.

Orthodox: "Consultation of Eastern and Oriental Orthodox Churches, Neapolis, Greece, 1988", in *Mission From Three Perspectives*. Geneva: WCC/CWME, 1989.

Stuttgart: "Consultation on Evangelism, Stuttgart, 1987", in *Mission From Three Perspectives*.

Tambaram II: "Dialogue and Mission: Issues for Further Study", questions approved at Tambaram consultation, January 1988, in *International Review of Mission*, Vol. LXXVIII, No. 307, July 1988, p.449.

Vancouver: *Gathered for Life: Official Report of the Sixth Assemby of the World Council of Churches, Vancouver, 1983*. Geneva: WCC, 1983.

Section II: Participating in Suffering and Struggle

1. Participating in suffering and struggle is at the heart of God's mission and God's will for the world. It is central for our understanding of the incarnation, the most glorious example of participation in suffering and struggle. The church is sent in the way of Christ bearing the marks of the cross in the power of the Holy Spirit (cf. John 20:19-23).

Participation in suffering and struggle in order that all may have life in abundance is therefore an essential part of any discussion of the theme:

> Your will be done
> Mission in Christ's way

All three elements — participation, suffering, and struggle — are important. Some people suffer but have ceased to struggle, and their suffering is ultimately meaningless. Some want to struggle but are not willing to endure the suffering necessary for achieving transformation. Suffering is not to be romanticized; rather it is to be overcome through struggle. It is inevitable in the struggle. The character of participation is determined by the nature of the suffering and struggle.

The followers of Jesus Christ are invited to participate with the people who are crushed in their struggle for the transformation of society.

I. Creative power

2. Within the ecumenical movement, power has been traditionally discussed in two ways. The first position has seen power negatively but has dealt with it in a "cynical" way. The second position has also seen power negatively and rejected it, pointing largely to its abuses (as was evident in Melbourne). The starting point for our discussion, however, was the opening towards an understanding of the creative capacity of power in working for "the good of the poor and their liberation from oppression".[3]

3. In our discussions the issue of power has emerged positively, since we concentrated on creative power. We located and studied power in the context of suffering and struggle, which we took to be the core of God's mission and will. This will was visible in the biblical understanding of humanity as being created in the image of God and sharing in God's power as co-labourers. This creative power is central for any understanding of the incarnation, which is the pre-eminent example of creative power — wrongly understood at times as the "power of powerlessness". For though the church was founded through the creative power of the cross, it was Pentecost which provided the creative power for building the community and organizing it through a common faith and understanding, suffering and struggle. It was this power which enabled the church to challenge all those who were gathered in Jerusalem to celebrate their

---

[3] *Your Kingdom Come*, report of the Melbourne world conference on mission and evangelism, 1980, p.210.

liberation from slavery but who had forgotten the liberation of others (Acts 2:5,9-11). The Holy Spirit therefore acted as a creative power to lead people to destroy the injustices in society with, as their horizon, the liberation of the whole of humanity so that the Spirit of the Lord should be on all peoples (Acts 2:17-21, Joel 2:28-32).

It is through the living out of this "memory of the future" (celebrating the coming reign of God *now*) that creative power fundamentally becomes the power to crush all structures which impede life and any missionary activity which escapes the painful realities of this world. Therefore we feel the main title of the conference should have included the full phrase, "Your will be done *on earth* (as in heaven)", rather than only the first part of it. By stopping at "Your will be done" we have left a false ambiguity which also risks an otherworldly misinterpretation of "Mission in Christ's way".

In this sense creative power is always in the context of justice, for the mission of God, we believe, is the mission of God in justice, cf. the biblical concept of *dikaiosune* (which includes the justice of God as well as justification, forgiveness and reconciliation).

4. Sometimes in ecumenical and ecclesial discourse the term "justice" has been limited only to mean distributive (sharing) and retributive (judgmental) justice. There has been a tendency to forget the fundamental aspect of justice as the founding, building and organizing of community: a community with people, a community with God, and a community with nature.

Such community is only possible as an expression of creative power when people struggle against those principalities and powers which defile the image of God in them. We see this creative power when the people burst out of their sealed-up tombs of occupation (Matt. 27:52,65). This is the new resurrection, a resurrection against the whole order of things which have killed or held people captive. This understanding of resurrection cannot be compromised, otherwise "justice community" is not possible. Therefore appeasement and reconciliation are not to be easily equated. Appeasement means losing the creative power of the gospel, whereas reconciliation is based on struggle and suffering, justice, and even conflict. This is how we see the creative power of prayer which is behind the theme of this conference, "Your will be done (on earth)".

5. Creative power is grounded in the brokenness of the crucifixion and the transformation of death to fullness of life. The eucharist, in which the central affirmations of Christian faith are celebrated, provides a constant

renewal of creative power for the church. The eucharist sustains people in their resistance and struggle against massive forces of injustice: security forces, low-intensity conflict and brutal oppression/repression. The attempts to crush the aspirations of the people cannot withstand creative power; this was particularly evident in the stories of Central America, Mountainous Karabagh, Namibia, South Africa and Palestine.

Creative power supports and sustains the building of community for justice. Truth-telling, communication, information-sharing, trust-building, training, telling the stories of the people, analysis and planning — all contribute to our understanding of how creative power sustains people in struggle.

6. The rising up of the people against injustice is the creative power of God for the people and for the whole world. Popular uprisings sustained by creative power, grounded in brokenness and hope and propelled by community-building, will transform the acts of the people into the justice God wills.

This suffering and struggle finds expression in non-violent direct actions, armed struggles where all means of non-violent resistance have been tried and crushed, or other means of confrontation, as the context requires.

The people celebrate, organize and share power in the midst of even the most violent attacks upon them. Creative power overcomes the brutality of death squads, detention centres, pacification programmes, forced relocations, and other means used to break the spirit of the people.

The rising up of the people, the suffering and struggle, the participation and celebration, all manifest the creative power that sustains new community for justice. The acts of the people become God's mission for justice through creative power.

7. The churches are invited then to recognize the creative power of God at work in the suffering and struggles of people's organizations. They are invited to recognize the energizing power of the Holy Spirit in the awakening, mobilization and resistance of people against the forces that diminish life. And they are invited to participate in these struggles as a missionary task to which they are called.

II. The power of resistance as a form of witness

8. *God became flesh in Jesus Christ and lived among the impoverished, participating in their suffering and struggle in order that all might have fullness of life.* As Jesus was sent, so he sent out the disciples to share the same suffering and to participate in the same struggles, bearing witness to

God's will to give life to all through Jesus Christ in the power of the Holy Spirit. As Jesus bore the woundprints because he faithfully dared to resist the powers of evil, so his followers are invited to resist these powers. The Holy Spirit is the comforter and animator for those who resist the forces of evil (Mark 13:9-11).

9. It is faith in God that has sustained people in resistance over the centuries so that they "conquered kingdoms, enforced justice, received promises, stopped the mouths of lions, quenched raging fire, escaped the edge of the sword, won strength out of weakness, became mighty in war, put foreign armies to flight. Women received their dead by resurrection. Some were tortured, refusing to accept release, that they might rise again to a better life. Others suffered mocking and scourging, and even chains and imprisonment. They were stoned, they were sawn in two, they were killed with the sword; they went about in skins of sheep and goats, destitute, afflicted, ill-treated — of whom the world was not worthy — wandering over deserts and mountains, and in dens and caves of the earth" (Heb. 11:33-38).

10. Resistance is an attitude of vigilance in the defence of life, so that the purpose of the God of life may be upheld — a combat to restore life sapped by distress, sickness, injustice and death.

Resistance becomes creative power when a community is formed and is actively engaged in struggle against powers of evil. Resistance is the refusal to accept the vision of society imposed by the oppressor; it is the envisioning of an alternative society, with equality, justice and love.

11. The exigencies of the situations against which resistance is directed determine the forms that resistance takes. Resistance can be expressed through forms such as picketing, hunger strikes, marches and demonstrations, sit-ins, strikes, songs, literature, art, boycotts, written protests, prayer vigils, etc.

The choice to resist and to effect change in unjust situations entails suffering. Christ's way demands sacrifices of us, for in his way confrontation and suffering are inevitable in the struggle against oppression and for social, economic and political justice. It requires great courage and abiding faith in God and God's people to risk this suffering.

Active resistance makes people aware of their dignity, and empowers communities. Even a small act of resistance can be the beginning of power and formation of community.

The church should articulate in words and participate in the struggle and suffering of those working for justice through different forms of resistance. It should cease justifying unjust structures and change its attitudes and structures to side with the poor, joining with them in resisting the powers of injustice, and helping develop a spirituality that comes from action locally and globally towards transforming this world.

12. People in different countries struggling and suffering under various forms of oppression are witnessing to the life-affirming mission of God by resisting the forces of oppression in many ways:

Militarism poses a great threat to the freedom and dignity of people around the world. It is a threat to life itself. As such the church is called to mobilize people in order to resist militarism through forms that are suitable in local, national and international situations — raising awareness, lobbying, and creating pressure groups.

Economic injustice at the global level has forced hundreds of millions of people in Latin America, Africa, Asia and the Pacific (and increasingly the north) into the external debt trap, providing no hope for a better life. Although, seemingly, borrowing is to improve life in these countries, it has the effect of impoverishing them by draining their resources. It augments the unjust social order, panders to the wants of the wealthy, and condemns the poor to perpetual servitude. When the people resist this, it often leads to violence and death — as in Venezuela this year.

Racism in all our countries is the manifestation of sin which divides and oppresses people on the basis of race and therefore has to be fought and resisted. It is the continuing experience of African Americans after two centuries and of immigrant groups in Western Europe. But it is the resistance of the oppressed people of South Africa which has again brought this evil to international attention. We urge the member churches to actively resist racism wherever it exists and to support the call of the World Council of Churches for comprehensive sanctions against South Africa.

The participants also discussed the exploitation by the affluent countries of poor countries through *transnational corporations* that spell danger and death to people. The Bhopal gas leak disaster of 1984, which left thousands dead and tens of thousands maimed and after four years still seeking justice, exemplifies the power of transnational corporations to escape liability.

13. Much time in group discussion was also given to several pressing national situations.

The people of *Namibia* have resisted colonization by the apartheid regime for seventy years. Their struggle for self-determination is now coming to a head. Churches, locally and internationally, need to exercise vigilance, lest the process be sabotaged even at this stage by the strategies of the South African government and others to maintain control.

After half a century of dispossession and oppression, the *Palestinians* have embarked on the intifada, and both claim and proclaim their right to self-determination. The independent state of Palestine has been recognized by 114 nations and a number of critical Jewish communities around the world.

In *Lebanon*, the very existence of the community is threatened by regional conflicts and international interests, through a war imposed on the people of that country. Communities are divided, and a prolonged war that brings suffering and misery shows no signs of abating.

Testimonies of effective resistance were heard also from Hong Kong, Mountainous Karabagh, Sri Lanka, South Korea, and other countries where situations of suffering in different forms exist. Participants expressed concern and solidarity with them in their resistance.

III. The power of culture and community

14. Culture and community have the power to transform suffering into struggle. *The Holy Spirit is sent to renew all our communities, convicting of sin, righteousness and judgment, so that our cultures may be transformed and people empowered to build just and caring communities.* It is the Holy Spirit who empowers people as they seek for justice, freedom and peace. It is the Spirit of God that gives life to all human communities.

15. Created in God's image, human beings are each born into a community — that is, a group of people in a particular place who need each other to define their identity, and who are bound to each other by a common language, common history, common sufferings and struggles, and common aspirations towards life in abundance. Such community may be a local human community or a community with a specific focus of concern.

Each community has a culture — by which is meant the totality of what constitutes its life, all that is essential for relationships among its members, and its relationships with God and with the natural environment. It is in relation to the community that people define their identity. Community and culture are inter-related as body and soul. The cultural dynamic is manifested in the daily life of the community and in each of its members.

While culture and community unite people, they may be absolutized and their power misused to exclude and oppress other people. This is true especially in situations where minorities have migrated to a new location, and this mechanism of exclusion acts in the majority community to discriminate against, exploit or oppress them. This is true also in the caste system in India. At the same time, this exclusion acts to reinforce the sense of community which the minority already experience among themselves. It is their own community and culture which empower them to struggle in their new environment. It is possible, though, for two or more cultures to live together in mutual respect and with justice and peace.

16. Cross-cultural evangelization has often entailed the imposition of cultural norms on the evangelized, besides bringing the good news of salvation. In some situations it is an ideological distortion of the gospel that has been imposed. In other places evangelization has been a means of breaking cultures. Precisely because of this, some communities have resisted the gospel. Other communities have received the gospel, and their cultures have been renewed and strengthened by the dynamic of the Holy Spirit working in them. The gospel has been experienced as a liberating force, breaking the power of oppressive aspects of culture. Culture as such does not constitute an absolute value — it has positive and negative aspects.

17. When a culture inspires its members to develop more fully their human potential, it becomes a God-given instrument for their spiritual growth, and should be affirmed by the churches. When such cultures and their communities are disrupted by changes imposed on them, violently attacked or oppressed — as in the case of the indigenous peoples of the Americas, Asia, Australia and Aotearoa/New Zealand, and in the case of oppressed peoples in Mauritania, Sudan, Eritrea and New Caledonia, among others; when tribal peoples, without political or economic power, are subject to assimilationist policies and the loss of their ancestral lands; when women are deprived of their basic human rights as equal citizens in any society; when the disabled are ignored or oppressed — in all of these situations, the churches must join with those who suffer and struggle.

18. While culture can have positive and negative aspects, community is essential for fullness of life. God in Trinity is a community of divine persons. Human beings are called to constitute life in the likeness of God, bound to one another in complete love. The unity/community which is God, established and maintained by love (agape), constitutes the plan for humanity. No individual person can constitute God's likeness alone. Just and loving interpersonal relationships are fundamental, for human life can reflect God's Trinitarian life — God's likeness — only in community,

obedient to the will of God. And God's will is justice, the fullness of life for all God's children, of every nation, race and gender.

19. For indigenous tribal peoples, the land of their birth, their ancestors, their history and their heritage is part of their personal and community identity, part of themselves. It is their existence, their life. They neither "possess" nor live on the land, but consider themselves an inseparable part of the land, enjoying the God-created beauty, the essential goodness of their unique part of the universe. The earth is the Lord's, and people receive it with joy and gratitude. Their sacred stories identify them with the holy places and events which occurred in the land the Creator has given them. To be deprived by violence or oppression of a people's ancestral land is to be deprived of identity, freedom, self-determination and the fullness of life. Yet this is the broken status of millions of human beings — of indigenous tribal peoples around the world and of other peoples dispossessed of their lands.

20. Most Christians have been kept ignorant of or remain indifferent to this situation. The churches need to speak with a prophetic voice, calling to the attention of all Christians and people of good will of all nations the plight of the dispossessed. In the Middle East great injustice has been done in the name of God, by misusing the holy scriptures as a justification for supporting Israel and its violent suppression of the human rights of Palestinians. The modern idol of "national security" results in the destruction or oppression of hundreds of Arab communities and thousands of families and individuals; this has been made possible by massive economic and military aid to Israel. The Israeli government since 1968 has attempted to force the indigenous people of Palestine to either submit to Israeli rule or leave their homeland.

Concluding invitation

21. Prefiguring the coming redemption of all peoples through Jesus Christ, God called the marginalized people in Canaan to resist the political and religious injustices of their day. As they were empowered by the announcement that God had declared them, the most defenceless, to be in the right, and were invited to use their creative power to build a just society in accordance with the will of God, so the churches are invited to reread the scriptures and to recognize that God is actively taking sides in history in order that suffering and struggling people in all places may have fullness of life. The churches are required to bear witness to the will of God that those who face suffering and death daily should have life, and to join with them in their struggle.

22. As the eternal word was incarnated not at the centre of power but among those who were scattered like sheep that have no shepherd, so the churches are invited to discover their mission incarnated among the suffering and struggling, resisting the powers of evil and, in the manner of Christ, bearing witness among them to the will of God to pull down the mighty from their thrones but exalt those of low degree, to set free those who are oppressed, and to invite the hungry and homeless to the feast.

23. As the Holy Spirit constituted communities among the poor and alienated, the widows and slaves around the Mediterranean world of the first century; as the Spirit has empowered suffering people over the centuries through faith to conquer kingdoms, enforce justice, receive promises,... win strength out of weakness, resist torture, refusing to accept release that they might rise again to a better life; as the Spirit empowers communities of suffering and struggling people today to use their creative power to resist racism, dispossession, imposed indebtedness, homelessness, exploitation and political oppression — so the churches are invited to recognize the wind and fire of the presence of the Spirit wherever the suffering cry out, and by participating in their struggles in the way of Christ, to become part of the good news for them, bearing witness that God wills for them and for all people, life in its fullness.

ACTS IN FAITHFULNESS

1. Palestine

24. We heard testimonies from Palestinian participants that the current struggle — the intifada — of the people is an authentic manifestation of creative power, the power of community and culture, and the power of resistance as a form of witness. This was also confirmed by a team visit to Palestine which witnessed the situation firsthand. The intifada is a liberation struggle which is transforming the Palestinians from victims to controllers and builders of their own destiny. This process has unified all sectors of the community, creatively empowering the people to grow in resolve daily as they resist the oppression and brutalities of one of the most sophisticated armies in the world.

a) *We recognize the creative power at work in the intifada, which has led the Palestinians to embark on a peace journey toward a two-state solution. Since we already accept the state of Israel as a reality, our focus is on the struggle for the state of Palestine.*

b) *We commit ourselves to full support of the struggle of the Palesti-*
nians, an end to their repression, an end to the occupation of their
land, the right of return, the right to self-determination, and the
establishment of an independent sovereign Palestinian state on Pales-
tinian soil. We call for the withdrawal of all Israeli forces from the
occupied territories in Palestine, Syria and Lebanon. In the interim,
we call for an end to military brutality and all repression, the
reopening of all educational institutions, and the release of all
political prisoners, especially children and youth.
c) *We differentiate between the state of Israel and Zionism on the one*
hand, and Jews and Judaism on the other. We therefore call on the
churches to commit themselves to educating their constituencies about
the reality of the situation through accurate information and exposure
visits to Palestine.
d) *We request that churches in the USA demand of their government that*
all forms of military and economic aid to the state of Israel be
withheld until the legitimate rights of the Palestinians are achieved.
e) *We request the WCC Commission of the Churches on International*
Affairs (CCIA) and the Commission on Inter-Church Aid, Refugee
and World Service's Middle East desk, in collaboration with the
Palestinian churches, to monitor progress on the above, and urge
WCC member churches to do the same; and we request them to share
information every three months concerning the progress made by the
churches in implementing the above.

2. Namibia

25. The testimonies from Namibians revealed deep fears that the
resistance of the people under the leadership of SWAPO, which resulted
in the implementation of the United Nations' Resolution 435 and a
monitored transition to independence and self-determination, is being
seriously threatened by the South African apartheid regime. We heard
with concern of continued maiming and killing of men, women and
children; lack of protective guarantees for the release of political prisoners; delays in the return of exiles and refugees, and fears for their safety;
and the inability of the small United Nations Transition Assistance Group
(UNTAG) force to monitor free and fair elections in the face of South
Africa's determination to maintain economic, military and political control of the whole of the Southern African region.

At this crucial stage, we commit ourselves to draw to international
attention the fact that free and fair elections in Namibia remain in

jeopardy unless and until South Africa's role in Namibia is minimized and eventually eliminated.

a) *We urge the WCC, in collaboration with the Council of Churches of Namibia and its member churches, to campaign for the withdrawal of the South African Defence Force and the demobilization of the South West Africa Territorial Force, and to coordinate and organize groups of prominent persons to visit Namibia in order to monitor the transition process.*

b) *We urge the WCC to request the United Nations to increase the UNTAG forces in Namibia during the period of transition to state-hood.*

c) *We commit ourselves to provide spiritual, moral, material and political support for programmes of repatriation, reconstruction and resettlement.*

d) *We request that this action be coordinated by the WCC Programme to Combat Racism (PCR), in collaboration with CCIA, the Commission on World Mission and Evangelism's Urban Rural Mission office (CWME/URM), Women in Church and Society, the Lutheran World Federation, and the All Africa Conference of Churches.*

3. Indigenous peoples: land and self-determination

26. Indigenous peoples' identity is linked to and dependent upon their relation to their ancestral lands and historical and sacred sites. The denial of their right to self-determination leads to the desecration of these lands and thus the catastrophic destruction of their environment, their liveli-hood and their spirituality.

The tragic plight of indigenous peoples of the Americas, Mauritania and Australia, and the struggles for self-determination and identity in New Caledonia and elsewhere in the world, call for justice and recognition — because the mission of God, we believe, is the mission of God in justice.

a) We commit ourselves and call on the churches and mission organiza-tions to recognize and respect indigenous cultures and help indigenous peoples to develop, organize and realize their full creative potential, and to support their claims for land and self-determination.

b) We commit ourselves to improve international and ecumenical com-munication networks, in order to help Christians make the link between indigenous people's land rights and fundamental ecological issues around the world, especially those related to nuclear testing, dumping of chemical and nuclear wastes, deforestation, dam con-struction and industrial pollution.

c) We request that PCR coordinate and monitor this action, in collaboration with CCIA, CWME-URM and indigenous peoples' movements.

4. Economic justice

27. Countries in the third world are increasingly plagued by the so-called external debt problem. They are groaning under the weight of loans that have been imposed on them during the last thirty years by the international monetary system, monitored by the rich countries. We consider this to be unjust in its origin, because it responds basically to the needs of the affluent societies for resources; it is immoral — and unpayable — because it continues to exploit the third-world countries as a new channel for the transfer of capital to the first world; and it is anti-evangelical because it subjugates and impoverishes entire countries, increasingly enriching those countries that are already rich.

a) *We request the WCC and its member churches to pressure organizations such as the International Monetary Fund and the World Bank, the governments of first-world countries and affluent classes to stop this cruel extraction of capital from developing countries.*

b) *We urge and commit ourselves to the establishment of a data bank through which detailed information can be disseminated to all concerned for action; such information should be translated into many languages, and a popular study guide which can be easily understood should be prepared.*

c) *We request the WCC and its member churches to facilitate a coalition with representatives of other religions in the third world to work together on this issue.*

d) *We request that this action be coordinated by the WCC Commission on the Churches' Participation in Development (CCPD), in collaboration with CCIA and CWME-URM, and that support and advice be sought from the churches and councils of churches in the third world.*

5. Lebanon

28. Mission in Christ's way integrates communities and resists all sinful attempts to exploit, destroy and break communities for selfish ends.

We have heard the testimonies of brothers and sisters from Lebanon, which is a victim of regional conflicts and the intervention of outside powers in the area. A war has been imposed on the people, exploiting religious affiliations for geopolitical goals and intentions. Although all communities in Lebanon insist on their will to co-exist and live in peace, the powers concerned will not allow Lebanon to exist as an independent state with a right to self-determination and sovereignty. Destruction and death are daily realities, affecting the communities in a drastic way. The attempt to break up the community and the country is being resisted through acts of love and understanding, as witness to God's concern for unity and integration.

We condemn and we call on the churches to condemn the actions of the exploitative forces that are responsible for the violence in Lebanon, threatening its territorial integrity and existence as an independent country, and offer solidarity with the suffering people.

a) We request the WCC and its member churches, in association with other like-minded organizations, to work out a programme of pressure on the super-powers and the United Nations Security Council to safeguard and ensure the territorial integrity and existence of Lebanon in its internationally recognized boundaries, and to support its independence.

b) We request that CCIA, in collaboration with CWME and the Middle East Council of Churches, work out and monitor a programme to disseminate to WCC member churches and other organizations accurate information on Lebanon and the witness of the churches in that country, and elicit expressions of solidarity.

6. The role of US churches

29. During this conference, representatives from many countries, including South Africa, Namibia, Palestine, Latin America, the Philippines and South Korea, together with African Americans and "border refugees", spoke of the suffering and struggle in their lands. They also reported on the dominating role played by some US institutions in their countries. This domination includes the extraction of their wealth, military intervention, attempts at political hegemony, and the creation of dependence. These acts are often carried out with the tacit complicity of churches, congregations and para-church organizations and sects in the USA, and are rationalized and justified through an ideology of domination conveyed through some US church programmes on evangelism and aid.

We believe that US churches represented at this conference are committed to the ecumenical sharing of resources and desire a deeper bond with others who struggle for justice in the USA and abroad. However, some US churches, para-church organizations and sects continue to support, both in the USA and internationally, ideologies and practices of domination through evangelism and aid programmes that promote and protect US interests. We call for an end to such practices and commit ourselves to expose them.

The struggle for justice in the USA is critical to many struggles for justice in other countries. Yet we know that ecumenical and denominational programmes for economic and social justice do not receive the necessary resources. We call for a new ecumenical fund equivalent to ten percent of the capital of the US churches to support programmes of urban, rural and women's struggles and for the critical struggles against racism. This fund would be administered by the National Council of the Churches of Christ in the USA in cooperation with its member denominations and their congregations.

* * *

The following text was presented to the final conference plenary on 31 May as an intervention from the floor and not as part of a report from any one of the sections. It received an affirmative indication from the great majority of voting delegates in response to the same question from the moderator used regarding the previous Acts in Faithfulness: "Does this speak for you?"

Armenia

This conference requests that the member churches of the World Council of Churches ask their respective governments to put pressure on Turkish authorities to admit the reality of the Armenian genocide.

We ask that the WCC appoint a group to visit the sacred sites of occupied Armenia, currently under Turkish occupation.

During the last seventy-five years more than two thousand churches and monasteries have been destroyed. We demand that the Turkish government commence the restoration and reconstruction of churches and monasteries.

We demand the freedom of occupied Armenia in Turkey and the right of the Armenian people of the diaspora to return to their homeland.

Next year is the seventy-fifth anniversary of the Armenian genocide. We ask that special attention (recognition) be given to this important anniversary at the Canberra assembly of the WCC, 1991.

Section III: The Earth is the Lord's

Preamble

1. We affirm that the whole creation belongs to the Triune God — every inhabited part of the earth (territory) and every piece of earth (land) is, and remains, God's. God has given the earth to the whole human family "to till it and keep it" (Gen. 2:15).

2. God calls us:
— to exercise our stewardship with justice;
— to maintain the integrity of creation;
— to use and share the earth's limited resources; and
— to sustain and fulfill the lives of all.

3. The affirmation of God's ownership of the earth challenges concepts and practices of ownership such as:

a) exploiting nature;
b) viewing land solely as a commodity;
c) claiming exclusive national ownership of respective parts of the earth; and
d) devising and maintaining cultural factors to protect privileges.

4. The affirmation of God's ownership of the earth can liberate us from the captivity of accumulating private property to the freedom of sharing, and challenge the presumption that humankind has the right to destroy the earth in the name of progress or national security. We are called to participate in God's reconciling work "for the fullness of time, to unite all things in him" (Eph. 1:9b-10a).

I. Stewards of God's creation

5. "The earth is the Lord's and the fullness thereof" (Ps. 24:1). If we confirm anew this confession today, the life and mission of our churches will be broadened and renewed. Psalm 24 declares that the ultimate authority over the earth is not kings and rulers, but rather Yahweh, the Lord, the liberator from Egyptian slavery. The Lord is the owner of the land. That land is the promised land, and remains promised land even after the tribes settled there — *terre promise et terre permise* (promised land and permitted land), as it has been called. The one who liberated and gave the land is revealed as Yahweh: "I will be as I will be." Yahweh will be there, even in times when the people do not like Yahweh's presence.

6. The psalm says that the Creator "founded [the earth] upon the seas" (Ps. 24:2), meaning "chaos". This is remarkable: in the midst of chaos which threatens life, the Lord secures a place for humanity. The foundations of creation are established and rooted in justice, as known from the experience of the Exodus. The psalm shows the close relationship between creation and covenant, and emphasizes the unbreakable connection between justice and the integrity of creation.

7. Therefore this confession becomes a prophetic critique for later kings and rulers. King Ahab, for example, and many of his successors, acted as if the earth were their own (1 Kings 21). To them and to us, this psalm says: remember David, who knew in faithfulness that "the earth is the Lord's". How have we acted; what do we see?

8. Reports from east and west and north and south indicate the prevalence of the abuse of creation. For example, an ecumenical team visited the district of Cottbus, near the German Democratic Republic's border with Poland. Here brown coal is obtained by means of strip-mining — with serious consequences for both humanity and the environment. Rural people who lived here for generations are today being forced to move in order to make room for excavation machines, which dig to a depth of thirty to one hundred metres. The ground on which people have lived is gradually being taken away.

The team reported on how the local church understands its mission in this situation. It gives guidance to the villagers in their process of mourning and taking leave, and the local minister acts as a liaison officer with the authorities. In the long term, a theological reflection on the stewardship of creation, the care of both humanity and nature and the use of energy, is being developed. Here the mission of the church is understood as giving guidance in a time of anxiety and seeking a place for people in their new situation. The theme: finding new life.

9. The same team reported on the pollution of rivers, seas, air and land in the Netherlands. This pollution is caused by the industries of several nations. Both secular and church-related groups are seeking a new lifestyle and developing means of education. Among them are the Franciscans, who combine their educational programme with a deep-rooted spirituality.

Seeing the situation in both countries, the team became convinced that these problems were related to those of many other people in the world whose desires and needs are subordinated to economic and political interests.

10. In our time we see how God's creation has been violated by the way we use the land, sea and space, the impact of modern agriculture and technology, and the massive production of arms. In each of these areas (except arms production) we recognize an ambivalence. On the one hand there is a proper use of the earth's resources, but on the other hand we witness the devastating abuse of God's creation. The reasons for this abuse are rooted in a turning away from the living God, the free reign of human greed, the misuse of power, the presence of fear and ignorance, and deception that hides the truth of creation's suffering.

11. In the face of this reality, we discover our need for repentance as we contemplate the meaning of the prayer, "Your will be done" — for we all, as individuals and as churches, share in the abuse of God's creation.

12. Mission in Christ's way must extend to God's creation. Because the earth is the Lord's, the responsibility of the church towards the earth is a crucial part of the church's mission. This mission brings the gospel of hope to all creation — a hope rooted in the resurrection of Christ. We are reminded that the early and undivided church stressed the deep unity between humanity and the whole of creation. In our church today we should share in prayer for the anxieties of this time. Our celebration of the Lord's Table should affirm God's redeeming love for all creation, and the breaking of the bread together should empower us to share the gifts of the earth with one another. This requires a change of lifestyle as a part of mission in Christ's way.

ACTS IN FAITHFULNESS

13. We have heard the stream of biblical affirmations that tell so powerfully that the earth is the Lord's. We have seen concrete examples of the violations of creation that threaten the foundations of all life. We have discovered how the abuse of creation and the reign of injustice reinforce each other.

14. Therefore, we commit ourselves and call on our churches to bring the power of the gospel and the hope of the resurrection to the sufferings of creation, extending God's active love for all the world. In our life and worship, we call upon the churches:

a) to affirm God's redeeming love for all creation in the celebration of the Lord's Table;

b) to urge its members to share the gifts of the earth with one another as we share in the breaking of the bread;

c) to promote a lifestyle that reflects our belief in the integrity of creation as part of our mission in Christ's way; and

d) to review their understanding and involvement in ongoing mission programmes in the light of the affirmation that "the earth is the Lord's".

15. We urge the churches to strengthen their cooperation with other organizations and groups who share a common commitment to the integrity of creation, and to strengthen their support of United Nations' programmes for the integrity of creation.

16. We commit ourselves and urge our churches to enter into the concrete challenge of defending the integrity of creation as a key dimension of mission in Christ's way. Specifically, this includes efforts to reverse the "greenhouse effect", to remedy the destruction of strip-mining, to halt the production and dumping of toxic wastes, to ban the hunting of endangered species, and to combat the pollution of the seas. In these measures we can draw strength from the international and ecumenical nature of our churches. Thus, we encourage the churches to enter pastorally into the suffering of people experiencing the effects of these calamities, and to enter prophetically into encounters with government and corporate authorities to courageously protect God's creation.

17. We see how children are affected and destroyed mentally and physically by the abuse of creation. By destroying them we destroy the best part of creation. How can the world be sustained if its future stewards are affected and destroyed before they can take over their biblical responsibility (cf. Luke 18:15-17)? We therefore call upon the churches to recognize our relationship to the world's children, whose future will depend upon our commitment now to safeguard the life of the creation.

18. To implement and evaluate these acts of faithfulness, we ask that the Commission on World Mission and Evangelism undertake a process of assisting the WCC member churches to re-evaluate their understanding of mission in the light of the affirmation that "the earth is the Lord's", and that a plan for gathering these concerns and carrying out these acts in faithfulness be prepared for the Canberra assembly of the WCC, 1991.

II. Towards a just sharing of the land

a) Realities

19. We have heard reports from different regions and communities about land-related problems in Brazil, South Korea, the Philippines and Taiwan, and have been informed about struggles of indigenous peoples for self-determination, especially in (but not limited to) the following

land-based communities: Australia, Aotearoa/New Zealand, indigenous nations of North and South America, the Pacific Islands, Palestine, the Middle East, South Africa and Southern Africa.

20. We have seen that around the world growing numbers of indigenous, poor *campesino*, homeless and disenfranchised peoples are being denied access to the land, while control over land is increasingly concentrated in the hands of a rich and powerful few.

We have seen that this has, and continues to, come about as a direct result of political and economic colonization, cultural and physical genocide of indigenous peoples, resource exploitation by transnational corporations, and repressive government measures on local, national and international levels, thus perpetuating unjust social structures.

And we have seen that the denial of land rights and access to the land is directly responsible for the destruction of indigenous nations and cultures, for a multitude of social problems causing great human suffering, and for the contamination and destruction of our sacred, God-given creation (Mother Earth).

b) Reflections

21. Reflecting on these historical and contextual realities and their implications, we have reached a common understanding and conviction that the injustices related to the land issue are derived from the fact that land ownership is in the hands of a few, whereas most people are deprived of it — the indigenous people, peasants, landless labourers, family farmers. Land must be liberated from its captivity, so that it can be shared and distributed justly.

We have focused on the following crucial problem areas for further reflection: (a) indigenous people's land rights; (b) land ownership and distribution; (c) land use and production; and (d) conscientization, organization and spirituality in movements of the landless people.

c) Biblical message: land is life

22. According to the biblical witness, the land ultimately belongs to God. In the jubilee tradition the land must rest periodically and be returned to its former stewards, therefore it cannot become a commodity. "The land shall not be sold in perpetuity, for the land is mine; for you are strangers and sojourners with me" (Lev. 25:23).

23. Land has been given to the human race (Ps. 115:16) for responsible use in solidarity with the oppressed and homeless. "The stranger who sojourns with you shall be to you as the native among you, and you shall

love him as yourself; for you were strangers in the land of Egypt: I am the Lord your God" (Lev. 19:34).

24. When the powerful few disobey God's will, God raises prophets who oppose them. "Woe to those who devise wickedness and work evil upon their beds! When the morning dawns, they perform it, because it is in the power of their hand. They covet fields, and seize them; and houses, and take them away; they oppress a man and his house, a man and his inheritance. Therefore thus says the Lord: Behold, against this family I am devising evil, from which you cannot remove your necks; and you shall not walk haughtily, for it will be an evil time" (Mic. 2:1-3; cf. Deut. 27:17).

25. The community of faith is secure in the hope that the poor and meek will be returned to the land. "But the meek shall possess the land, and delight themselves in abundant prosperity" (Ps. 37:11; cf. Matt. 5:5).

26. In the early church as well as today, the believers, gathered into a sharing community, bear testimony to the will of God. "There was not a needy person among them, for as many as were possessors of lands or houses sold them...; and distribution was made to each as any had need" (Acts 4:34-35).

27. It is affirmed that the fruits of the land should not be unfairly distributed: "It is the hard-working farmer who ought to have the first share of the crops" (2 Tim. 2:6).

28. Finally, the God who establishes the reign of justice for the marginalized, is praised: "[the Lord] who keeps faith for ever; who executes justice for the oppressed; who gives food to the hungry. The Lord sets the prisoners free" (Ps. 146:6b-7; cf. Luke 1:52-53).

29. Therefore, if God stands on the side of the poor (Ps. 109:31), who can overcome them (cf. Rom. 8:31-33)?

30. As Christians we are learning that the landless, the uprooted and those who have to shelter among the rocks (cf. Job 24:4-8) experience the loving presence of God, and follow God's will in communities of mutual support. For example:

— Landless farmers in Brazil organize their struggle for land through *acampamentos* (encampments), in which the cross is always at the centre.

— North American indigenous peoples seek not ownership of the land but jurisdiction as caretakers, thus affirming the biblical principle of not selling the land.

31. As Christians concerned with the will of God in relation to land, we must direct our church and organizational resources to support the

resistance and networking of people struggling to defend or to win back the land to which they have rights.

32. We reaffirm the Melbourne report:

> The poor are already in mission to change their own situation. What is required from the churches is a missionary movement that supports what they have already begun, and that focuses on building evangelizing and witnessing communities of the poor that will discover and live out expressions of faith among the masses of the poor and oppressed.
>
> The churches will have to surrender their attitudes of benevolence and charity by which they have condescended to the poor; in many cases this will mean a radical change in the institutional life of the missionary movement. The churches must be ready to listen to the poor, to hear the gospel from the poor, to learn about the ways in which they have helped to make them poor.[4]

ACTS IN FAITHFULNESS

33. As evidenced by the previously mentioned biblical teaching about the just sharing of land as the will of God, we affirm that mission means to support the struggle for a "just sharing of land" in concrete actions.

34. Regarding *indigenous people's land rights*, we call upon the WCC and its member churches:

a) to return church lands taken from indigenous peoples and to divest church assets in corporations exploiting indigenous lands;

b) to be active in repealing and opposing the enforcement of colonial and artificial borders and repressive measures that disenfranchise indigenous peoples and dispossess them of their lands, waters and ways of life; and to offer concrete support to indigenous communities, nations and organizations engaged in struggles to obtain self-determination and jurisdiction over their ancestral lands;

c) in relation to the indigenous peoples of North America: to support the struggle of the people of Havasupai in the Grand Canyon/Red Butte area in Arizona as they work to protect their ancestral homelands against rape and exploitation by uranium mining; to support the struggle of Alaska's indigenous peoples to dismantle the Alaska Native Claims Settlement Act (PL 92-203) and to return the jurisdiction in Alaska to the indigenous traditional governments; and to support the struggle to resist forced relocation of the Navajo (Dineh) and Hopi peoples of the Big Mountain area of the Four Corners;

---

[4] *Your Kingdom Come*, report of the Melbourne world conference on mission and evangelism, 1980, p.177.

d) to support the Palestinians' right to self-determination and to a homeland;

e) to directly participate in the struggle to dismantle the system of apartheid in South Africa and to support the right of the South African people to self-determination;

f) to support the struggle for indigenous land rights in Australia and to call for the absolute protection of indigenous sacred sites from desecration by corporate and government entities;

g) to support the Brazilian indigenous people, particularly the Yanomani Indians in the Amazon, in their struggle against transnational corporations that deprive the people of land rights and destroy the forest;

h) to give attention to the suffering and struggle of indigenous peoples seeking self-determination in the Pacific, particularly in New Caledonia, Tahiti, Hawaii, Palau and the Marshall Islands;

i) to actively oppose the "celebration" in 1992 of Columbus and five hundred years of colonization, and to support the 1992 commemoration of five hundred years of resistance by the indigenous peoples of North, Central and South America; and

j) to take up the issue of indigenous peoples and their struggles for self-determination and survival as a standing programme within the WCC structures, and to create a Commission thereon; this to be considered and brought to the Canberra Assembly of the WCC, 1991, for implementation.

35. Regarding *land ownership and distribution*, we call upon the WCC and its member churches:

a) to stand in solidarity with landless people in their struggles, organizations and movements to occupy land for their sustenance and survival; and

b) to engage in a global strategy for a genuine land reform programme controlled by its beneficiaries, beginning with the sharing of church lands with the landless and homeless.

36. Regarding *land use and production*, we call upon the WCC and its member churches:

a) to confront the technological imperialism of national and transnational corporations in their exploitation of lands, displacement of small farmers, contamination of the environment, and exploitation of land labourers living under inhuman conditions;

b) to call governments owning grain reserves to accountability for a just sharing of food;

c) to formulate conditions and criteria for an ecological economy that serves sisters and brothers in need and not the greed of a few living in abundance, based on the spirit of justice, peace and the integrity of creation; and

d) to call Christians particularly in the third world and in industrialized nations to commit themselves to the just use of land, on the basis of a renewed theological understanding of the covenantal partnership between God, God's people and and communities in struggle.

37. Regarding *conscientization, organization and spirituality in movements of landless people,* we call upon the WCC and its member churches:

a) to promote an information exchange to make churches and Christians conscious of these problems as being their own, in cooperation with related ecumenical church bodies, people's organizations and mass media at local, national, regional and global levels;

b) to strongly support church bodies and people's organizations struggling for land rights and just distribution of land resources;

c) to develop a rich biblical spirituality that inspires, strengthens and sustains the people's struggle for overcoming the causes of unjust sharing of land; and

d) to promote regional and global sharing of experiences among leaders and grassroots members of small farmers' organizations and landless peasants' movements in their struggle for land and survival, such as in the Philippines and Brazil.

III. Called to be peacemakers

38. Refugee movements in many parts of the world are no longer "an isolated deviation from the norm" but have "become a characteristic of contemporary world politics" (WCC Central Committee, 1981). As such they are a result of the lack of justice and peace in the present world, and therefore challenge the churches to a particular peace-making ministry with regard to this issue.

39. We heard reports and experiences from many different situations in which refugees and migrants had to leave their countries. An ecumenical team report about the situation of Mozambican refugees in Swaziland and Zimbabwe was heard, as well as reports about modern forms of slave and "flesh" trade.

We heard about increasingly restrictive immigration policies, including detention, deportation and violation of human rights in Western Europe and North America, and learned that many individual Christians and congregations in the receiving countries are not sufficiently aware of the many refugees nor of the root causes of refugee movements. As a result, the responsibility for refugees is usually left in the hands of special agencies and other action groups.

40. In the light of the discussion, we commend to churches, mission boards and individual Christians the following steps of a peace-making mission:

a) That Christians and churches have a "Samaritan mission" (cf. Luke 10:25-37), in which we would:

— learn to *see* the victims and then offer whatever material aid is needed by them;

— provide protection for them; and

— assume a ministry of advocacy for them.

b) That Christians have a "prophetic mission" in regard to refugees and migrants, to:

— diagnose the root causes, which include militarism, the struggle of the super-powers for influence, civil wars, transnational corporations, poverty, land issues, the destruction of nature, the abuse of religion, racism, oppression, economic pressures, etc. — all of which are expressions of personal and structural sin reflecting our lack of commitment to the mission of Christ;

— disclose the unjust political and economic structures and our own involvement in them as churches, as individual Christians and as responsible citizens, and repent for our continued involvement;

— build up lobbies for and with refugees and migrants in the receiving countries, and demand appropriate actions against the root causes; and

— denounce militarism as a threat to the peace and integrity of creation.

c) That, together with the "vision of the city to come" (cf. Rev. 21), we should "migrate" towards that city. Churches and Christians are called to develop ways for "migrating" together with the strangers in their midst. Here we are to consider obedience to God's own mission:

— The existence of these people is God's challenge to us; they are God's messengers to us.

— Therefore we must listen to what they have to tell us; they in turn need to listen to our stories and to dialogue on equal terms.

— We must be aware that refugees are people who have suffered the loss of their identity and therefore need a kind of healing ministry.

— Let us exchange our cultural values with them.

— Let us move together towards that "city of peace". We are aware, however, that on our way there are stumbling blocks such as nationalism and ideology, where we put ourselves first instead of God. We should pray and work for a societal order and for legislation that is based on the conviction that "the earth is the Lord's", and that strangers and citizens must co-exist as guests on God's earth and at God's table. We should be ready to die for the sake of justice and peace.

— Let us create a situation of co-existence in which all partners can share their faith on equal terms, and let us renounce all worldly power in this dialogue.

ACTS IN FAITHFULNESS

41. We have heard both from earlier WCC affirmations, and more recently from members of the team which visited refugee camps in Zimbabwe and Swaziland, of the enormity of the refugee problem and of the human suffering resulting from it.

42. We affirm that mission starts with the Triune God who, according to the scriptures, loves (Deut. 10:18) and protects (Ps. 146:9) the strangers, who in Jesus Christ identified with them (Matt. 25:35-43), and who called us to be God's migrant people towards the city to come (Heb. 13:14).

43. We therefore commit ourselves to drawing attention to the individual and collective selfishness and intolerance in human hearts which results in hostility towards strangers, racism, and nationalistic arrogance, and to the insistence of the gospel that change can and should be effected there.

44. We urge the churches to denounce militarism by:

a) pressing for the stoppage of the exportation of arms from their own countries;

b) challenging educational institutions to set up peace education programmes; and

c) calling on all institutions in their own countries to cease the glorification of wars and militarism.

45. We commit ourselves to establishing grassroots consultations and educational programmes on the refugee issue, and to support efforts to achieve empowerment and self-determination, for example, in regard to the people of Palestine and in Southern Africa and Central America.

46. We challenge the churches to identify, address and seek to eliminate the causes of the uprooting of people, and also to establish a new and comprehensive definition of "refugee" on an international level. We furthermore ask the local churches to facilitate and encourage

encounter and dialogue among refugees, migrants and local people, and to give attention in Bible study, preaching and teaching to the fact that issues like flight, migration, homelessness, exile and the search for a continuing city (Heb. 13:14) belong to the most central traditions in the Bible.

47. These efforts should be examined at the Canberra assembly of the WCC, 1991. Further we ask that some victims be invited to that assembly, together with representatives of refugee communities, to enable a just dialogue with the view to formulating a programme for action.

IV. Stewardship of the earth and human cultures

48. Stewardship of the earth in response to God's entrusting the earth to the human family, to share its resources and sustain the life of all, implies the unity of humankind and the goal of a renewed human family as one inclusive community. With the famous affirmation: "There is neither Jew nor Greek, there is neither slave nor free, there is neither male nor female; for you are all one in Christ Jesus" (Gal. 3:28), St Paul emphasizes that in Christ all barriers are broken down — in the sense that racial, religious, social and sexual differences can no longer be the pretext for discrimination and division. Participating in God's mission, the church has not only to *proclaim* that: it has to *live* it.

The divisive effect of the differences within the human family has to do with our cultures. As human creations, cultures reflect both faithful answers to God's will and human sin. Cultures play a crucial role in the identity and survival of ethnic groups. They represent a collective memory through which, by means of customs and codes, languages and arts, regulations and rites, songs and stories, values are preserved and handed down to the next generation. Yet while these elements of a culture provide a basis of belonging together, they often tend to exclude others. Thus God's will for one inclusive human family is violated. There are elements and factors in our cultures which justify social hierarchies and discrimination or which cement oppression. They must be discerned and denounced.

In the discussion we related the question "what cultural factors are at work that justify discrimination?" to different situations represented in the group.

49. On the basis of the report of an ecumenical team visit to South India, we dealt with the implications of the caste system there — that centuries-old hierarchical system which divides the Indian population into

four castes with hundreds of sub-castes. Castes are social levels which are mutually subordinate and exclusive. The worst effect of this hierarchical structure is on the millions of "outcastes" who do not belong to a caste at all and who nowadays call themselves Dalits (broken, downtrodden). Thousands of years ago this system was set up by a group which had political and religious power as an instrument of keeping that power. By introducing the religious criteria of purity over against pollution, those not belonging to the lowest of the four ranks of castes became "untouchables" — perceived as being so polluted that caste people must avoid all contact with them. The Dalits have therefore had to live in settlements separated from the main part of the villages, even today. The religious concept of *karma*, which supposes one's present life to be the result of a previous life, made the members of lower castes and the outcastes accept their fate as unquestionable. The example of the Indian caste system shows that certain religious beliefs as elements of a dominant culture can play a destructive role and must be denounced as such.

50. Koreans in Japan, offspring of war-industry labourers brought to that country during the second world war, live under permanent pressure of the monopoly claim of the dominant national culture. Force was used to suppress their language, their names and their customs. Though for decades they have had to endure fingerprint registration along with other aliens, recently they have begun to resist this demeaning practice. Christians in Japan have committed themselves to support Koreans in that country in their struggle against this oppression; similarly they support the struggle of the Burakumin (the outcastes of Japanese society) for human dignity.

51. In some countries, political ideology does not permit the practice of any religion, as in Albania. The people of such countries need our support in persuading their governments to respect the right to religious freedom.

52. In some Latin American countries — even where people of indigenous cultures such as Quechua, Aymara, Maya, etc., are the majority — indigenous people suffer under the Western cultural arrogance of those who are in power. Their culture is condescendingly called "native culture", indicating that this might be attractive for tourist entertainment but not essential for the integrity of the multicultural nation. Coca, which was used for traditional religious rites and for medicinal, social and cultural purposes, is now being exploited in a multi-billion-dollar business controlled primarily by foreigners. This phenomenon is destroying the earth's ecology (through deforestation and the use of pesticides that destroy the earth's natural life-giving substances); it further

oppresses the indigenous people, and leads to the destruction of countless lives.

53. In Aotearoa/New Zealand, the ecumenical body of churches is committed to develop a bicultural partnership of the Maori (indigenous) and Pakeha (white) communities, and to give integrity to the covenant of the nation, "Te Tiriti o Waitangi" — whereby both partners are given equal value and respect and share equally in decision-making and the resources of the nation. It is necessary to conscientize the dominant Pakeha culture at all levels and to actively support the self-determination of the Maori.

54. Another example of a bicultural (or even multicultural) setting was noted in Britain. There, the growth of black-led churches testifies to the racism inherent in British society. Black people suffer rejection and alienation in church and society. Black-led churches are both a response of black people to the painful rejection and racism within the dominant churches, and a rejection by black Christians of cultural and religious assimilation. Black-led churches have built up their faith communities in which they seek to affirm their equality, participation, identity and cultural values. As autonomous partners they can become a fruitful challenge for the "mainstream" churches towards mutual enrichment.

55. There are certainly countries where none of the examples mentioned above would apply. However, exclusion and subjugation on grounds of sexual difference are practised to at least some extent in almost every country, of which *sati* (immolating the widow at the funeral of the dead husband) — still practised in isolated cases in India — is perhaps the most extreme. While some countries already have legislation to ensure equal opportunities for men and women, it is common knowledge that good legislation alone will not overcome traditional patterns that favour male domination. A whole network of cultural factors handed down through the centuries ensures general acceptance of the supposedly inferior status of female members of a given community. These factors and mechanisms range from "good manners" to habits and customs. Access to means of acquiring knowledge, gaining self-esteem and actively taking part in decision-making processes have generally been taken for granted and held as an unquestionable necessity for males in a given community; females, however, have to overcome enormous hurdles before being unconditionally accepted.

This exclusion and subjugation of women in male-dominated societies is often apologetically attributed to a supposed physical or psychological incapability of "the weaker sex" and justified by certain passages from the scriptures. Religious beliefs condition the minds of most people towards unquestioningly accepting and even glorifying the dormant, dependent and docile status ascribed to women, thus contributing towards cementing and perpetuating this form of exclusion and subjugation. Ordination of women was taken as an example in this regard. Agreement could not be reached on the question of how the denial of ordination to women by some churches should be understood in the light of the theme of this subsection. While such denial was generally held to be discriminatory, some voices pleaded for a view that allows for justification of such denial on theological grounds.

ACTS IN FAITHFULNESS

56. As a consequence of our affirmation that "the earth is the Lord's", we must denounce and unmask all elements of our cultures that perpetuate or produce discrimination and division. We affirm the unity of human-kind and therefore commit ourselves to a sincere endeavour to develop models of inclusiveness. The voiceless and dehumanized need to be encouraged to take the initiative in questioning exclusive structures, affirming their having equal rights, and demanding the redressing of cultural injustice that fractures the human community, counting on God's promise of a renewal of the human family.

57. Efforts by the victims of exclusion and subjugation to regain dignity must be affirmed, as well as the endeavour to find an inclusive language. The extent to which this could be a common concern with people of other faiths should be explored.

58. As part of this search for an inclusive sustaining community, we commit ourselves and urge our churches to affirm and encourage the endeavours of the Dalits to question and challenge the caste system in India which keeps that sector of Indian society in a perpetual state of dehumanization. The concern and engagement of the churches in India in this pursuit should receive the undivided support of the WCC and its member churches. The National Council of Churches in India should be asked to report on this issue to the Canberra assembly of the WCC, 1991.

59. We commit ourselves and urge our churches to reread the scriptures from the perspective of the marginalized, especially women.

60. We commit ourselves and urge our churches to engage in efforts to discern, unmask and overcome factors that cause, maintain and perpetu-ate the subordination of women in church and society. Resources and human efforts should be systematically invested in promoting forms of communication and models of inclusiveness that enable the women in our

churches to regain their integrity and be undisputed partners in actively shaping the contemporary world. We request the WCC to include the question of the ordination of women in the agenda for the Canberra assembly of the WCC, 1991.

61. Given the fact that the production and traffic of cocaine has reached a high level of global destruction, this has become a moral, cultural, social and economic issue of great urgency. We denounce its demonic character and commit ourselves and urge our churches to find ways to resist it and to stop the continued growth of this "global cancer".

SUMMARY OF SECTION III ACTS IN FAITHFULNESS

62. We have heard the stream of biblical affirmations which tell so powerfully that "the earth is the Lord's". We recognize our responsibility to the world's children whose future life will depend upon our commitment now to safeguard the life of creation.

We call upon all member churches to review their understanding and involvement in their ongoing mission programmes in the light of the affirmation that "the earth is the Lord's".

We affirm that mission means to support the struggle for a just sharing of land and resources in concrete actions, and we call upon the World Council of Churches and its member churches:

a) to return church lands taken from indigenous peoples and to divest church assets in corporations exploiting indigenous lands;

b) to take up the issue of indigenous peoples and their struggles for self-determination and survival as a standing programme within the WCC structure, and to create a commission thereon; this to be considered and brought to the Canberra assembly of the WCC, 1991, for implementation;

c) to offer concrete support to all landless peoples in their struggles, organizations and movements to reclaim and occupy land for their sustenance and survival;

d) to engage in a global strategy for a genuine land reform programme controlled by its beneficiaries, starting with the sharing of church lands with the landless and homeless;

e) to promote regional and international sharing of experiences and strategies on both leadership and grassroots levels among organizations of the landless and disenfranchised such as peasants, indigenous peoples, small farmers, refugees, etc.; and

f) to identify, address and seek to eliminate the causes of the uprooting of people and to establish a new comprehensive definition of "refugee" on an international level; and to ask local congregations to give attention in Bible study, preaching and teaching to the fact that issues like flight, migration, homelessness, exile and the search for a continuing city (Heb. 13:14) belong to the most central traditions in the Bible.

To implement and evaluate this Act in Faithfulness we ask that the Commission on World Mission and Evangelism undertake a process to assist the WCC member churches in re-evaluating their understanding of mission in the light of the affirmation, "the earth is the Lord's", and that a plan for gathering these concerns and carrying out this Act in Faithfulness be prepared in relation to the Canberra assembly of the WCC, 1991.

Section IV: Towards Renewed Communities in Mission

Introduction

1. The call for renewed communities in mission comes to us at a time when the forces of destruction dividing the human community seem to have become more active than ever. Throughout the world, humanity is threatened by division because of the restrictive affirmations of group identities and allegiances to a race, class, nationality or religion: the economic gap between north and south is growing constantly wider. And we see the disintegration of the sense of community expressed in anonymity and alienation as a result of progress in technology and communication. In view of the worldwide resurgence of individualism we feel the need not only to reinstate the Christian idea of community, but also to reformulate it in the light of a renewed understanding of the Holy Trinity. In this context, the conflict experienced in relation to this resurgence of individualism adds a further dimension to the struggle of "communities of resistance".

Everywhere in the world there are clear signs of a new thirst for community. Everywhere we see forms of community life as people strive for political and social freedom. A keen sense of community can be discerned among those who are struggling for justice, especially the poor and the marginalized.

2. In the church today we are witnessing the rediscovery of the dimension of community in the faith, as well as new ways in which to express it in its life and witness. On completely new lines, and on a level never previously achieved, research is being carried out on the community nature of the church.

The need for community is both profoundly human and profoundly Christian. This is the setting in which we reaffirm that it is God's firm purpose to unite all human beings in a single community.

3. God created the world and gave it to all humankind to use and to share in faithfulness. Here in God's world the church is called to be a living sign and instrument of God's will. It is also the way of the cross which leads through the liberating struggle against suffering. It is a community of sharing, which affirms the fullness of life in the image of the Triune God. Through the eucharist, the church is sent into the world to be the body of Christ, broken and shared for the world. The presence of the risen Lord in the power of the Holy Spirit enables us to break down barriers and renew structures and thus be the signs of the presence of the reign of God on earth.

In the church the quest for community is carried on in a great many ways and for a variety of reasons. Here are some examples: neo-charismatic communities, the church of the poor (base ecclesial communities) and the large number of African independent churches. Some communities have come into being by way of resistance, in solidarity with the struggles of the poor, outside the confines of the confessional traditions. All this makes the unity of Christians a most urgent question and a priority for the church. In many places these experiences have given the church a new credibility in the midst of a divided world; it has attained a maturity, an integrity and a new identity as a "community of love" — a community of love which demonstrates the power of God present in the struggles of the poor as they confront their powerful oppressors.

4. Because of their very variety, however, these living communities are not always in harmony with each other. Their variety is both ambiguous and full of promise.

We must recognize the gap separating the fullness of a renewed humanity such as God has promised in Jesus Christ from what we actually experience today. It is God the Spirit who alone creates, judges and unceasingly renews communities.

In trying to respond to the call inviting us to renew our missionary communities, we propose to distinguish three dimensions of this renewal.

1. Popular religiosity and the faith communities of the poor

We think particularly of the renewal movements which have long existed among the poor. Ecumenical discussions on mission, however, are only now beginning to take them into account. These movements contain a significant potential for a renewed understanding of mission within the struggles for liberation and change towards greater justice. They have much to teach us about mission through the vigour of their faith and their indigenous cultures.

2. Christians across frontiers

New forms of exchange of personnel and of multi-directional sharing are developing. But we note a trend towards perpetuating or even increasing the tradition of sending personnel from the north to the south. It is important in this context to look immediately for new guidelines and criteria to match our shared ecumenical affirmations and to eliminate the demonic forces of racism within our structures.

3. International relations of churches in mission

For more than a quarter of a century the quest for new models to express genuine partnership has been on the agenda of the WCC. Many excellent ideas have been expressed but not a great deal has happened. This is why there is a clear and urgent need for a renewed call to commitment and action.

I. Popular religiosity

a) Characteristics

5. In exchanging our experiences we have seen that much of the vitality and evangelizing dynamism of the Christian faith is expressed in a variety of popular expressions of religion (Pentecostal churches, base ecclesial communities, African independent churches, etc.). Despite their significance and numbers, these expressions of Christian faith are seldom included in our discussions and ecumenical sharing.

Popular religiosity is a universal phenomenon. It exists in both the southern and the northern hemisphere. We know, for instance, that in the north there are marginalized sectors, people with no voice in their society, ethnic minorities and counter-cultures similar to the popular religious communities in the south.

These communities often express their faith independently of the official churches. We consider this situation a reaction against the unfortunate identification of evangelism and colonization: this identification has often led to a denial in the name of the gospel of the people's right to self-determination and has frequently led even to genocide. This has left no room for the indigenous peoples' expressions of faith and struggles for liberation. The institutional churches are often incapable of incorporating these popular expressions of religious faith; they confront and even oppose them, and in so doing protect the interests of the middle classes.

In other situations, as in the Orthodox and some other traditions, these popular forms of religious expression have found a place within the liturgical and doctrinal framework of the church.

b) Culture, identity and faith

6. Despite the variety of these communities and the differences among them, we note that they have a number of common features which are significant for the renewal of the Christian community in mission:
— the importance of community life;
— the importance accorded to the concrete reality of everyday life (fertility of the land, health, sexuality, work, etc.);
— the affirmation of the collective identity of the people or of groups;
— the use of religious language which is more communal and symbolic than rational; and
— the importance of the festive aspect of religious life.

The presence and reality of these communities requires us to affirm that proclamation of the gospel of Jesus Christ cannot and must not conform to the domination of a specific cultural, political and economic model.

7. The theme of gospel and culture needs to be dealt with as a matter of urgency today, and popular religiosity is an important part of this. Missionary practice and the letters of the apostle Paul teach us that gospel preaching must respect all cultures and be incarnated in them. The Christian faith can neither live nor find expression in worship outside these cultures without becoming meaningless for the peoples to whom it is addressed. The question then arises: how is the specificity of the Christian faith to be maintained in the midst of many cultures? This is a complex question and we have been able only to note that our opinions differ. Together we can say that the reference to Jesus Christ, his words

and deeds, in the light of the fullness of life of the reign of God, must be the criterion enabling us to evaluate and understand these cultures. The gospel of Jesus Christ must become incarnate in every culture, while retaining the freedom to judge whether this or that form of religious expression and culture is a help or a hindrance to fullness of life for human beings, who are all created in the image of God.

This criterion also applies to non-Christian expressions of popular religion, for these are an integral part of the history and identity of the peoples and as such must be respected. In the north and the western world in particular, but also in other regions, a civil religion (which covers social, political and economic factors) is becoming a form of popular religiosity. This phenomenon must be carefully studied in connection with gospel and culture and with regard to its effects on society.

8. We acknowledge that in some contexts religious movements become the agents of division and sectarianism among the people; often they develop a non-ecumenical spirituality, far removed from the needs of the people and even cutting the people off from the popular struggle. Here the churches must promote a genuine spirituality in the service of life in all its dimensions, for everyone and in unity.

9. These many expressions of religious community among the poor challenge us to rethink and renew our traditional ecclesiological concepts on at least three levels:

— the value of the church's presence manifested in the form of a community, in line with the Acts of the Apostles and the Epistles of St Paul and St John;

— the importance and development of lay participation (by men, women, young people and children) as active agents in the life of the church and in evangelism; and

— a real and profound understanding of the relation between ecclesiology (forms of the church) and pneumatology (experiences of the Holy Spirit); the emphasis lies on the living experience of the Holy Spirit which leads not only to conversion and personal sanctification but also to recognition of the Spirit as the motive power of a living church.

It is the responsibility of the ecumenical movement to be a witness in every context to what is specific to the Christian faith as a liberating and reconciling faith.

ACTS IN FAITHFULNESS

10. We have heard stories of popular religiosity and movements among the poor in different parts of the world. We affirm that they have

enormous potential for the renewal of the church and human com-
munities. We also note the destructive effects of certain forms of popular
religiosity, for instance when applied by the rich to justify their oppres-
sion of the poor. Therefore we commit ourselves to stimulate our
churches:

a) *to promote the wider sharing of the experiences and challenges of*
   these popular movements and to encourage greater intercultural
   dialogue among them;

b) *to promote specific studies about the relationship between gospel and*
   culture in different contexts; and

c) *to promote through the WCC Programme on Theological Education*
   the incorporation of the study of popular religiosity into the curricula
   of theological formation.

11. We acknowledge that our churches and mission organizations have
neglected the significance of popular cultures and movements. We call
ourselves and our churches to repentance and to revise our mission
strategies so that they will not violate the values and ways of living of the
people. We ask the churches and institutions concerned to question the
coming celebration of five hundred years of the so-called discovery of the
Americas, to transform the celebration into an opportunity for a critical
review of the past, and to call for the celebration of the destroyed
cultures.

II. Crossing frontiers in mission

a) Biblical and theological basis

12. As Jesus was sent by God into the world, so are all Christians sent
out by Christ to socio-economic, cultural, racial as well as geographical
frontiers for mission in the power of the Spirit (John 20:21).

Across these diverse frontiers in mission, Christians celebrate and
witness to God's intention made manifest in Christ for the salvation of all
people. They seek to testify to God's reign that transcends all boundaries,
and to build a renewed human community freed from slavery to sin and
all forms of oppression (Eph. 2:12-22).

Mission is the essential task of every local community. Therefore the
many frontiers within our own local congregations must be bridged as we
dare to proceed to other frontiers.

13. The first frontiers we cross are often at our very doorsteps, where
we learn about and are engaged in mission with our neighbours and
friends in a spirit of love, service (Mark 10:42-45) and identifi-

cation (1 Cor. 9:19-26). But, following the mandate of Christ, we are also called to go out as witnesses to the ends of the earth (Matt. 28: 18,19).

While all Christians are called to cross various frontiers in mission in their local context, the church, from time to time, sets apart and sends some across cultural and geographical frontiers. These "missionaries" bring to focus and clarity the missionary vocation of the whole people of God everywhere.

Whether as individuals or in groups, whether through words, deeds or their very lives, the people of God are called to build bridges across the various divides in human community such as race, class, sex and ideology. Thereby we proclaim Christ's self-emptying love on the cross, where he "has broken down the dividing wall of hostility... that he might create in himself one new man in place of the two, so making peace" (Eph. 2:14,15).

14. Crossing frontiers in mission demands profound sensitivity to the cultures and values of others, a posture of incarnational dialogue, and identification with people in their struggles for justice, freedom and human dignity, all of which arise out of a life of prayer nurtured by the scriptures (Luke 11:2-4).

Though in mission we carry the spiritual treasure of Christ in the midst of our weakness like "common clay pots", we acknowledge that the presence of God, the power of the Spirit and the pattern of Christ go with us as we cross frontiers in mission.

While affirming our option for identification with the poor, we observe that the communities of the poor themselves are becoming more and more the bearers of mission.

b) Principles and priorities

15. Mission across frontiers is based on two fundamental principles: promoting unity among all Christians, and strengthening local communities.

Mutuality and respect need to be ensured between those who are sent and those who receive them.

Exchange of persons in mission across frontiers must help build vibrant local worshipping and witnessing communities.

Communication and cooperation with the church in the place where a person is sent in mission is an essential prerequisite. Denominational heritage and responsibility for mission in the area of the local church must be respected so that "all in each place" may seek together to fulfill the purpose of God in mission. In places where the church is not present, the local culture and heritage must be respected as well. Active proselytism aimed at gaining members from another Christian church is contrary to the spirit of Christ.

We have come to discover the joy of multi-directional exchange of persons in mission. This needs to be enhanced, particularly facilitating movement of persons from south to north and between south and south, with an equitable sharing of all resources.

While long-term cross-cultural missionary service needs to be further promoted, several new and creative forms of exchange of persons between churches on a short-term basis are being explored. Such attempts must be encouraged and made more ecumenical. Experiments in new and creative ways of sharing people in mission across frontiers must be supported. This would imply discovering the mission potential of people such as immigrants, refugees and asylum seekers who travel across frontiers; they can be seen as sent by God for witness and renewal of communities.

Persons cross frontiers in mission not merely to go to "get a job done" or to assist a partner church in a particular task. Rather they are sent and received as persons, to share all that they are and their denominational and cultural heritage, to affirm and share life in Christ in all its richness.

c) People crossing frontiers in mission

16. Those who engage in mission across frontiers need qualities such as: profound sensitivity and openness rooted in spirituality, respect for the cultures and values of other people, willingness to learn and overcome frontiers at home, ability to engage in mutually beneficial dialogue, and a sincere longing for building and renewing community. A commitment to ecumenism is also an imperative.

People who cross frontiers in mission must have a deep understanding of racial and ethnic identities and be able to handle hidden prejudices within themselves and others even before they leave their home context. This is already experienced by multi-racial communities.

Extended preparation, including in the use of scripture and through appropriate training and cross-cultural orientation, is required.

In order that mutual understanding among Christians across frontiers may be increased, exchange visits among members of local congregations of two or more churches in different cultural contexts may be explored. But such short-term visits must be carefully planned; proper orientation, adequate exposure to the local situation and processes of evaluation, interpretation and reporting on return must be ensured.

As far as possible, exchange visits should be planned multi-direction-ally. The WCC member churches must be encouraged to undertake greater sharing of professional mission personnel between churches in all directions in order to reflect the global and ecumenical nature of partner-ship in the gospel. It is important, too, that support be given for enhancing greater south-to-south exchange of personnel.

The WCC should be asked to develop means and instruments for planning, resourcing and monitoring the ecumenical sharing of personnel in mission.

ACTS IN FAITHFULNESS

17. We believe that every crossing of frontiers by Christians, both locally and globally, has the potential for participating in the process of seeking justice, peace and the integrity of creation. Therefore, we commit ourselves and shall sensitize others to become the agents of the whole gospel of Jesus Christ, involving both proclamation of the good news, as well as participation in the liberation struggles of the poor and the oppressed. In that process, we affirm that the communities of the poor are themselves the bearers of the gospel.

18. We affirm that as far as possible all sharing of resources and personnel in mission should be undertaken ecumenically and that even bilateral relationships should be placed within a wider ecumenical framework. We also recognize the need to emphasize the exchange of people among the different regions in the south. Therefore we enlist our member churches and the WCC to develop appropriate structures of ecumenical sharing of persons for mission where priorities are estab-lished, resources are shared, and monitoring and accountability are ensured around a common table.

III. International relations of churches in mission

a) Vision

19. The structures of the churches' international relations in mission must be such that they help us to share our joys and our sorrows, our talents and our needs in a way which makes no one only a donor and no one only a recipient.

Each of our churches has gifts to offer and needs to satisfy. We must all contribute to the changes in the structures of missionary institutions in both north and south, made necessary by the vision of sharing in universal communion.

Such new — and renewed — structures will give concrete expression to the churches' commitment to mission in Christ's way.

b) *Characteristics*

20. If these new and renewed structures are to be a sign of the reign of God as we perceive it, they should have among their characteristics the following:
— recognition that all God's gifts are common property;
— mutual acceptance of one another as partners;
— recognition of cultural diversity as an enrichment of sharing;
— equal access to sources of information;
— transparency;
— joint planning and implementation of policies;
— openness to sharing of non-material resources such as theological reflections, liturgies, hymnologies, new forms of spirituality, life-styles, etc., as well as financial resources; and
— acceptance of mutual accountability and correction of anything that proves ineffective or inadequate.

c) *Obstacles*

21. If this is to be made a reality, the churches must take account of the obstacles that stand in the way of this new vision and remove them. Among these we may mention:
— the application in our missionary relations of ideologies and pre-judices which lead to situations of injustice, oppression, poverty and dependence;
— psychological resistance to change of any kind;
— bilateral relations which exclude any ecumenical dimension;
— paternalism in all its forms, including the tendency of some people in the churches of the south to expect outside help even for things they can do themselves;
— confessional and denominational models which exclude all but sister churches;
— proselytism, with its aggressive and manipulative element;
— the priority given to financial factors, with the resulting consolidation of the power of the rich to the detriment of the poor; and
— ideas and strategies which leave no room for cultural diversity.

d) Guiding principles

22. As we search for models to incarnate our vision of renewed missionary relations, we affirm some guiding principles which could inspire attempts at practical application:

— commitment to acting together wherever a common approach is required;
— priority to relations from church to church rather than from church to missionary society or agency;
— promotion of a global vision of mission in which the fullness of the reign of God is proclaimed and genuinely experienced;
— transparency in relations and in the sharing of responsibilities; and
— promotion of power-sharing and genuine reciprocity in all decision-making.

We are looking for models which reflect the guiding principles outlined above: for example, transformation of a missionary society through the transfer of power and funds to a common governing body in which all the partners — in both north and south — can share on a footing of real equality.

What we would like to see is a great variety of experiments attempting to put these principles into practice and thereby strengthening ecumenical activities at all levels (local, national and international).

ACTS IN FAITHFULNESS

23. We have heard the call for a new concept of sharing in which all who have been marginalized on grounds of sex, age, ethnic origin, disability, economic situation or political allegiance, as well as the homeless, the refugees, the asylum-seekers and the migrants, will participate on an equal footing in all decision-making and all activities. Thus, for example:

a) the churches, councils and networks should create ecumenical structures for this purpose at national and regional levels; and
b) steps should be taken to ensure equitable representation of women and young people on decision-making bodies.

Consequently, we urge the member churches of the WCC to make additional funds available for educating and equipping the people of God for mission in a way that will transform missionary relations.

24. We have heard that certain agencies with their partners have undertaken to review and revise the existing forms of resource sharing. We pledge ourselves to encourage our churches and agencies to carry out similar evaluations with a view to setting up common decision-making structures and ensuring reciprocal sharing in mission. We commit our-selves to participate in international relations only when these work for the advancement of local ecumenism and encourage the use of existing ecumenical bodies, or create new ones where these are lacking, so that we work together in all areas of mission.

Recommendation

25. As a sign of openness to change, we recommend that the churches, agencies, missionary societies and ecumenical bodies should in a spirit of sharing transfer at least ten percent of their mission and development funds through *ecumenical* channels, in order to give local churches the capacity to engage together in mission.

The Worship Life
of the Conference

Jean Stromberg

> We are marching in the light of God
> We are marching in the light of God!
> Oo! We are marching in the light of God.

Following a large wooden cross, the participants of the World Conference on Mission and Evangelism emerged from the closing worship singing the South African freedom song and moving to the rhythm of the accompanying drums. In the wide plaza in front of the chapel the song continued spontaneously as participants who had gathered from every region of the world embraced each other and said their farewells. It was in many ways an appropriate conclusion for a conference which had explored mission in Christ's way: the company of God's people, following the cross, preparing to move on to their places of service in the world.

It was also appropriate that the conference ended as it had begun — in worship. From the moment that the first call to worship sounded through the sanctuary of Trinity Baptist church, a Southern Baptist Church adjacent to the university campus where the opening worship was held, the worship life gathered together the conference's prayers for the will of God to be done on earth in a liturgical context, provided occasion for the celebration of the rich diversity of gifts, cultures and languages of God's people, and space for experiencing through our senses and actions our commitment to mission in Christ's way.

Planning for the worship life in San Antonio

The ecumenical worship experience over the last few years has been an exceedingly rich one. Nine years ago at the World Conference on Mission

---

● Jean Stromberg is assistant to the general secretary of the WCC.

and Evangelism in Melbourne, Australia, an international team of musicians and liturgists had gathered materials from all parts of the world to express the theme, "Your Kingdom Come"; short liturgical responses in many different languages, the use of facilitators and instrumentation from various cultures were central elements in the worship experience.

Three years later in Vancouver, building on the Melbourne experience as well as that of other ecumenical gatherings, there was a strong affirmation of the experience of ecumenical worship. The necessity for wide participation of God's people and a keen sense of the vocation of prayer were two fundamental understandings of those who planned for the worship at the Assembly. The possibilities for using choirs and varied cultural instruments as aids to facilitating the worship of all the people assumed new dimensions. The sense of space for worship was greatly enlarged; it was not only that the use of a tent as the place of worship provided a different kind of physical space, but also that worship, the expression of the whole people of God in praise and adoration, assumed larger proportions and more fundamental significance to the ongoing search for unity.

Various ecumenical meetings in recent years have made use of the experience of Vancouver and have pushed further the development of our ecumenical worship experience. In the Sharing of Resources meeting in El Escorial and in recent Central Committee meetings the use of symbolic actions and an even wider gathering of materials from every part of the world have enabled many to see that the sharing together in the life of God is a profound experience of the koininia of the body of Christ. For many persons, their participation in ecumenical worship has been a foretaste of the kingdom community and of the unity we seek.

In this tradition and experience of worship the international planning team for San Antonio worship assumed their mandate: to plan for participatory, inclusive worship, which would enable the large group of participants to worship as one across confessional, cultural and linguistic lines. Within that mandate the team was concerned to integrate the worship life with the programmatic discussions of the conference and to deepen the understanding and exploration of the conference theme through participation in a liturgical life of prayer, song, readings and actions.

The team gave primary importance to the vocation of prayer. A ten-day prayer calendar was prepared for use in churches before and during the conference. A local committee established and maintained a prayer vigil during the days of the conference, praying by name for the participants and for the churches and countries from which they had come, and interceding for the special requests which the participants brought from their various situations. It was also in prayer that the team could offer the worship plans and preparations, knowing that these could be only a framework to enable the expressions of spirituality of those who were gathered, an offering that the Spirit could use to the glory of God.

Daily worship services

It was in the daily worship services that the conference became a family, gathering each morning in the university chapel. The services followed a similar structure each day; within that pattern there was variety of movement and language, of people and of symbolic actions. Because no interpretation was possible in the chapel, there was a minimum of spoken words during the time of reflection. The orders of service were printed each day in the four official languages and many other languages were used in the singing, prayers and readings.

The central image of growth with its rich imagery of planting, nourishing, pruning, waiting for the harvest, gathering the fruit, provided continuity as well as focus for the daily worship services — in song, in scripture, in symbolic actions and visual symbols. This image, central to the Christian experience, was chosen because of its particular appropriateness for missiological reflection and action. A brief description follows of the development of this image in the focus of each daily worship service.

Flowers will bloom in the wilderness

The first of the daily worship services opened with the prophet Isaiah's vision of what God will do: "Flowers will bloom in the wilderness! The desert will sing for joy!" It is from the announcement of the vision that all things follow: that women and men are called to participate in God's mission of making flowers bloom out of dry land; that we are called to mission in Christ's way in the planting, growing and bearing of fruit of the message of the gospel in all of life. The starting point for our faithfulness in mission is the announcement of what God intends for all humankind and for all creation.

Each person upon entering the chapel was given a small wooden bowl containing soil which provided a focal point for reflection upon John the Baptist's call to "prepare the way of the Lord". Symbolic of the wastelands of individual lives, of communities and of our world, the soil from individual bowls was gathered into large clay pots to be made ready for the planting of seeds. In response to the prayer, "Prepare a way, O Lord, in the desert, in our deserts, for Christ to come, and make all things new", the participants sang "Your will be done, O Lord; Your will be done on earth".

Unless a seed falls into the ground and dies....

In the second daily worship the participants held the wooden bowls which contained seeds for reflection on the mystery of life out of death: "Unless a grain of wheat falls into the ground and dies it remains alone; but if it dies, it bears much fruit." Gathering around large clay pots of soil, the participants remembered and named saints and martyrs of this and every age whose lives, like seeds, had dropped to the ground yet whose witness has borne fruit. It was a moment of prayer in dedication and surrender to the will and purpose of God for "we cannot know the glory of Christ's resurrection if we do not have the fellowship of his sufferings".

Acknowledging that "we cannot expect to gather the kingdom's harvest if we do not sow the kingdom's seed", the participants then planted their seeds in the large clay pots, praying: "In us and through us, may your Spirit proclaim: Christ has died, Christ is risen, Christ will come again."

Like a tree planted by the rivers of water

In the gospels, Jesus affirms that he is the light of the world; that he is the life-giving spring of water. Our Lord speaks of his own life as given for our nourishment.

Part of the calling to mission in Christ's way is to nourish lives with the water and the light of life so that the seed of truth may take root in all hearts. During this service, participants used the wooden bowls to water the small plants that had sprouted in the large clay pots or to hold lighted candles which they placed around the plants.

Every branch that bears fruit is pruned

The promise of growth and of bearing fruit is accompanied in scripture by the warning that every branch that does not bear fruit is cut off and cast into the fire. Every branch that bears fruit is pruned. Pruning is a necessary part of growing; it is also God's action, so that the plant may bear much fruit.

During the pruning of a large tree at the front of the chapel, participants were invited to write on paper what should be pruned in their own lives, in our several societies and in our world. In a processional exit, the pruned branches were carried out of the chapel and cast into a fire; participants then cast their written "prunings" into the fire.

Behold how the farmer waits for the land to yield its crops

"Think of a farmer: how patiently he waits for the precious fruit of the ground until it has had the autumn rains and the spring rains! You too must be patient." ... Participants joined in a litany of waiting with the prophets of old: Isaiah and Jeremiah, Amos and Hosea who believed that God is a God of justice; with the women of the Bible: Sarah and Hannah and Elizabeth and Mary, who looked forward to new life and new beginnings; and with Jesus in the garden, who asked his disciples to wait with him.

Participants held empty bowls as a focus for this meditation. In the letter to the Philippians Paul tells us that Christ, "not counting equality with God a thing to be grasped, emptied himself". Mary Magdalene saw the empty tomb; today we speak of empty stomachs, empty pews. Participants reflected on the relationship between emptiness and waiting.

Sharing the bread of life

Mission in Christ's way calls for the sharing of life — of companionship and of bread. Nourished by the bread of life, Christians are promised the companionship of Christ who walks beside us and before us. "Because you broke bread and shared it," the participants prayed, "we will do so too and ask your blessing." With the story of the walk to Emmaus as the context, participants received pieces of bread and were encouraged to share with others their own stories of how their eyes were opened to faith as they walked to the Bible study groups.

The fruits of the Spirit for the people of God

The seed sown in faith and nurtured in love, the plant pruned and tended with discernment, bears fruit. The seed of the gospel bears the fruit of the furthering of God's kingdom. The seed of faith, nurtured by the Spirit, enables us to bear the fruits of the Spirit in our lives. The fruit is the goal of our mission; it is also the witness that our mission is done in Christ's way. During this last of the daily worship services, fruit was shared among the participants as a sign of sharing all our gifts and lives, so that God's will may be done on earth.

Walking the way of the cross

An early morning worship event, focusing on suffering in our world and its relationship to our commitment to "mission in Christ's way", was planned as a meditation walk through the university campus, incorporating stops for personal as well as communal reflection and action. This event, on the third day of the conference, came, in the liturgical development, between the planting of seeds with the remembrance of the martyrs and the nourishing of new life. In this important space, between

Golgotha and Pentecost, is the death and resurrection of our Lord. The worship team wished to give special consideration to these events in relation to our discipleship and to our faithfulness in solidarity with those who carry crosses today.

"Walking the way of the cross" brought the two parts of the conference theme together in a powerful way: nowhere does the prayer "Your will be done" ring more powerfully than in Christ's prayer in Gethsemane; nowhere does the call to mission in Christ's way express itself more eloquently than in the taking up of one's cross to follow Christ.

Over a period of three hours, a continuous flow of persons, each at his/her own pace, around 800 in number, moved quietly, solemnly at times, through the walk. A meditation guide, with reflections from persons in many parts of the world, enabled a focusing of thought on the themes of each of the meditation places.

Meditation on the life of Christ: Participants paused first in front of large murals which pictured scenes from the life of Christ illustrating how his life was lived in solidarity with the poor and the oppressed. These actions of Christ led directly to the giving of his life on the cross. The call to Christians to take up the cross is a daily challenge to the ways in which we live our lives as well as to the great moments of choice. "If the Lord's disciples keep quiet," the women of the Iona Community have written, "the very stones will shout aloud: take up your cross and follow me." Participants were invited to mark their foreheads with ashes in the sign of the cross to indicate their commitment to living the way of the cross.

Meditation in Gethsemane: The words of Jesus, "Not my will, but yours be done", written in many languages, surrounded the second place of meditation. Participants were invited to contemplate the struggle of Jesus in Gethsemane to pray this prayer to his father. Can we pray for God's will to be done on earth without reflection on and commitment to the personal and communal cost of that prayer? The death of Jesus reminds us of the lengths to which God "was prepared to go," Dan Madijan SJ has written, "in forgiving us, in bearing our rejection, in sharing our sufferings".

Meditation on scourging and mocking: Pictures of suffering and oppression and sounds of war and violence made vivid the powers which mock God's reign and which continue to impose suffering and oppression on people. Participants were invited to carry, together with others, a large wooden cross, to feel the weight and the burden of that cross. A meditation poem by Pierre Griolet contrasted the real cross of Jesus with those "carefully polished" crosses which hang on the wall. Yet still today the "sign of the cross is being engraved on human flesh right in our midst. And we see nothing!"

Meditation in the judgment hall: The walls of the "judgment hall" were covered by the names of those who have been condemned for their kingdom actions. Voices read continuously from long lists the names of those who have been condemned to die because of their faith. Persons were invited to write on the walls the names of those whom they have known who have suffered for righteousness' sake.

Even today, the meditation guide noted, Jesus is condemned to death: when people cry for freedom, and they are accused of being terrorists; when people speak out the truth, and they are accused of being traitors; when people do good, and they are accused of being self-seekers; when people fail to lift up their voices in support of truth.

"I am afraid ... of that life which does not come out of death, which cramps our hands and retards our march. I am afraid of my fear and even more of the fear of others, who do not know where they are going, who continue clinging to what they consider to be life, which we know to be death!" Julia Esquivel wrote during her exile from Guatemala.

As participants left the judgment hall, they passed by a bowl of water and a towel. "When Pilate saw that he was gaining nothing, but rather that a riot was beginning, he took water and washed his hands before the crowd, saying, "I am innocent of this man's blood, see to it yourselves." The meditation guide posed the question: What is our responsibility as Christians in the judgment halls of our world? Can we wash our hands of this responsibility? One of the seminary students, Julie Pierce, wrote of her response to these questions: "Privileged and protected, yet unable to wash my hands of responsibility. The towels around the bucket of water were shouting at me. I wanted to touch them — to see if they were damp from use or just arranged to look as if they had been used. Am I called to join Pilate in the washing of hands? No! Mission in Christ's way means taking responsibility."

Meditation on nailing: The sound of nails being hammered into wood echoed strangely across the university campus in the early morning hours. These sounds were reminders of those who are being crucified today by unjust economic policies, by military and political oppression, by discrimination, by unfettered greed, by the denial of basic human needs.

A nail, handed to all participants as they approached this meditation area, was sign both of that which has the power to hurt as well as that which has healed us. The Christian tradition includes the understanding that Jesus "was pierced for our transgressions, he was crushed for our iniquities; the punishment that brought us peace was upon him". Participants were invited to write personal or communal sins and to nail the paper to the large beam of wood, in this way acknowledging that "by his wounds we are healed".

Meditation on forsakenness: In the world today there are many "forsaken areas"; the large photographs which surrounded this meditation place showed some of these, but many experiences of forsakenness can never be captured by a camera. The words of Zephania Kameeta, Namibia, express that forsakenness: "Why, O why Lord? Why do you seem deaf to our doleful cries?" Jesus himself cried out: "My God, my God, why have you forsaken me?"

Participants were invited to reflect on this experience with all their senses. Wine mixed with vinegar was offered as the taste of bitterness of forsakenness. Participants who were willing were blindfolded and led by others along the way, experiencing more fully the sense of helplessness and aloneness.

Meditation by the cross: The reading from Isaiah included the words, "Because of his affliction he shall see the light in fullness of days; through his suffering, my servant shall justify many, and their guilt he shall bear..." Participants were invited to kneel at the cross and to meditate on the meaning of the cross for mission in Christ's way, in their own lives, in their society and in the world. Upon leaving the meditation area, participants were reminded of their baptism as they washed the sign of ashes from their foreheads.

Meditation on resurrection: An icon of the resurrection as well as contemporary depictions of the resurrection from various parts of the world pointed to the hope of the resurrection for mission in Christ's way. A reflection from K.H. Ting, China, reminded participants: "The resurrection truth tells us that it is through loss, poverty, suffering and death that life is attained, in nation as well as in church. It tells us life does not depend on power, wealth or property but on the risen Christ, the Lord of Life, who is also the ascended Christ, sitting at the right hand of God and upholding the universe by his word of power."

Reflection on shared bread: The meditation walk ended by a simple breakfast of water and tortillas as an act of solidarity with those for whom a single piece of bread must suffice for today as well as a reminder of the millions who cannot be confident of getting any food. "Shared bread is the experience of people as community, and therefore," as Samuel

Rayan, India, has written, "the experience of God; it is communion at once human and divine. A central concern of Jesus is to promote table fellowship and get people to share bread and life."

Concluding worship

While no statement could reflect the richness of the shared experience of the conference, participants read together in the closing worship a litany of commitment which attempted to gather together some of the affirmations of the conference:

Leader:	That we worship one God,
	Father, Son and Holy Spirit,
	In whose image we are made,
	To whose service we are summoned,
	By whose presence we are renewed,
All:	This we believe.
Leader:	That it is God's will
	That the world should be saved
	And not despoiled by imperialism, violence, apathy, oppression, pollution,
	Or any other mask of human greed,
All:	This we believe.
Leader:	That it is central to the mission of Christ
	To participate, by word and action, in the struggles of the poor for justice,
	To share justly the earth's land and resources,
	To rejoice in the diversity of human culture,
	To preserve human life in all its beauty and frailty,
	To witness to the love of God for all people of the earth, and to invite all to share that converting experience.
All:	This we believe.
Leader:	That through the power of the Holy Spirit,
	The persecuted shall be lifted up and the wicked will fall,
	The hesitant prayers and hidden actions of God's people shall change the course of human history,
	The ancient words of Scripture shall startle us with fresh insight,

All: This we believe.

Leader: That God has called the church into being
          To be the servant of the kingdom,
          To be a sign of God's new order,
          To celebrate in the streets and fields of every land
          the liturgy of heaven,

All: This we believe.

Leader: That all the words this conference addresses to the churches,
          God addresses first to us,
          That all the acts of faithfulness require to be made incarnate
          in our life, work and witness,

All: This we believe.

Leader: That Christ, fully aware of our differences,
          Prays that we may be one
          So that the world may believe,

All: This we believe,
          And to this we are committed
          For the love of God,
          In the way of Christ,
          By the power of the Holy Spirit. Amen.

As the participants — women and men of all ages, lay persons and bishops from every region of the world — emerged from the chapel at the conclusion of the final worship service, they carried in their hands the wooden bowls which had accompanied the daily reflections on the purposes of God in mission: the preparation of the soil, the seed sown and nourished, the new plant pruned that in the fullness of time it may bear fruit.

These bowls which had been passed from hand to hand during the week were now, in the last liturgical act of the conference, to be taken by each participant. But the bowls were not to go empty. Participants were challenged in the closing service to consider the seeds which God had sown within the conference, seeds of personal commitment to Jesus Christ, seeds that could bring new life to the mission, evangelism, social action and worship of the churches to which the participants returned.

After a period of silence, participants moved out of the pews to receive seeds in their bowls, visible reminders of the personal commitments which they had made before God and of their mutual commitments in the acts of faithfulness.

And so the worship, and the conference, ended. But the ending was also a beginning, the beginning of the liturgy after the liturgy. The exit from the chapel was also an entry, an entry into the world to places of service and ministry, to mission in Christ's way.

"Will you be my People?"

Sylvia Talbot

I will be your God. Will you be my people? Some years ago in a
Methodist conference Bible study session Harrell Beck, with great flair
and imagination, told the story of the creation, ending with a reminder
that the question: "Will you be my people?" is answered each day
according to the way we go about finishing the work God has begun. It is
that work we gather to consider. And, I have been asked to reflect a little
on what this has meant to me in my own life and work.

I belonged to the community of God's people before I even knew it,
and have never wanted to be outside it. As a member of a community
called Lutheran, I was helped to forge a faith that continues to mature. As
I grew up, I had ample evidence that God is real. For one thing, coming
from a Caribbean island as I do, God's presence is unmistakable in the
beauty and mystery and magic of the everyday world. Love was in
abundant supply and sharing was, and still is, a common family practice.
In times of family crisis, help came from unexpected sources, and that
was always interpreted as help coming from God. I had learned early to
rely on God. Because help in time of need came in the shape of men and
women, God being present to us through others, I internalized the
importance of being that kind of help, God being present to others
through me.

As I recall, my congregation was not active in the life of the community except as members were active individually. Only on mission
Sundays was social outreach emphasized by focusing on the needs of
people in faraway lands. Demands on church members related mostly to
what we could do to keep the church open, active and interesting, and

---

● Sylvia Talbot is vice-moderator of the WCC Central Committee. This meditation was
given at the opening worship of the conference.

what we could do for people in need. I learned from the selective way scripture was used that mission was charity, and, therefore, I developed a keen sense of responsiblity for doing the charitable thing. Somehow, I got the notion that Christianity was to be practised on a personal level only, and thus a good Christian was one who did kind things for people. The church community of my youth was a comfortable experience — affirming, happy, non-threatening — but it lacked challenge.

Of course, I know now that the missionary intention of the church goes far beyond what I grew up believing. The prophets of the Old Testament are quite clear about the work God wants done and to know a Jesus who was sent not only to bind up wounds, but also "to announce that captives shall be released and the downtrodden shall be freed from their oppressors" points clearly to the nature of our mission.

Many people, events and experiences helped to shape my understanding of what it really means to be God's people. Two are important enough to share. The first was the experience of living and working in a community of the Church of the Brethren in Puerto Rico, many of whom had been conscientious objectors. It was the first time I had met real, live people who had the courage to say "no" to national policy they perceived to be contrary to God's will. Their rejection of violence, combined with alternative ways of serving their country through teaching, agriculture and providing health care, influenced my thinking. I became conscious, not only of the need to question societal values, but also of the responsibility to understand and use alternatives to those values.

Another significant milestone on my journey of faith was my introduction to the African Methodist Episcopal Church on marrying one of its pastors. My social consciousness was awakened and disturbed as we worked together in ten different countries. I identify with the suffering this community of people has endured (and continues to endure) from the massive attack on their personhood and dignity. I never cease to marvel at the depth and genuineness of their faith. Their songs of praise tell their story. My faith has been nourished and strengthened in this community. My faith journey has been influenced as much by their faith as by their suffering and pain. I feel their pain and I know the intimate details of their struggle because it is also my struggle.

Witnessing to God's design

But I am a part of a much larger struggle, as well. I also know intimately the travail of countries trying to make available a better life for their people. It is not expressed in the same words, but it resonates with the promise of "life in all its fullness". Powerlessness and injustice dominate the everyday lives of millions of people. Majorities and minorities in countries across the world experience an inability to influence or change their social reality, whether it is grinding poverty, war, the burden of national debt, or repression. The problems are complex and formidable. Their resolution depends not only on national will, but more importantly on the unselfish interest and sense of justice of the global community.

On the other hand, there are those who relentlessly pursue their agenda of domination and control. Their policies and activities are self-serving and self-preserving.

We Christians cannot believe that this is God's world and still remain unconvinced that, individually and collectively, we must enter into the struggle to change the reality of poverty and powerlessness wherever they exist. But I am also aware of another reality. The church, acting in the society, is not always recognized, understood or accepted. There is a lot of confusion in the minds of people, inside and outside the church, about the witness of the church. Does the church only speak through its official channels? Are lay members still the church outside the sanctuary? Are church members witnessing as they become involved in the life of the community?

I was once so incensed by a newspaper article that criticized the church for not doing anything about the increasing rate of what was then called "children born out of wedlock", that I dashed off a letter to the editor outlining clearly what indeed the church was doing through teachers, nurses, women's groups and a host of other people. I knew well because I was deeply involved in that work. To my surprise, my letter was published on the front page of the Sunday edition, with comments that started a useful dialogue in that community about our witness as a church.

The struggle for justice and human dignity persists, and much of that struggle is played out within the church community. Both the powerless and the powerful are represented in the church community with perceptions that are certainly incompatible. No wonder the church finds it so difficult to make a credible witness! Perhaps that is why the discussions that take place formally and informally in conferences of this nature are so important. The international conference is an arena where awareness is heightened and the possibility of solidarity becomes real.

Being God's people makes some demands on us. I continue to discover that to be God's people is to experience kinship with others and with the rest of creation *and* to accept responsibility for them. To be God's people is never to be neutral in the face of exploitation and oppression of our brothers and sisters. Rather, it is to do what Yahweh asks of me "only this, to act justly, to love tenderly, and to walk humbly with (my) God" (Mic. 6:8). To be God's people is to be God's partners. It is an intentional shaping of one's ministry to bear witness to God's shalom — justice, freedom, peace, wholeness. The expectation overwhelms me, and to process it all is a life-consuming struggle!

You may feel the same way. There must be times when, like me, you feel the call to Christian discipleship too demanding and too costly. The temptation is to cower in the corners of inadequacy because the task seems so big and we are so small. This experience is not new. It is the experience of Elijah. But Elijah heard the same voice we hear when we stop long enough to listen to God. It did not come in the wind, not in the earthquake, not in the fire — no great fanfare, just the whisper of the conscience of a person of faith slightly off centre asking: "What are you doing here?"

That question has been asked of me more times than I care to admit — at times when I know risk-taking to be more appropriate but I am too timid to act; at times when I have withdrawn in the face of personal tragedy or adversity believing that my experience has nothing to say to anyone else; at times when I allow myself to believe that injury to another human being or to this earth is inevitable, and, therefore, it does not occupy top priority on my agenda; at times when my perceived power-lessness allows me to accommodate injustice and tyranny. It is at these times that I gratefully borrow some words of a prayer left to us by Howard Thurman:

> God I need you, when the path to take before me lies,
> I see it, courage flees, I need your faith.

The story of Elijah did not end by emphasizing his weakness, but instead, Elijah is reformed, endowed with new strength and purpose, and again becomes God's instrument. So it could be for us. We are challenged to realize that God empowers us constantly to act in obedience to God's will.

Using power positively

From the perspective of a member of an oppressed group, God's will is quite clear. One does not read the Exodus story without identifying with the Israelites saved through God's intervention. One does not hear the story of the bent woman straightened by Jesus without some excitement about the possibilities open to those who experience bentness. The words of the creation story about being made in God's image and about God's creation being good are not considered an idle tale. It does not seem far-fetched to conclude that God does not intend that people starve to death in a world capable of sustaining them, or that some people use selfishly more resources than they are entitled to. God does not intend that some people be denied full freedom and dignity. Is it the lack of clarity or the lack of will that prevents God's people from acting in obedience?

Some Christians have a clearer discernment of God's will than others. They do not succumb to the feeling of powerlessness. They do not allow evil to remain unnamed. They choose to take risks for the sake of a more just and humane society. I am enriched and empowered in a marvellous way by their witness. We could look at four examples of power being used, not to control, or to subjugate or to destroy, but to heal, to teach, to enable. I see in this type of witness discernment of God's will and God's power.

The power of presence

First, there are those who use the *power of presence* to call attention to injustices and inequities and to the exploitation and tyranny in our global society. I think of the eloquent testimony to the power of presence by a group of women known as the mothers of Plaza de Mayo in Buenos Aires who week after week walk in a silent vigil to call the attention of their government and of the world to the disappearance and torture of their loved ones. There is something extraordinarily powerful about the power of the presence of the powerless in the presence of power!

I remember the anti-apartheid group of Christian women in Frankfurt standing in solidarity with political prisoners in South Africa. Some years ago, when I stood with them in a symbolic gesture, their weekly vigil had entered its fourth year. Just standing there on this busy street with the name of Nelson Mandela written boldly on a placard hanging around my neck, I felt truly yoked, both to the people of South Africa in their struggle and to the German women in theirs. The women shared with me their joy in noticing a remarkable difference in the way people reacted to them now and how they reacted when they first started.

I have discovered recently what the power of presence means in the lives of women who are victims of sexual or domestic violence. Being present with a woman who has just been abused, that is, being there for her — supporting, comforting, affirming — enables her to reach deep within herself for the strength to survive and recover. But it does something else. Being in solidarity in a deeply personal way with others helps me to understand better their reality and to be more passionately committed to changing that reality. To understand this is to understand the passionate commitment of people involved in the sanctuary movement, the peace movement and other work that confronts the threat to the survival and vitality of people.

While some Christians continue to debate the appropriateness of different forms of witness, other Christians are making their witness public and visible to express clearly what their faith says about matters of vital importance to our existence. The presence of Christians in places where decisions are being made is as critical as our presence in places where people hurt. Until we understand that, internalize it and act on it, how will we really be able to represent or reflect Christ in our lives?

Through my work in public health, I began to see clearly that all the kind, wonderful things we did as a church did not affect the high infant mortality rate. They did not prevent children getting sick with the same illness over and over again. They did not prevent women from seeking abortions out of a sense of despair and hopelessness. People still had no jobs, therefore had no food, and some lived in such dilapidated houses and had so many problems that the resources available to a small congregation could not help. There must be times when a Christian presence where policy decisions are being made is of greater benefit to people who suffer injustices and inequities.

I have been challenged on many occasions about my own decision to serve as a minister of government. For some, it was a questionable way of witnessing, yet, as minister of health, I was able to ensure that thousands of children received better health care, that the community was protected by legislation governing sanitation and the pharmaceuticals made available to them, that people received information to help them make wise decisions about their health, and more.

There are, of course, many other ways of witnessing I would consider more inappropriate. One is our giving out of our abundance to people in need instead of giving out of a conviction that they are entitled to benefit, too, from the abundance in the world. When we give in that way it is without any concern whether that need has been met and the situation changed. On the global level, president Diori Hamani of Niger summed it up well when he complained to the rich, Western nations: "You save us from drowning, but you prevent us from reaching the riverbank."

Where does mission in Christ's way take us? Are there problems that are not properly ours to address as Christians though they affect our neighbour or our world?

Someone asked a friend of mine, who was in a protest march against the unwise use of pesticides on farms in California, what was a good Christian like her doing in the march; to which she countered, what's a good Christian like you doing on the sidelines!

The power of words

Second, there are those who use the *power of words*, aware that doing flows out of knowing. Preaching has always commanded pride of place in the hierarchy of church activities and perhaps that is as it should be. It has a critical function in equipping God's people for ministry. As William McClain says: "Preaching is not small talk about little things. It brings together God's word and human needs. It calls for a decision for or against Jesus Christ." How much we need good preaching to help us on our journey!

Words are powerful. I am sometimes critical of our propensity to resolutions and statements, especially when they are not followed up by action. Yet, I know that when the Christian community speaks with a common voice against a travesty of justice, or to advocate justice and peace, its voice is heard. Our words confront the words of the powerful and carry power if we speak God's truth. Statements and resolutions offer hope to people in difficult and life-threatening situations. They testify to that.

The impact of the policy statements of faith groups and ecumenical organizations on current issues is still to be assessed, but they are important to the life of the church and to the community. When the church acts in this way it helps to dispel the notion that its interest is mainly other-worldly.

Words animate and motivate and encourage when through stories, poetry and song, people can tell of the power they claim as God's people.

And what of the words we speak to each other? How powerful they can be in bringing to fruition the unity, the wholeness, the justice we seek! I still think the most important words I speak are those I use to teach in my Sunday school class trying to share experiences, beliefs, information that could be helpful in making Jesus Christ known to young people.

As the spouse of a pastor and now a bishop, the weight of the responsibility to say the right thing has always weighed heavily on me. There are always opportunities to influence, to inform, to encourage, to challenge. My style has been one of challenge and so it would be quite unlike me to allow this opportunity to challenge you escape me. Perhaps, in these next years when we strive to achieve the goals of the Ecumenical Decade of Churches in Solidarity with Women, some special attention could be given to equipping the spouses (here I am thinking primarily of women) of pastors and bishops and other officials of the church for their distinctive ministry.

The power of association

Third, there are those who use the *power of association*. The value of networks and coalitions and movements is well-known now. We are no longer deterred by the enormity of the tasks. In the story, Elijah was made to realize that he was not alone in the struggle. Like him, we are discovering the host of witnesses determined and ready to work with us for this just, caring and peaceful society we envision.

There is a song that recognizes this power of association:

Just one hand can't tear a prison down,
Just two hands can't tear a prison down.
But if two and two and fifty make a million,
We'll see that day come 'round.

One of the groups I have invested a lot of time and energy in is Church Women United here in the USA. Because of our diversity, we have been forced to find ways to cross barriers. We have discovered the wisdom of joining forces not only with Christians, but with whomever pursues the same goals. I do not believe that God entrusts God's work only to people calling themselves Christians.

There is increasing awareness that we must not only advocate on behalf of people who are poor and powerless, we must also join forces with them in changing those values, attitudes and structures that keep them captive. In solidarity we find common ground for the unity of effort needed to transform the dominance-dependency relationship into one of mutual respect and empowerment. In solidarity, we nurture and support one another.

The power of prayer

Fourth, there are those who use the *power of prayer*. Prayer is an essential discipline of the Christian and it may seem unnecessary even to mention it. But there is a special significance about public prayers. For example, in 1983, when about three thousand Christians gathered in

Washington, DC, to hold a witness for peace on Pentecost, they made the headline news. Over two hundred of them were arrested for holding a peace vigil inside the Capitol. The news stories intimated that Christians were becoming a threat to the government policy of military build-up. The society was taking notice of praying Christians!

Prayer was always at the top of the agenda during the 1960s and 1970s when the civil rights movement in the United States was at its height. No action was taken without prayer, and I have been told that on many occasions when physical injury was certain, they would pattern their prayer after Jesus' prayer in Gethsemane: "If it is your will."

For over one hundred years, hundreds of thousands of women across the world come together on World Day of Prayer to pray for one special concern in the world, hoping to discern what God is saying to us. Who is to say what the value is of this global movement that binds together into one people of such diversity?

When we pray we "tap the well-springs of faith", from that source comes our power and courage. Those on the frontline, in direct confrontation with the powers of evil and destruction, testify to the power of prayer to hear God in the din of struggle and to enable them to witness with courage and integrity.

In this imperfect world we human beings have fashioned, I hold to the vision of shalom. I thank God for you and others in the company of witnesses on this journey of faith. I pray that our words, our actions, our experiences will invite others to faith. As we leave here, may we be energized, enriched, enlightened and empowered so that we can be counted among those on mission in Christ's way.

Address by the
Conference Moderator

Anastasios of Androussa

Human pride, in its individual, social or racial expression, poisons and destroys life in the world at large or in the small community in which we live. The human will obstinately exalts its autonomy. Loneliness is on the increase, nightmares multiply, fears mount up. Old and new idols are being erected in human consciousness. People dance around them. They offer them adulation and worship them ecstatically. But at the same time, every so often, new, sensitive voices speak out for a just and peaceful age. New initiatives are being taken; a new awareness of worldwide community is growing.

In our ecumenical gatherings all of these facts come to light, sometimes alarming, sometimes hopeful. Our problems overwhelm us. We describe them and try to solve them. But when we think we have solved one, three new ones spring up. Our mood keeps swinging, like a pendulum, between hope and despair.

In this world the faithful continue to pray: "Thy will be done, on earth as it is in heaven", proclaiming, quietly but resolutely, that above all human wills there is one will that is redemptive, life-giving, full of wisdom and power, that in the end will prevail. The choice of subject for our meeting is essentially, I think, a protest and a refusal to accept that which militates against God's loving design, and at the same time an expression of hope and optimism for the future of the world.

● Bishop Anastasios of Androussa is professor of the history of religions at the University of Athens, acting archbishop of the Orthodox Church in East Africa, and moderator of the WCC's Commission on World Mission and Evangelism.

Reality and expectation

In the prayer "thy will be done, on earth as it is in heaven", the firm certainty prevails that the Father's will is *already a reality*. Countless other beings, the angels and saints, are already in tune with it. The realization of God's will is not simply a desire; it is a fact that throws light on all the rest. The centre of reality is God and God's kingdom. On this the realism of faith is grounded. On this ontology is based every Christian effort on earth. To some, to mention "heaven" might seem anachronistic. We usually look for immediate answers, down-to-earth and realistic — according to our own fixed ideas. We forget, however, that contemporary science and technology have made important leaps forward with regard to a material heaven. A few decades ago we sought to solve humankind's communication problems by using wires stretched out over the earth's surface. Later on we used wireless waves, still following the surface of our planet. With the new technology, however, we have discovered that we can communicate better above the earth, by sending wireless waves heavenwards. So in our theological, ecclesial and missionary thinking, if we turn our sight once more to the reality of "heaven", about which scripture speaks constantly, we shall certainly find new answers to the world's problems and difficulties.

Our church has not ceased to look in that direction, with prayer and festival affirming the supremacy of God's will. For this faith to clarify the mass of problems that oppress us, the two ideas that form our theme need to be looked at in combination. I shall attempt a first synoptic approach, drawing on the Orthodox tradition of twenty centuries.

1. "Thy will be done." In the prayer our Lord taught us, this petition follows two others, with which it forms a group: "Hallowed be thy name, thy kingdom come, thy will be done." The chief characteristic of the three is the eschatological perspective. They all begin to be realized here below, in order to be perfected in the glory of the kingdom that is to come.

The verb of the petition is in the passive voice. Who exactly is the subject of the action? A preliminary answer says: God. In this petition God's intervention is sought for the implementation of his will, for the establishment of his kingdom. He has the initiative, he carries out his own will. The chief and decisive role in what happens to humankind and the whole universe belongs to God.

A second interpretation sees God's will being done on earth through humankind's conformity with God's commandments (cf. Matt. 7:21, 12:50; John 9:31). We are called to "do" the Father's will. It is a question of the point of view that is expressed in the insight that permeates the Old Testament and in the continuity that is a dominant feature of Jewish literature. In it our participation in the fulfilment of God's will and the necessity of obedience are emphasized.

There is, however, yet a third interpretation, a composite one, that sees as subject of the action both God and human being, that considers that the divine will is realized by divine-human cooperation. Thus the two preceding views are intertwined. Certainly, so that his will may be done, God's intervention is essential. But we, by conforming to his precepts that express God's will in the here and now, contribute to the foretaste and coming of the kingdom in historical time, until its final consummation at the last day.

"On earth as it is in heaven." In this appendage we can perhaps distinguish various closely connected aspects: ethical, social, missionary, ecumenical, and a further one, which we will call realistic. They sum up graphically most of what Chrysostom was saying: "For he did not say, 'thy will be done in me or in us'; but 'everywhere on earth,' so that error might be done away with and truth established, all evil be cast out, virtue return and so nothing henceforth separate heaven from earth."[1] The prayer that our Lord put on our lips and in our hearts aims at a more radical change: the "celestification" of the earth. That all persons and all things may become heaven.[2]

By the phrase "thy will be done", of the Lord's prayer, we beseech the Father that he will bring to completion his plan for the salvation of the whole world, and at the same time we ask for his grace that we may be freed from our own will and accept his joyfully. And not only we as individuals, but that all humankind may have fellowship in his will and share in its fulfilment.

2. After Pentecost this prayer on the church's lips is highlighted by the facts of the cross and the resurrection. It becomes clear that the divine will has been revealed in its fullness by the word, life and sacrifice of Jesus Christ. Each member of the church is called thenceforth to advance in its realization, "so to promote 'the' Father's 'will', as Christ promoted it, who came to do 'the will' of his Father and finished it all; for it is possible by being united with him to become 'one spirit' with him."[3] Christ is made the leader of the faithful in realizing the divine will.

The prayer "Thy will be done" is at the same time our guide in Gethsemane, at the decisive point in the history of the new Adam, our first-born brother. "My Father, if this cannot pass unless I drink it, thy will be done" (Matt. 26:42). This prayer, in which the conformity of the human to the divine will reaches its culmination, illustrates *on a personal level* the meaning of the phrase "thy will be done" of the Lord's prayer. For all those who determine to be conformed to God's will, who struggle for its realization on earth, the time will come to experience personally the pain, grief and humiliation that often accompany acceptance of God's will.

Christ's repetition of "thy will be done" in the context of the passion also illustrates the second option of our theme, "Mission in Christ's way".

Mission in Christ's way

By this expression we often tend to concentrate our attention on some particular stage in Christ's life, e.g., the passion, the cross, his compassion for the poor, etc. It is certainly not strange to put particular emphasis at times on one aspect, especially when it is continually being overlooked in practice. But the theological thinking and experience of the catholic church insist on what is universal *(to kath' holou)*. The same is true of the person of Christ. This distinguishes the outlook and feeling of the one, holy, catholic and apostolic church from the schismatic, sectarian thinking that holds to that which is only a part. In this theological connection I would like to indicate five central points.

1. *Trinitarian connection and relationship.* Jesus Christ is seen in a continuous relationship to the Father and the Holy Spirit. He is the *apestalmenos* of (who was sent by) the Father. The Holy Spirit clears the way for him, works with him, accompanies him, sets the seal on his work and continues it forever. Through Christ's preaching we come to know the Father and the Holy Spirit. But even the preaching of Christ would remain incomprehensible without the enlightenment of the Holy Spirit, impossible to put into effect without the presence of the Paraclete.

In every expression of Christian life, but especially in mission, the work of Christ is done with the presence of the Holy Spirit; it is brought to completion within historical time by the uninterrupted action of the Holy Spirit. The Holy Spirit "recapitulates" all of us in Christ. He forms the church. The source and bearing of our own apostolic activity resides in the promise and precept of the risen Lord in its Trinitarian perspective: "'As the Father has sent me, even so I send you.' And when he had said this, he breathed on them, and said to them, 'Receive the Holy Spirit'" (John 20:21-22).

The Christ-centredness of the one church is understandable only within the wider context of Trinitarian dogma. The one-sidedness of the Western type of Christocentrism was often caused by the restriction of the image of Christ to the so-called "historical Jesus". But the Christ of the church is the eternal word, "the only Son, who is in the bosom of the Father" (John 1:18), who is ever present in the church through the Holy Spirit; risen and ascended, the universal Judge, "the Alpha and the Omega, the first and the last, the beginning and the end" (Rev. 22:13). The faith and experience of the church are summed up in the phrase: the Father, through the Son, in the Holy Spirit, creates, provides, saves. Essentially, mission in Christ's way is mission in the light of the Holy Trinity, in the mystical presence and working together of Father, Son and Holy Spirit.

2. *Assumption of the whole humanity.* One of the favourite terms that Jesus Christ used to describe himself was "son of man". Jesus is the new Adam. The incarnation of the word is the definitive event in the history of humankind, and the church has persisted in opposing any Docetist deviation. "Incarnate by the Holy Spirit and the Virgin Mary" remains the credo of faith. In his conception lies the human contribution, by the wholehearted acceptance of the divine will, in obedience, humility and joy, by his mother, the most pure representative of the human race. "Behold, I am the handmaid of the Lord; let it be to me according to your word" (Luke 1:38) was her decisive statement.

The absolute distinction of matter and spirit — as imagined by representatives of ancient Greek or Indian thought — is rejected, and humanity is raised up as a whole. Jesus Christ is not only the saviour of souls but of the entire human being and the whole material-spiritual creation. This is as hard for classical thought to understand as the Trinitarian dogma. Often indeed an attempt is made to simplify or pass it over. But then mission loses all its power and perspective. Christian mission does not mean taking refuge from our materiality, in one way or another, for the salvation of mere souls, but the transforming of present time, of society and all matter in another way and by another dynamic. This perspective demands creative dialogue with contemporary culture, with secular persons stuck in the materialism of this world, with the new options of physics about matter and energy and with every variety of human creation.

3. *The radically and eternally new element: love.* Christ overthrows the established forms of authority, wisdom, glory, piety and success, traditional principles and values, and reveals that the living centre of all is *love*. The Father is love. The Son is love incarnate. The Spirit is the inexhaustible power of love. This love is not a vague "principle". It is a "communion" of persons. It is the supreme Being, the Holy Trinity. God is love because he is an eternal trinity, a communion of living, equal,

distinct persons. The Son reveals this communion of love *(koinonia agapes)* in the world. In it he is not only the one who invites, but also the way.

Closely bound up with love are freedom, justice, liberation and fellowship of all humankind, truth, harmony, joy and fullness of life. Every sincere utterance and endeavour for these things, anywhere in the world, in whatever age and culture, but above all every loving, true expression of life, is a ray of God's grace and love. Jesus did not speak in vague and philosophical language about these great and holy things but revealed them in power by clear signs and speech, and above all by his life.

Among the many surprises that Christ held in store was the fact that he *identified himself with the humble*, the simplest of the people. From among those he chose his companions and apostles. And in the well-known saying about the universal last judgment he directly identified himself with the despised, the infirm, the poor, the strangers and those in distress in the whole world. "As you did it to one of the least of these my brethren, you did it to me," he says, having "all the nations" assembled before him (Matt. 25:31-46).

This course remains determinative for his church, his mystical body, for all ages. For this, it constitutes, in its authentic form, the most benevolent power that fights for human dignity, worth, relief, the raising up of every human being throughout the length and breadth of the earth. Concern for all the poor and those unjustly treated, without exception — independent of race or creed — is not a fashion of the ecumenical movement, but a fundamental tradition of the one church, an obligation that its genuine representatives always saw as of first importance. "To the extent that you abound in wealth, you are lacking in love," declares Basil the Great, criticizing the predilection of many for a "piety that costs nothing".[4] He did not hesitate to call a "robber" not only the person who robs someone, but also the one who, though able to provide clothing and help, neglects to do so. Tersely he concludes: "You do injustice to so many, as many are those you could help."[5] The modern fact of the world's integration extends these judgments from the individual to the collective plane, from individuals to wider conglomerations, to peoples, the rich nations. The saints of the church did not simply speak for the poor, but, above all, shared their life. They voluntarily became poor, out of love for Christ, who made himself poor, in order to identify with him.

4. *The paradox of humility and the sacrifice of the cross.* From the first moment of his presence in humanity Christ makes *kenosis* (self-emptying)

the revelation of the power of the love of the Triune God. He spends the greater part of his human life in the simplicity of everyday labour. Later, in his short public life, he faces various disputes and serious accusations. The power of love is totally bound up with *humility*. The opposite of love we usually call hatred. But its real name is egoism. This is the denial of the Triune God who is a koinonia (communion) of love. Therein also lies the drama of Lucifer, that he can do everything except be humble. And that is precisely why he cannot love. Christ destroys the works of the devil (1 John 3:8), and ransoms us chained in our egoism, by accepting the ultimate humiliation, the cross. By this humility he abolishes on the cross demonic pride and self-centredness. In that hour the glory of his love shines forth. We are redeemed.

Christian life means continual assimilation of the mystery of the cross in the fight against individual and social selfishness. This holy humility, which is ready to accept the ultimate sacrifice, is the mystical power behind Christian mission. Mission will always be a service that entails acceptance of dangers, sufferings and humiliations, the experience of human powerlessness and at the same time of the power of God. Only those who are prepared to accept, with courage and trust in Christ, sacrifice, tribulation, contradiction and rejection for his sake, can withstand. One of the greatest dangers for Christian mission is that we become forgetful in the practice of the cross and create a comfortable type of a Christian who wants the cross as an ornament but who often prefers to crucify others than to be crucified oneself.

5. *Everything in the light of the resurrection and eschatological hope.* The first precept of the universal mission is given in light of the resurrection. Before the fact of the cross and resurrection Jesus had not allowed his disciples to go out into the world. Unless one experiences the resurrection, one cannot share in Christ's universal apostolate. If one experiences the resurrection, one cannot help bearing witness to the risen Lord, setting one's sights on the whole world. "All authority in heaven and on earth has been given to me. Go, therefore, and make disciples of all the nations" (Matt. 28:19). The first sentence takes our thought back to "on earth as it is heaven" in the Lord's prayer. Authority over the whole world has been given to the Son of man, who fully carried out the Father's will. He is the Lord, "who is and who was and who is to come, the Almighty" (Rev. 1:8). The faith and power of the church are founded precisely on this certainty. Cross and resurrection go together. To conform one's life to the crucified life of Christ involves the mystical power of the resurrection. On the other side, the resurrection is the

glorious revelation of the mystery and power of the cross, victory over selfishness and death. A mission that does not put at its centre the cross and resurrection ends up as a shadow and a phantasy. As do simple people, so also the more cultivated, who wallow in wealth, comfort and honours, come at some moment of crisis face to face with the implacable, final question: what happens at death? In this problem that torments every thinking person in every corner of the world the church has the task of revealing the mystery of Christ's word: "For this is the will of my Father, that every one who sees the Son and believes in him should have eternal life; and I will raise him up at the last day" (John 6:40).

I recall a personal experience, in an out-of-the-way region of western Kenya. We arrived at night at a house that was in mourning. The little girl, stricken mortally by malaria, was lying on a big bed, as if sleeping peacefully. "She was such a good child. She was always the first to greet me," whispered the afflicted father in perplexity. We read a short funeral prayer, and I said a few words of consolation. Alone in the room of the school-house where we were staying, by the light of the oil lamp, with the sound of rain on the banana leaves and zinc roof, I remembered the events of the day. Away in the darkness a drum was beating. It was in the house of mourning. In my tiredness I wondered: why are you here? There came confusedly to my mind the various things that are spoken about in connection with mission: preaching, love, education, civilization, peace, development. Suddenly a light flashed and lit up in the mist of my tired brain the essence of the matter: You bring the message, the hope of resurrection. Every human person has a unique worth. They will rise again. Herein lies human dignity, value and hope. Christ is risen! You teach them to celebrate the resurrection in the mystery of the church; to have a foretaste of it. As if in a fleeting vision I saw the little African girl hurrying up to greet me the first, as was her habit, helping me to determine more precisely the kernel of the Christian mission. That is, to infuse all with the truth and hope of the resurrection; to teach them to celebrate it.

What our brothers and sisters in the isolated corners of Africa and Asia or in the outskirts of our large and rich cities long for, in their depression and loneliness, is not vague words of consolation, a few material goods or crumbs of civilization. They yearn, secretly or consciously, for human dignity, hope, to transcend death. In the end they are searching for the living Christ, the perfect God-man, the way, the truth and the life. All, of whatever age and class, rich or poor, obscure or famous, illiterate or learned, in their heart of hearts long to celebrate the resurrection and the "celestification" of life. In this the prospect of a mission "in Christ's way" reaches its culmination.

Fullness and catholicity

The consequences of such a theological understanding are many-sided. The important units, among which will be groups of problems critical for our time in the days that follow, have already been fixed: (1) turning to the living God; (2) participating in suffering and struggle; (3) the earth is the Lord's; (4) towards renewed communities in mission. Already, much study, leavened with prayer, has taken place in small and larger groups, in conferences and congresses. The third part of this summary report will turn on only two axes.

1. "Thy will be done", as it is repeated by Christ himself in Gethsemane, helps us to overcome a great temptation: *the tendency for us to minimize the demands and cost of doing God's will in our personal life.* It is usually easier for us to rest in the general, in what concerns mostly others.

a) But the will of God, as it is revealed in Christ, is a single and indissoluble *whole* ("... teaching them to observe *all* that I have commanded you"). "Thy will be done" entire, not by halves. The various so-called corrections that have at times been made to make the gospel easier and the church more acceptable or, so to speak, more effective, do not strengthen but rob the gospel of its power. While waiting at a European airport a couple of years ago there came into my hands a leaflet in which, framed between other things, was written: "Blessed are those who are rich. Blessed are those who are handsome. Blessed are those who have power. Blessed are the smart. Blessed are the successful. For they will possess the earth." I thought to myself: How many times, even in our own communities, do we prefer, openly or secretly, these idols, this worldly topsy-turvy representation of the beatitudes, making them criteria of our way of life?

The name of the city in which this meeting of ours is taking place reminds us not only of San Antonio of Padua to which the toponomy refers but also of St Anthony the Great, one of the universal church's great personalities, who traced a model of perfect acceptance of God's will. This great hermit, in perfect obedience to "if you would be perfect, go, sell what you possess and give it to the poor, and you will have treasure in heaven; and come, follow me" (Matt. 19:21) went out in an adventure of freedom and love, which led to the outpouring of a new breath of the Spirit in the church at a time when it was in danger of compromising with secular power and the spirit of the world.

In the midst of our many socio-political concerns we have to bear in mind and act on the understanding that "this is the will of God, your sanctification" (1 Thess. 4:3). Our *sanctification*, by following the divine will in all things, in our daily obligations, in our personal endeavours and in the midst of many and various difficulties and dilemmas. The simplistic anthropology that encourages a naïve morality by passing our existential tragedy by does not help at all. Human existence is an abyss. "I do not do what I want, but I do the very thing I hate... I see in my members another law at war with the law of my mind and making me captive to the law of sin which dwells in my members" (Rom. 7:15-23). Many of us, in critical situations, while we easily say "thy will be done", in practice add: "not as thou wilt, but as I will". This overt or secret reversal of the divine will in our decisions is the main reason and cause of the failure of many Christian missions and initiatives. The hard inner struggle for purification and sanctification is the premise and mystical power of the apostolate.

The carrying out of God's will in the world will always be assisted by *continuous repentance*, so that we may be conformed to the model of Christ and be made one with him. That is why in the Orthodox tradition monasteries have special importance, above all as centres of penitence. Everything that accompanies this struggle — worship, work, comforting the people, education, artistic creativity — follows, as a reflection of the spiritual purification, the transforming personal experience of repentance. The quest for new types of communities that will serve the contemporary apostolate must be closely bound up with the spiritual quest in the contemporary social reality for concrete forms of communities that will live out thoroughly, on the personal level, repentance and longing for the coming of the kingdom. The critical question for a mission in Christ's way is to what extent others can discern in our presence a ray of his presence.

b) Conformity to God's will does not mean servile submission or fatalistic expectation. Nor is it achieved by a simple, moral, outward obedience. Joyful acceptance of God's will is an expression of love for a new relationship in the Beloved; it is a restoration of humanity's lost freedom. It means our communion in the mystery of the love of the Holy Trinity, communion in freedom of love. Thus, we become "partakers of the divine nature" (2 Pet. 1:4). Conformity to God's will is in the end a sharing in what the Orthodox tradition calls "uncreated energies", by which we reach theosis, we become "good by grace".[6] The most blessed pages of Christian mission were written out of an excess of love for Christ, an identification with him.

c) The church continually seeks to renew this holy intoxication of love, especially by the sacrament of the holy eucharist — which remains the pre-eminently missionary event — everywhere on earth. In the divine liturgy the celebrant, as representative of the whole community, prays: "Send thy Holy Spirit upon us and upon these gifts here present." Not on the gifts only, but we beg that the Holy Spirit may be sent "upon us" also, so that we may be "moved by the Spirit". The whole prayer moves very clearly in a Trinitarian perspective. We beseech the Father to send the Spirit to change the precious gifts into Christ's body and blood, and in receiving holy communion we are united with him; we become "of one body" and "of one blood" with Christ, that we may bear the "fruit" of the Spirit, become "God's temple", receivers and transmitters of his blessed radiance.

The enthusiasm for the *acquisition of the Holy Spirit*, which is of late much sought after in the West, has always been strong in the East, but in a sober Christological context and in a Trinitarian perspective. The church's experience is summed up in the well-known saying of St Seraphim: "The purpose of Christian life is the acquisition of the Holy Spirit." And the saint continues: "Prayer, fasting and almsgiving, and the other good works and virtues that are done for Christ, are simply, and only, means of acquiring God's Holy Spirit."[7] This presence of the Holy Spirit has nothing at all to do with spiritual pride and self-satisfaction. It is at bottom connected with the continual exercise of penitence, with holy humility. "I tell you the truth," wrote a holy monk of Mount Athos, Starets Silouan. "I find nothing good in myself and I have committed many sins. But the grace of the Holy Spirit has blotted them out. And I know that to those who fight sin is afforded not only pardon but also the grace of the Holy Spirit, which gladdens the soul and bestows a sweet and profound peace."[8]

2. The fact that the will of God refers to the whole world, the whole universe, *excludes any isolating of ourselves in an individual piety*, in a sort of *private Christianity*.

a) The will of God covers the whole human reality; it is accomplished in the whole of history. It is not possible for the Christian to remain indifferent to historical happenings in the world, when faith is grounded on two historical facts: the incarnation of the word and the second coming of Christ. The social, human event is the place in which the church unfolds. Every expression of human creativity, science, technology and the relationships of persons as individuals, peoples and various groupings are to be found among its concerns. We are living at a critical, historic juncture in which a new universal culture, the electronic culture, is taking shape. The natural sciences, especially bio-medicine, genetics, astronautics, are creating and posing new problems. Half of the earth's population is crushed into huge urban centres; contemporary agnosticism is eating away at the thought and behaviour of the city-dwellers. The passage from the "written" to the "electronic" word is opening up undreamed-of possibilities for the amassing of a whole universe of increased knowledge and creating a new human thinking. A new world is emerging. A new sort of human being is being formed. The church, the mystical body of "the one who is and was and is to come" has a pledge and a duty to the march of humanity in the future, the whole society in which it exists as "leaven", "sign" and "sacrament" of the kingdom that has come and is coming. What the church has, it has to radiate and offer for the sake of all the world.

But if one temptation is for us not to see the universal duty when we pray "thy will be done", the reverse is for us to be occupied only with universal themes, indifferent to concrete reality; to be too sensitive to certain situations and indifferent to others. (To speak, for example, constantly about injustice in such-and-such a publicized region and be indifferent to injustice in Europe, as, for example, in Albania, where four hundred thousand Christians are oppressed, deprived constitutionally of every expression of faith, even of the elementary right to have a church.)

In various corners of our planet, want, disease, oppression, injustice, the raw violence of arms, oppress millions of our fellow human beings. All of these are cells of the same body — the great body of humanity to which we belong. Their suffering is the suffering of Christ, who assumed the whole of humanity, and the suffering of the church, his mystical body. It is — must be — the suffering of us all.

The prophetic voice, both for the immediate and actual and worldwide, remains always the church's obligation, even if it annoys certain people who do not wish to touch any unjust establishment. In many situations, within and outside, the church is obliged today to speak in the way of the biblical protest: Woe to those who talk about justice but who in practice seek only their own right and their own privileges. Woe to those who rejoice, crying "peace, peace", but forge the fetters of the defenceless. Woe to the rich nations that continually celebrate freedom and love, but by their policies make the developing peoples poorer and less free. Woe to those who appear as God's lawyers and representatives, making a mockery — deliberately or unintentionally — of what is finest in humanity, the witness of Jesus Christ.

b) But still the gospel cannot remain the possession of only certain peoples who had the privilege of hearing it first. By putting on our lips the prayer "thy will be done", the Lord "bade each one of us who prays to take thought for the ecumene" (John Chrysostom). [9] God's will, as it was fulfilled and revealed in Christ, has to be made known in every corner of the earth, in every cranny of the world, in every expression of our contemporary many-centred civilization. A world missionary conference like our own cannot relegate to a footnote the fact that millions of our fellow men and women have not heard, even once in their lives, the Christian message; that hundreds of races still, after twenty centuries of Christian history, do not have the gospel in their mother tongue.

Distinctions between Christian and non-Christian nations are no longer absolutely valid in our days. In all nations there is a need for re-evangelization in every generation. Every local church finds itself in mission in its actual geographical and cultural territory and context. But its horizons, outside the place in which it is active, must extend in the catholic church "from one end of the earth to the other". Despite cultural differences, all of us face more or less the same basic human problems. All the local churches, expressing the life of the "one, holy, catholic and apostolic church", are in a state of mutual interdependence and inter-change, on both receiving and sending. The distinction between sending and receiving churches belongs to the past. All should, and can, both receive and send. In proportion to the gifts (charismata) that every local church possesses (personnel, knowledge, expertise, financial resources) it can contribute to the development of the worldwide mission "to the end of the earth" (Acts 1:8). It is time for every Christian to realize that mission is our own obligation and to take part in it looking to the whole of humankind. Just as there is no church without a worshipping life, so there cannot be a living church without missionary life.

c) Those outside the Christian faith, who still have no knowledge of the will of God in its fullness, do not cease to move in the mystical radiance of his glory. God's will is diffused throughout the whole of history and throughout the whole world. Consequently it influences their own life, concerns them and embraces them. It is expressed in many ways — as divine providence, inspiration, guidance, etc. In recent times in the ecumenical movement we have been striving hard for the theological understanding of people of other faiths; and this difficult, but hopeful, dialogue very much deserves to be continued at this present conference.

Certainly for the church, God's will, as it was lived out in its fullness by Christ, remains its essential heritage and contribution in the world. But respect for others will not be a so-called agreement on a common denominator that minimizes our convictions about Christ, but an injus-tice, if we are silent about the truth that constitutes the givenness of the church's experience; it is another thing, the imposition by force, that is unacceptable and has always been anti-Christian. A withholding of the truth leads to a double betrayal, both of our own faith and of others' right to know the whole truth.

Jesus Christ went about doing good among people of other faiths (let us recall the stories of the Canaanite woman and the centurion) admiring and praising their spontaneous faith and goodness. ("I say to you, not even in Israel have I found such faith", Matt. 8:10.) He even used as a symbol of himself a representative of another religious community, the good "Samaritan". His example remains determinative: beneficent service and sincere respect for whatever has been preserved from that which was made "in the image of God". Certainly in today's circumstances our duty is becoming more clear and extensive: a journey together in whatever does not militate against God's will, an understanding of the deepest religious insights that have developed in other civilizations by the assistance of the Spirit, a cooperation in the concrete applications of God's will, such as justice, peace, freedom, love, both in the universal community and on the local level.

d) Not only the so-called spiritual but also the whole physical universe moves in the sphere of God's will. Reverence for the animal and the vegetable kingdoms, the correct use of nature, concern for the conservation of the ecological balance, the fight to prevent nuclear catastrophe and to preserve the integrity of creation, have become more important in the list of immediate concerns for the churches. This is not a deviation, as asserted by some who see Christ as saving souls by choice and his church as a traditional religious private concern of certain people. The whole world, not only humankind but the entire universe, has been called to share in the restoration that was accomplished by the redeeming work of Christ. "We wait for new heavens and a new earth in which righteousness dwells" (2 Pet. 3:13). Christ, the Almighty and Logos of the Universe, remains the key to understanding the evolution of the world. All things will come to pass in him who is their head. The surprising design, "the mystery of his will", which has been made known to us "according to his purpose", is "a plan for the fullness of time, to unite all things in him (*anakephaleosasthai ta panta en ô Christô* — according to another translation: 'bring everything together under Christ, as a head'), things in heaven and things on earth" (Eph. 1:9-10). The correspondence with the phrase of the Lord's prayer is obvious. The transforming of creation, as victory over the disfigurement that sin brought to the world, is to be found in the wider perspective and immediate concerns of Christian mission.

Through all the length and breadth of the earth millions of Christians of every race, class, culture and language repeat "thy will be done, on earth as it is in heaven." Sometimes painfully, faithfully and hopefully; sometimes mechanically and indifferently. But we seldom connect it intimately with the missionary obligation. The conjunction of the two phrases "thy will be done" and "mission in Christ's way" gives a special dynamic to our conference. Understanding the missionary dimensions of this prayer will strengthen in the Christian world the conviction that mission is sharing in carrying out God's will on earth. And, put the other way round, that God's will demands our own active participation, working with the Holy Trinity.

By sharing the life of the risen Christ, living the Father's will moved by the Holy Spirit, we have a decisive word and role in shaping the course of humankind. The Lord is at hand. The history of the world does not proceed in a vacuum. It is unfolding towards an end. There is a plan. God's will shall prevail on earth. The prayers of the saints will not remain unanswered! There will be a universal judgment by the Lord of love. At that last hour everything will have lost its importance and value, except for disinterested love. The last word belongs to Christ. The mystery of God's will reaches its culmination in the recapitulation of all things in him. We continue to struggle with fortitude. We celebrate the event that is coming. We enjoy a foretaste of that hour of the last things. Rejoicing in worship. With this vision. With this hope.

Lord, free us from our own will and incorporate us in your own. "Thy will be done."

NOTES

[1] John Chrysostom, "Commentary to Saint Matthew the Evangelist", Homily 19, 5. *P.G..* (= J.P. Migne, *Patrologiae Cursus Completus, Series Graeca*, Paris), Vol. 57, col. 280.

[2] Origen, "On Prayer," XXVI, 6, *BEPES* (Library of Greek Fathers and Church Writers, Athens), Vol. 10, p.279.

[3] *Ibid.*, XXVI, 3, p.277.

[4] Basil the Great, "To those who become wealthy," *BEPES*, Vol. 54, p.67.

[5] Homily on "I will pull down my barns", 7, *BEPES*, Vol. 54, pp.64-65.

[6] Maximos the Confessor, "On various questions...," *P.G.*, Vol. 91, col. 1084AC, 1092C.

[7] P.A. Botsis, *Philokalia ton Roson Neptikon* (Philocalia of the Russian Vigilents), Athens, 1983, p.105.

[8] Archimandrite Sophrony, *Starets Silouan, moine du Mont-Athos* (translated from Russian into French by the Hieromoine Symeon), Sisteron, 1973, p.318.

[9] Chrysostom, *ibid.*, col. 280.

Mission Issues for Today and Tomorrow

Eugene L. Stockwell

Seventy-nine years... Seventy-nine years ago next month some 1200 representatives of mission boards and societies gathered in Edinburgh, Scotland, for a major mission conference, launching the ecumenical movement of this century.

Seventy-nine years later we meet here in San Antonio, heirs of a great and complex history, trying as did our forebears to seek a contemporary faithfulness in Christian mission for our day as they did for theirs.

Seventy-nine years... how short a time in God's reckoning! Yet how enormously different is our day from 1910. At Edinburgh, fully 99 percent of the participants came from North Atlantic countries. They looked out at a world beyond their own, aiming at "the evangelization of the world in our generation". Edinburgh was an overwhelmingly Protestant, white, male gathering, shaping a mission from the West to the rest.

At San Antonio, about 70 percent of the delegates come from areas to which the mission societies at Edinburgh sent missionaries. Here we come from all corners of the world, representing all continents, all major races, female and male alike, Orthodox and Protestant, in a city largely Roman Catholic. Here we welcome consultants designated by the Vatican. Here we welcome guest-participants from other great religions. Here we come to assess who we are as a Christian faith community and to try to understand under God's will what we are to be and do today in a mission in Christ's way.

Gone, thank God, are many political dominations of 1910, as new nations have thrown off the shackles of colonialism to assert their independence and shape their own destinies.

● Eugene L. Stockwell retired in July 1989 after having served as director of the WCC's Commission on World Mission and Evangelism since January 1984.

Gone, thank God, is the simplistic reading of history that sees Christian development as the inexorable forward progressive march of humankind.

Gone, thank God, is the pretentious ignorance that the best is in the west.

Gone, thank God, is the cultural pride that is blind to the age-old beauty of mind, experience and spirit of what so many glibly called "pagan".

Gone, thank God, is the false identification of the mission of God with the mission of the church as we know it, as well as the identification of the church with the kingdom of God.

What a world of difference between 1910 and 1989! But, lest we gloat, what a complex, threatened, pain-ridden world we still live in!

Present is economic oppression of every sort — with massive foreign debt destroying the fabric of hope and life across much of the earth.

Present is the impending threat of global annihilation in an instant of thermonuclear catastrophe, or in expanding ecological suicide.

Present is massive human pain — much of it so unnecessary — caused by war, torture, hunger, the uprooting of peoples, the ruthlessness of greed, the insensitivity of pride, the gulf between the "haves" and the "should-haves".

Present, still, is a Christian community that seems endlessly divided, mocking Christ's prayer "that all may be one".

Present, still, are churches that live to themselves, that assume that mission is an option when convenient, that portray evangelization as a prescription for success, forgetting the cross, and talking of institutional church growth as if it were biblical.

More hopefully, however...

Present, also, is the shattering of old idols of success and prosperity, of dreams of peace without justice, of life without struggle, of achievement without love, of satisfaction without self-giving.

Present, also, is a growing awareness that the good of all entails unity, not uniformity, diversity with respect for difference.

Present, also, is a growing humility that knows that human power has limits, that technology will not save us, that vulnerability is our human condition.

So here we are, at San Antonio, gathered beneath a prayer — "Your will be done" — seeking to find a mission that is not ours, but is God's; a "mission in Christ's way". How great an opportunity! How daunting a task! How strange that God might convene us here to seek God's will and to move us towards a new commitment to Christ's way!

The mission of Christians and of the Christian church is founded on God's mission, on the Trinitarian action of God the Creator in Jesus Christ through the Holy Spirit. God sent his Son into the world, in an act of supreme self-giving and unbounded love. As children of the same God we are likewise sent, in self-giving and love, to align our lives and communities with the overarching witness of the Holy Spirit who seeks ardently to reunite all people, countries and nature in God (Eph. 1:9-10).

We are called to repentance — individual and collective — for our sin of rejection and stubborn disobedience.

We are called to conversion to Jesus Christ in our personal lives, in our communities, and in the structures of society, that we may discover life abundant.

We are called to witness to the Holy Spirit in our midst.

We are called to share what we have received from God with all the peoples and nations of the earth, respectfully and with sensitivity to culture and diversity. In a word, the church is called to a mission in Christ's way — no more, no less.

Often the church has in the past, and in our time, engaged in a mission that by no stretch of the imagination could be seen to be "in Christ's way".

— Too often the church has confused proclamation with words alone, forgetting the integral witness of worship, deed and life.

— Too often the church has confounded witness with the imposition of a gospel wrapped in cultural trappings that obscure the living Christ.

— Too often the church has threatened hell in the name of heaven, focusing on a future heaven at the expense of an earth God loved so much that to it he gave his only Son.

— Too often the church has stressed numerical growth rather than spiritual depth, power rather than the vulnerability of the cross.

— Too often the church has spoken words of justice and righteousness, but ignored or persecuted those who lived out true justice.

We are here at San Antonio to say a resounding "no" to that kind of mission.

Only nine years ago, at the last World Council of Churches' world mission conference, in Melbourne, Australia, the ecumenical community explored the meaning of Jesus' prayer "your kingdom come". The kingdom was seen to be intimately related to a "preferential option for the poor". The gospel is indeed good news for the poor, though to the rich it may augur seemingly bad news of loss of power and prestige. The kingdom of God turns conventional values upside down and reveals

God's will in unexpected, demanding ways. Here in San Antonio we pursue the kingdom theme under the following phrase of the Lord's prayer, "Your will be done", and in Christ's way of living out God's will shall we seek guidance to our contemporary obedience.

Our fundamental clue to a mission in Christ's way continues to be the experience of the poor — the poor in wealth and the poor in spirit. The major mission conferences of this century have not always grasped that fact, but in recent years it has been ever more evident that the poor are at the heart of the matter. Was it not always so? Jesus himself, his disciples and closest followers, were poor, terribly poor in material terms, yet found their wealth in God. They were not stranded on useless definitions of who is poor. The rich may debate who is poor and who is not, but those who have no home, no food, no power, no hope — they know they are poor. Our sophistry about definitions fools nobody but ourselves.

What is so notable in recent years, and so surprises us in comfortable church structures, is that even as we say that "God has exercised a preferential option for the poor" we have been surrounded by the fact that many of the poor have exercised a preferential option for the Christian community, the church. Where is the vitality of Christian faith most vitally expressed these days? In European cathedrals? In comfortable suburban US neighbourhoods? In New York, London, Bonn, Moscow, Tokyo or Geneva? We find this vitality in struggling black communities in South Africa, in Latin American desperately poor neighbourhoods and basic ecclesial communities, in Indian villages, in Chinese renascent house churches, in Pentecostal communities (whatever their name) who trust the Spirit in every detail, in human rights movements, in women's movements for just emancipation, in all those unexpected "Nazareths" from which we so easily expected nothing at all. I am indebted to a US theologian, Larry Rasmussen, professor at Union Theological Seminary in New York, for a renewed insight into this reality. Hear some of his phrases:

— "More and more, Christianity is a faith of struggling peoples who are recasting it amidst those struggles."
— "All liberation theologies... insist that justice is the moral test of God-claims and spirituality. They are profoundly oriented to public life, and they push for the kind of Christian faith that would help end massive suffering."
— "Almost all the new voices in theology are voices of emerging peoples who are driven to toss off the heavy layers of fate and circumstance, and who press justice as a matter of faith..."

It is to such justice that Dom Helder Camara, that great Roman Catholic apostle of the poor in Brazil, refers:

> When I was in Japan I met one of the greatest robot inventors... I thought, God must be happy that there are co-creators like this among human beings. But I thought of my people in Recife, too.... I had a prayer in my heart that God would let this Japanese robot-creator meet my people, and that that would give him the idea that the fantastic progress that he has in his head and hands should serve first of all to make the poor less poor, and not the rich more rich.

Lest we be too presumptuous or sentimental, all of us here at San Antonio are rich. We will eat today; the poor will not. We know where we will sleep tonight; the homeless do not. Competent medical assistance is nearby; for the poor it hardly exists. Our children have a fair chance to receive an education; the poor cannot count on such a chance. We can spend ten days talking about a mission in Christ's way; the poor have little privilege to talk beyond the daily struggle for life.

We enter into the issues of this conference seeking God's will and way. We dare not claim too much, we must not dare too little. What are some of the critical issues with which we must wrestle at this time in the history of our world and of the Christian world mission?

The relation of unity and mission

Among the many important issues of our day that might be highlighted at this time, I choose four that seem of special importance for Christian mission today. The first is the *relation of unity and mission* and its particular characteristics today.

Much has been said and written about unity and mission, to a point where the literature on the subject becomes repetitive. Most comments are based, rightly, on Jesus' high-priestly prayer: "I do not pray for these only, but also for those who are to believe in me through their word, that they may all be one; even as thou, Father, art in me, and I in thee, that they may be in us, so that the world may believe that thou hast sent me" (John 17:20-21). But in the history of Christianity we have generally commended belief in Jesus while we have destroyed the unity of the body of Christ to a point where no one who remotely knows about Christianity is in any doubt that Christians are divided, split into a thousand and one churches, sects, groups and communities. This is a scandal, pure and simple.

What is more, the role of Christian mission in this situation is ambiguous at best. There was a time when it could be argued that Christian mission across the world highlighted the scandal of division and hence encouraged unions of churches that hitherto, out of European or North American histories, had been divided. The Church of North India, the Church of South India, the United Church of Christ (Kyodan) in Japan, and many other unions, give eloquent testimony to this reality. Divisions back in the so-called "sending nations" did not forever have to be perpetuated. None of these unions are perfect, but all point to a relationship of unity and mission that is not purely spiritual, but that in fact has brought Christians into a visible, concrete, unity of life and worship in communities of common purpose.

But how far we are from the unity for which Christ prayed! We thrill to the concept of "one universal church, catholic and apostolic" but, to be honest, in this very gathering none of us would point to all of us and say we are that. The World Council of Churches has over three hundred member churches, Orthodox and Protestant, all Christian, each separated from the others. Beyond World Council membership is the large Roman Catholic Church, and a host of churches — ecumenical, evangelical, Pentecostal, etc. — which earnestly testify to Jesus Christ but which cannot remotely be said to testify by their life and being to the full unity of the church, of Christ's body on this earth. Nor can we here. I have many hopes for this conference and its follow-up — but if I were to hope for only one thing, only one result, it would be that as we commit ourselves to God's will in a mission in Christ's way we might encourage the Christian churches of the world towards a new unity, visible and real, so that in the specifics of our worship, living and witness, the world might know that we are what Jesus prayed for: one.

Allow me to speak a word, from my Protestant viewpoint, to my fellow Christians of other histories. To my Roman Catholic friends I want to say a word of profound thanksgiving for the Second Vatican Council, for ecclesial base communities of immense importance in their witness, for missionary congregations of sisters, brothers and priests whose identification with the poor and whose missionary witness is superb. Of course I have my problems with some of your hierarchical structures and with some of your ethical positions, which I know you hold to out of deep biblical and theological commitment, as surely you have problems with some of mine. But I hope that some day — alas, not here at San Antonio — you and I, in the name of the one Christ we worship, can partake together, at one eucharistic table, of the elements of the body and blood of our Lord.

To my Orthodox friends I want to say a word of profound thanksgiving for your great treasure of witness across centuries, for the effort to be faithful in understanding and theology to what is truly "orthodox", for the liturgy that you celebrate as a missionary event, for steadfast witness under unbelievably difficult and oppressive systems of government in many parts of the world. But I hope that some day — alas, not here at San Antonio — you and I, in the name of the one Christ we worship, can partake together, at one eucharistic table, of the elements of the body and blood of our Lord.

To my friends who, with difficulty, I group together as "conservative evangelicals", knowing that no one likes that depiction, I turn out of a conviction that I, as most of us in this conference, believe we are "evangelical", committed to the evangel, the gospel, and want to be part of one Christian family with you. To you I want to say a word of profound gratitude for pressing us all to understand the basics of Jesus' message, for your intense awareness of human sin and your liberating search for true salvation, for your insistence on biblical truth and your insistence on personal morality. But I hope that some day — alas, not here at San Antonio — you and I, in the name of the one Christ we worship, can accept each other, more than we do today, as fellow Christians. I hope that our common definition of sin is not limited to individual life but to community and collective life as well. I hope that together we will struggle for human rights for all God's people, that we will be united in preserving all humanity and all earth from the powers of media perversion and the worship of success. I hope the day will come when we will not be confronted with an "ecumenical" mission conference in May at San Antonio and an "evangelical" conference in July in Manila, all in the name of the same Christ, but that we might be truly one in the Lord, that all may believe. We must work for that, earnestly. Faithfulness to Jesus Christ requires it in our day.

But at present, probably our greatest efforts must be in our local communities. My daughter recently sent me a "covenant" worked out by several churches in a single community (Allentown, Pennsylvania) that for me makes unity come alive. These were Episcopal (Anglican), Lutheran, Presbyterian, Roman Catholic. At a very local level they made certain agreements over a period of two years. I cite some of these agreements:

— to pray for one another;
— to engage periodically in joint worship;
— to try to understand each other's heritage and beliefs;
— to work together for social justice;
— to enter into joint action projects for the community;

— to strive towards "not doing individually what we could do together";
— to evaluate biannually their commitment to each other.
I think that such local commitments, anywhere in the world, can mean more than pious statements of conferences such as ours. Unity and mission must be local. Here is an attempt, important but imperfect, to manifest unity at a local level, and to relate it to mission in Christ's way. It is of no small moment that these Allentown churches conclude their agreement by saying: "We dedicate ourselves to these objectives and ask the blessing of Almighty God on this covenant that we may be faithful to the agreement to his honour and glory." Can we at San Antonio do as much? Can we, as we return to the myriad situations we here represent, begin to establish the concrete, specific, workaday agreements that will make unity and mission more than documents of a conference? I hope that San Antonio will move us, and the churches of the world, in that direction.

Gospel and culture

A second important mission issue of our time is summed up in the phrase "gospel and culture". Though the relationship between the Christian gospel and human cultures is as old as the gospel itself, in recent years there has been a growing sensitivity to the many ways in which the church and missionary movements have all too often violated or disdained human cultures that themselves are part of God's creation. Many evangelistic efforts, however sincere or well-intentioned, have run roughshod over people's customs and cultures, often allied to military and colonialist powers. With shame we recall the destruction of indigenous cultures across five centuries in the Americas in the name of civilization and evangelization, or the alliance between some missionaries and "gunboat diplomacy" in China in the nineteenth and first half of the twentieth centuries. More recently, much evangelism and mission has been tied to the economic and technological domination by Western powers. Today, an "electronic evangelism", that falsely offers a "pure and simple gospel" fashioned for transmission worldwide in a high-tech studio somewhere in Dallas or elsewhere, is but a more recent evidence of the same phenomenon, as if such a "gospel" can be inserted into any human culture without reference to the complexities and beauties of a particular cultural experience through which God's Spirit was always at work.

Thus the 1983 Vancouver WCC assembly called all of us to look again at the whole issue of Christ and culture in the present historical situation.

It is easier to note the crucial importance of the relationship of gospel and culture than it is to suggest ways to secure a creative inter-relationship of the two. There have been many efforts in this direction, and here I would pay special tribute to the consultation on gospel and culture in 1978 of the Lausanne Committee's theology and education group (the Willowbank report), which struggled with this issue from an evangelical perspective. There are many creative efforts in liturgy, music and the arts to reverse erstwhile Western cultural impositions. Less noticed perhaps, but of much importance, are the efforts in Western countries to disentangle expressions of faith from idolatrous "ways of life" where civil religion and "patriotic nationalism" have been assumed to be Christian.

Two current needs are (1) to challenge the strong impact of secularistic, technological, consumerist, and often militarist, cultures that spread across the globe, frequently masquerading as "Christian", and (2) to seek to affirm the many cultures of the poor who, often in suffering, evidence marks of grace and beauty that are surely gifts of the Spirit. A recent book, *The City of Joy*, by the French author Dominique Lapierre, tells in compelling fashion of a Calcutta slum where tragedy and grinding oppression reigned, but even more compellingly relates the magnificent and stirring triumph of the human spirit over even the worst of circumstances. From the ignominious slum of that "city of joy" there is much to learn about how the gospel and the cultures of the poor can interact and learn from each other.

What can emerge from San Antonio on this issue? There was a time when in the planning of this conference it was proposed that one of the sections of the conference be specifically on gospel and culture. It was decided, rightly or wrongly, not to do that, but rather to recognize that gospel and culture issues permeate the work of every section of the conference. To confine this matter to one area of our work seemed to release the rest of the conference from its impact.

If there is one area among many I would lift up in this connection it is the relationship between our understanding of the gospel and the place that women have in society and in the church. Age-old cultures, along with ancient theologies, have combined frequently to subjugate women so firmly and so long that even some of the most obvious discrimination against women is accepted as "cultural" and hence somehow acceptable. Here is surely an area where a better understanding of the gospel can help us to realize that some traditional cultural patterns violate the elemental human rights of women. Jesus knew better, and in the face of the patriarchal systems of his day did much to honour the dignity of women, but many who follow him fail to do as much. A more profound understanding of the relationship of the Christian gospel and culture should lead us towards greater justice for women in both society and the church.

Parenthetically, it has been instructive (and disconcerting) that in trying to move the composition of this conference towards a membership that would roughly equal half women and half men time and again the churches proposing delegate nominations would simply refuse — there is no other word for it — refuse to give as prominent a place to women as they would to men. Justifications offered for this unwillingness abound, but the fact remains. The issues of gospel and culture are not far from us; we sense their impact right here.

Christian relationship to people of other great religious faiths of humankind

A third issue that I wish to raise for your thoughtful consideration is that of the *Christian relationship to people of other great religious faiths of humankind*. This is not an easy subject for Christians to discuss, for many assume that the only stance to take is that all persons of all other faiths should, must, will become Christians. I am sure that those of these other faiths present in this conference, whom we warmly welcome here, are not convinced that conversion to Christianity is their only alternative if they are to be faithful to God's will.

Let us, as Christians, be clear on where we stand. We believe in one God, revealed in Jesus Christ, fully and for all humanity. We believe that the greatest joy, the fullest understanding, the salvation to which humanity can aspire, is in Jesus Christ. We believe that the Holy Spirit is at work everywhere and among all peoples (not just among Christians) to bring about God's unfathomable purposes for all humanity, and for eternity. We believe that the Holy Spirit witnesses to Jesus Christ. We also believe that God has provided all of us with a world of immense plurality and diversity, not by accident but by intent, a cosmos wherein the purposes God intends are being worked out to bring all to fruition and perfection in God.

Yet on this global planet, so fragile, so small within the bounds of the entire universe, so beautiful, we find ourselves as Christians living as neighbours with many fellow human beings, many of them very poor, who have a deep commitment to faiths we find strange, alien, different. Our neighbours find us equally strange, alien, different. Those who are Muslims, Buddhists, Hindus, Jews, Zoroastrians, Jains, etc., are not created by another God than the One we worship. They are our sisters and brothers, flesh of our flesh, life of our life. Time and again they espouse great ideals and live by them, something we Christians often fail to do. Time and again they provide insights into the purposes of divinity that many of us Christians fail to see and appropriate. What are we Christians to make of all of this?

At the WCC Vancouver assembly it was acknowledged that in all great religions there is a true search for God. What that assembly was unable to say was that perhaps, just perhaps, in that search some might find God! In 1938, at the Tambaram (Madras, India) conference, which was a predecessor conference to San Antonio, there was a great debate about the relationship of Christians to other religions. Hendrik Kraemer, with his "biblical realism", spoke of a discontinuity between Christianity and other religions. Asians, especially, disagreed, knowing out of daily experience that God was not absent from the lives of many who were not Christians but who often lived lives of extraordinary beauty and kindness.

Fifty years after the 1938 Tambaram meeting the WCC called together another group at the same place, in January 1988, to relook at these issues from a contemporary perspective. We were clear that respectful dialogue with persons of other faiths is both necessary and a Christian imperative, all the more so because of religious intolerance and fanaticism in all religions. In such dialogue, surely we expect Christians to state their faith forthrightly, without compromise, affirming Jesus Christ as Lord of all. We know there will be disagreements. We know that full unity with persons of other faiths is still beyond the horizon of our view. We know that God, through the Holy Spirit, has much yet to teach us even about our own faith as others question and challenge our beliefs. We wander in a wilderness where there are some signs, but much uncertainty. We affirm that mystery is part of our life, our very being, our circumstance, our search. But also we know that if we seek God's will, in what for us is a mission in Christ's way, there are some givens. One is that the world is small and full of diversity, God-given. Another is that the needs of humanity are not divided among religions, but human need for life, for meaning, and for hope is surely one. Another is that eternal salvation is not for us to determine, but for God to determine in God's own way and time, and we can trust God for that. At the very least, we who take the name of Christ may well be more humble about our views of God's purposes and more certain of God's eternal care and love than so often we exemplify in our relations to persons of other faiths, those whom God created, as God did us, to be an integral part of God's creation on this earth.

Recently, Dr Pauline Webb, a distinguished Christian leader in Britain and an ecumenist of long experience, faced forthrightly the question so often posed as Christians think about their relations to people of other faiths: "Is Jesus the only way?" Her answers I would like to make my own. She gives three possible ones: "yes", "no" and "I don't know". The context of her answers is, she says, that "the greatest division in our world today is not between those of different faiths but between those who have faith and those who have no faith at all; those who hope and those who despair; those who believe that life has an eternal destiny and an ultimate meaning and those who fear that all is meaningless and will end only in death and destruction."

Her "yes" to the question of whether Jesus is the only way is a personal statement of faith best put in the words of John Wesley: "I trust in Christ, in him alone for salvation." Jesus is the only way by which most of us have found the way to God, and we will commend him to all others who seek the path of faith. But in our encounters with people of other faiths we cannot deny that many of them have arrived at having a profound relationship to God. We feel compelled to say, "No, Jesus is not the *only* way" if that is taken to mean that all who do not name the name of Jesus have lost the way, have no passport to heaven. Then comes the "I don't know" answer. Dr Webb says:

> Just as I am convinced that we have been right about our faith and the unique revelation God has given us in Jesus, I am learning too that we have often been wrong about the other faiths, and have written off as heresies or heathen many ideas that were actually distortions of what those faiths truly teach.

In the face of our checkered Christian history of arrogance and intolerance we have little standing to decide who will be saved and who will not. God's purposes are so much broader than ours. We can leave to God the decisions about ultimate salvation, and meanwhile we can share our treasured faith in Jesus Christ with sensitivity and conviction while opening ourselves also to God's gifts of grace so evident in the faith worlds of many religions on earth.

It is my hope that this conference will not miss the chance to express some such stance, thus encouraging the worldwide Christian community towards new expressions of Christian faith and respect that our divided world so urgently needs.

The defence of life

There is a fourth issue I want to lift up, not so easy to describe. My Latin American friends would probably describe it as *"the defence of life"*. Others would speak of "community". Within the World Council of

Churches' current planning it might be categorized under the heading "justice, peace, and the integrity of creation". I find it hard to describe in words, but easy to feel in personal terms.

— I remember the mother of eleven children in Chile who did not know how to work enough hours to feed her family.
— I remember the Chinese friends who worked endless hours but wanted to find more meaning in life than they so far had experienced.
— I remember the Mozambique miners in South African gold mines who worked to support their families but died far from home.
— I remember the Russian Christians who for their defence of basic human rights ended up in wretched Siberian labour camps.
— I remember the Palestinian youth who threw a stone and harboured a bullet in his body.
— I remember a Pacific island woman who, when her child turned to jelly, knew intimately what nuclear devastation meant.
— I remember the homeless New York mother who wandered the streets in search of, for her, a non-existent home.
— I remember Jesus, a refugee, a Nazarene nobody, a criminal by laws that made him outcast.

What brings all this together? I suspect that it is a search for humanity, for respect for the highest creature God has created, the human being. I believe that mission has something to do with respect for that person, that community of persons God deigned to create, to sustain, to love to the utmost.

What is the essence of this issue? It is the issue of life itself, of life abundant, seen most clearly through the eyes of the poor. What we are about here, at San Antonio, is no small matter. We are not here to fuss about minor ideas, about bureaucratic arrangements, about complaints (valid or otherwise) that we may have, about theological niceties we may enjoy. We are here about God's people, about God's purposes for human beings, about God's love for all humankind. Nothing less. So we come to San Antonio with some specific concerns, which emanate from our major concern. We are here to say, once and again, that life for all matters.

— It matters for Nicaraguan peasants who have too long felt the assaults of "contras" from beyond their borders.
— It matters for Japanese "Buraku" who have never known what life is truly meant to be.
— It matters for Maori men and women in Aotearoa (New Zealand) who affirm their cultural identity.
— It matters for Indochinese refugees who know not where to turn.

— It matters for Turkish migrant workers in Europe who try, against all odds, to find a new life.
— It matters for a comfortable suburban American who long ago lost any sense of meaningful living today.
— It matters for anyone who is persecuted for religious beliefs and longs for the freedom to worship in peace.
— It matters for you and me, for our children and our grandchildren, who wish for a better day, a fuller life, a more serene and just planet in which we might live and move and have our being.

There is no point in talking about "mission in Christ's way" and doing God's will if we cannot bring it down to the everyday matters of daily living, daily experience, daily relationships to the basic issues of justice that make the critical difference between life and death.

It seems presumptuous to single out four issues in the midst of the host of concerns delegates to this conference urgently bring to our tables of discussion. I believe these four issues are universal, contemporary, pressing. But whatever the issues of the day, forever we are faced with the imperative of God's will and a mission in Christ's way that Jesus so magnificently exemplified. Would that we might here in San Antonio rededicate ourselves to Jesus Christ and thread our way through these issues and many others, confident that at least our firm intention is a faithfulness to the God who is revealed supremely in Jesus Christ and to whom we ascribe all glory and honour, now and evermore.

Address by the General Secretary

Emilio Castro

I have been asked to make my presentation in the form of a testimony — not so much in biographical terms as with reference to the main theme of our meeting:

YOUR WILL BE DONE
MISSION IN CHRIST'S WAY

The first thing to note is obvious: we are praying the Lord's prayer; we are speaking to God. We are talking about his will, not ours. Prayer is the hidden well-spring of our faith and action; often it is the only form of protest left to us. In face of injustice or accident or the incomprehensible there inevitably wells up from the depth of our being an almost despairing protest or question: "Why? How could it happen?" In other situations our prayer is an anticipation of possible action. Precisely because reality is so harsh we are called to affirm that this visible reality is not the ultimate one and that we are engaged in mission specifically to challenge and transform it. Prayer is openness to God's resources. When the apostle Paul tells us that our struggle is "not against flesh and blood but against the principalities and powers of darkness", he is reminding us of what we know from experience. To try to transform this world in the direction of the kingdom of God is a task far beyond our human strength, but it is a task in which we are not alone, a task in which God himself is engaged.

The church has rightly incorporated the instruments and working methods of modern science into its missionary practice. Thus, as the Western churches sought to fulfill their missionary responsibility, Western science and technology have been transported as an integral part of it

---

● Emilio Castro is general secretary of the WCC.

to all regions of the globe. But more than that, these churches applied the rule of "efficiency" to their own life, applying the techniques of social service in the life of their congregations. As a result of this twofold quest for efficiency — in mission and in service — they developed structures of all kinds for service at home and throughout the world without realizing that they were bypassing the sense of mystery, the essential community of prayer, and transmitting cultural values disguised as gospel values! When diakonia ceases to be service by the congregation, when it is no longer centred in the prayer of a committed community, it loses its spiritual dimension, it grows away from its roots and, in becoming secularized, forfeits its humanizing power. This is why it is so important that both this conference and the next assembly of the World Council of Churches should be centring their thinking and their quest for action around a prayer: here in San Antonio, "Your will be done"; in Canberra, "Come, Holy Spirit — Renew the Whole Creation". Both cases reflect an awareness of a reality that sustains, inspires and challenges us — a reality beyond our immediate perception that gives meaning to all our human activity. "Out of the depths I cry to thee, O Lord" — out of the reality of our limitations and despair. But also, "Lord, I believe; help thou my unbelief". In the knowledge of God and the sureness of his presence we dare to look to the present and the future, crying, "your will be done" and placing ourselves in the service of that will.

While the first thing to note is the spiritual or, if you will, the mystical and deeply liturgical nature of our missionary existence, the second thing that impresses itself on my mind is the tremendous risk we run in speaking of the will of God. We have all recently been stirred by the storm unleashed by a book against whose author a death warrant has been pronounced in the name of God. If we look at our own Christian history we have inquisition and counter-inquisition to remind us that the claim to know and to be executing God's will has very often turned out to mean serving our own ends and our own will, and has been used to justify crimes of all kinds against our neighbour.

Think of the tragic experience of Jim Jones and his congregation who moved from California to Guyana where they ended up committing collective suicide. Think of the religious groups who, in the name of God's will, refuse to have anything to do with the benefits of modern science. Think of the flagellants who every holy week castigate their own bodies in the belief that they are thus doing God's will. Fanatics of the right or of the left, or whatever ideological complexion, how often we fall into the trap of our own arrogance. Let us remember as the year 1992 approaches — the anniversary of the "discovery" of America in 1492 — how easily mission became bound up with colonization, evangelization with domination, obedience to God's will with empire. In the course of our history, the idea of a manifest destiny awaiting a particular nation in virtue of a divine design has been used to justify atrocities.

It is dangerous to speak of God's will. We can only guard against the dangers by reminding ourselves of the penultimate nature of our existence and the provisional character of our judgments. On the one hand we must enter into history with all the seriousness of the ultimate things. Our day-to-day decisions, the way we treat our neighbour are significant for our eternal destiny because in that neighbour we meet Jesus Christ, God incarnate. But at the same time, we enter into history in the knowledge that the one who came to us in Jesus Christ is the one who, at the end of history, will come to judge the quick and the dead, to bring his purifying fire and to establish a new measure of judgment that is beyond our historically limited understanding. Here we have the root of Christian opposition to the death penalty. We cannot admit irreversible sentences in our finite history because in doing so we are usurping a final judgment which God has not entrusted to his creatures.

"Your will be done" constantly reminds us of a different objective reality and of our own subjectivity. In practice we can guard against misconceptions of God's will through ecumenical dialogue, not only with other Christians but also with other cultures and religions. Within the community of faith, fraternal dialogue among ourselves can correct us and prevent us from falling into sectarian fanaticism of one kind or another. This is perhaps the most important ecumenical experience of recent years. The fact of being together challenges us. It does not relativize us in the sense of making us lose the dimension of the ultimate, but it does make us human, it does bring us back to the level of what we are meant to be: unworthy servants submitting the offering of their worship and work to a judgment higher than our own. Thus the encounter with other confessions prevents us from clinging to caricatures of one another and pronouncing anathemas; at the same time it also reduces the ever-present danger of fanatical sectarianism. But better still, the ecumenical fellowship enables us to discern the will of God as a purpose in history transcending any national and cultural perspectives. At one and the same time it corrects and inspires us. This is why we are trying together to hear a message on justice, peace and the integrity of creation that will show their inter-relatedness and the real challenges that call for our united witness. This is why we have accepted it as God's will that we challenge the structures of power in our own society, whether it be the power of big business or of the state, ideology or personal dictatorship. Ecumenical solidarity is fundamental to seeking to discern God's will and to do it in obedience.

We are also helped by the reality of an ecumenism wider than interchurch ecumenism. The Christian churches, and the World Council of Churches in particular, are well aware that they live in a world where people are motivated in their search for a more worthy society by different ideologies and other religious views of the cosmos. Any claim to absolute validity for our convictions will show that we worship not the transcendent God but our own idea or image of him. The search for God's will, which for Christians means studying the gospel text amidst the tensions and ambiguities of given moments in history, calls for dialogue, mutual criticism and constant reconsideration of positions. The right to criticize, which is a fundamental expression of freedom, must be guaranteed for everyone. Only then will the tentative truth, which we postulate as God's will, be desacralized and consequently purified and placed in the service of God's purpose of liberation. To recognize the tentative nature of our statements is to affirm that as we discuss and hold dialogues and together seek to establish a society of greater liberty and justice we are guided by the Spirit of God, the Spirit of freedom, who helps us to discern error and affirm common values in our life together, as we listen to each other's witness. Consequently, God's will, to which we consecrate our existence, is to be sought in the gospel text read in the encounter with peoples who confess other creeds. This subjects us to constant scrutiny and correction, so that we are naturally in the witnessing situation of those who are called to give account of the hope that is in them, in dialogue and service to all human beings.

The difficulty we have in discerning God's will, the traps laid for us by our own arrogance and selfishness, which make us mistake our own will for God's will, can be overcome by fellowship among churches in the ecumenical movement, by witnessing dialogue with people of other philosophical and religious convictions. But above all they are checked by constant reference on our part to the person of Jesus Christ.

This is why the second phrase of our theme is so useful: "Mission in Christ's way". It calls us to search the gospel for God's will; that will which can be seen day by day in concrete situations as the spirit of Jesus Christ encounters the human realities in the midst of which we bear witness to his life and mission. A truth, a will expressed once and for all in the life of Jesus Christ, but prophetically present here and now in real situations.

Here, then, we have a third thing to note: when we pray for God's will to be done we are praying for the full revelation of what has already been made flesh and reality in the life, death and resurrection of Jesus Christ. We Christians cannot talk about a will of God in general terms as something to be discerned in history or nature, apart from the fundamental, revolutionary and unique fact of our experience: the presence of God in Jesus of Nazareth. Jesus and his disciples pray in anticipation for the fulfilment of that saving, liberating will of God that was to be fully manifested in the cross of Jesus Christ. In the words of the letter to the Hebrews:

> In many and various ways God spoke of old to our fathers by the prophets; but in these last days he has spoken to us by a Son, whom he appointed the heir of all things, through whom also he created the world. He reflects the glory of God and bears the very stamp of his nature, upholding the universe by his word of power. When he had made purification for sins, he sat down at the right hand of the Majesty on high (Heb. 1:1-3).

And as the first letter to Timothy tells us, in the second chapter:

> This is good, and it is acceptable in the sight of God our Saviour, who desires all men to be saved and to come to the knowledge of the truth. For there is one God, and there is one mediator between God and men, the man Christ Jesus, who gave himself as a ransom for all, the testimony to which was borne at the proper time (1 Tim. 2:3-6).

Ever since Jesus Christ, the key to our history, we know that nothing in the creation is outside the liberating will of God. When we pray "Your will be done", we stand before the mystery of his will fully manifested in history. After having prayed with tears of blood in Gethsemane "Not my will, but thine, be done", Christ was able to say on the cross, "it is finished". This central affirmation of our Christian faith provides the necessary corrective to guard against any ideological reductions of the faith or liberalizing affirmations of human good will in general. It gives a specific sense to our mission. We derive from, and we point towards, an historic episode with universal scope: God in Christ reconciling the world to himself. Ever since the life, death and resurrection of Jesus Christ we know the saving, liberating will of God, made manifest in the creation, confirmed in his providence towards all the peoples of the earth and coming to us as a summons, calling the whole of history towards the shalom of the kingdom, the God who is coming.

This central, fundamental affirmation of our Christian existence can be valid only in a situation of dialogue and relations with our neighbour. It is not a statement that can impress itself objectively on human minds. Because it is related to a life history that in the gospel culminates in the affirmation of the resurrection and the presence of the Holy Spirit, we are obliged to live out our confession in interaction with other living faiths, in dialogue with the questions raised by contemporary scientists, and in confrontation with the powers of oppression and death.

The history of Jesus Christ has to be told at the frontier, where we venture into unknown territory. It cannot be told without reference to ecclesial experience, the living tradition of the church — but neither can it be told without the experience of the Spirit of God at work among human beings. This explains the capital importance of the study now being carried out by the WCC's Commission on Faith and Order on "Confessing the Apostolic Faith Today". Because we come from Jesus Christ, we have there a constant point of reference that is central and essential to our mission.

We acknowledge that others are engaged in God's mission even without knowing the name of Jesus. Christians fighting for freedom and justice find themselves working side by side with people who confess other religious creeds, or who find it impossible to react to the dimension of mystery that we call faith.

We rejoice to see that the cause of God's kingdom has other advocates besides those we find within the Christian church. We rejoice to discern the manifestations of God's Spirit in people whose lives are a demonstration of love and service which shames and inspires us. But none of this removes the specific responsibility that lies with us as the people of the faith, to contribute to the total spiritual wealth of humanity through the proclamation of Jesus Christ, the reference to his life, his passion and his resurrection. When all is said and done, this is the unique contribution we have to make.

Mission in Christ's way is mission that springs from prayer, mission that contemplates in all humility the mystery of God's saving will, but that also points in wonder to the Lamb of God who takes away the sins of the world. To speak the name of Jesus, to proclaim the gospel — call it what you will — in our proclamation of God's will the inevitable and fundamental centre is Christ.

But since God's sovereign will has been perfectly fulfilled in Jesus Christ, this means we have a criterion to guide us as we seek to interpret his will in the present. We have been taught to pray "in Jesus' name". This is the filter that will ensure that our prayer is purified by the Spirit, by the person of Jesus. But equally, in the other direction, when we seek to interpret God's will in the real world of history, there too the "name" — the criterion — of Jesus Christ has to be fundamental in controlling and determining our actions.

In the life and teaching of Jesus of Nazareth we find that priority is always given fundamentally to the neighbour. In Jesus there is total disregard of self. In his baptism he places himself in the ranks of sinners so that with them he can assume the whole human condition. At the other extreme, on the cross, the crowd shouted: "He saved others; he cannot save himself." He did not think of himself, nor did he want to, precisely because he was concerned for the salvation of the thief beside him, for his mother and the disciple at the foot of the cross, for the crowd that did not understand him — precisely because he was dying for others. If the will of God that I proclaim and try to carry out in my daily life centres on my own good, on asserting my own power, on seeking my own advantage, then it is not God's will in Jesus Christ. The church only has a right to exist as a servant people: "As my father sent me, so I send you."

But in Jesus we see something else more clearly still: that in giving priority to his neighbour rather than to his own life, he gives priority above all to the marginalized, the poor, children, the sick, to known sinners, to those who have no power. The dynamic of mission in Christ's way must always start from the marginalized sectors of society and move upwards towards the domes of power. It is from the starting point of the poor that the fabric of God's kingdom will be woven. Here we have to acknowledge the tragic experience that has emerged from our mission in the last two centuries: churches that started out in the service of the poorest sections of society and that gradually rose with them to occupy positions of power in that society, forgot that the dynamic of their mission must return once again to serving first of all the powerless. Today the poor come to us in the drug addict or the dissident, in the economic migrant or the political refugee, in the lonely person who cannot find a place in our competitive society, or in the victims of that society. The church has learned to speak of the priority God gives to the poor. But we have done so with a bad conscience and we have tried to find ways and means to justify our position of wealth. Yet the problem is not our own justification: it is a matter of recognizing the dynamic of the kingdom, the liberating and restoring will of the Father made fully manifest in Jesus Christ, in his concern for the least of his fellow beings. It is a matter, then, of our living as a people of faith together with those who are today the bearers of God's promise of liberation. There can be no question of idealizing the poor; sin is also present in those who are the victims of our collective and individual sin. But we do have to recognize that God recommences the struggle for his kingdom through those who are passed over by the centres of power in our society.

The particular feature of God's will made manifest in Christ, which calls us to forget ourselves and put the poor at the centre of our vocation of service, is that it also states that the poor and the marginalized are called to assume responsibility; they are equipped to stand up and take their destiny into their own hands. It is striking that in the gospel, Jesus, in his relations with all those who come to him, whether they are seeking health or forgiveness, responds to them with a word that heals and liberates but, above all, restores:

> "Go and sin no more" (John 8:11).
> "Rise, take up your pallet and walk" (Mark 2:9).
> "Go, show yourself to the priest" (Mark 1:44).
> "Today salvation has come to this house" (Luke 19:9).
> "Follow me, and I will make you fishers of men" (Matt. 4:19).
> "Come to me, all who labour and are heavy laden, and I will give you rest" (Matt. 11:28).

but:

> "Take my yoke upon you, and learn from me; for I am gentle and lowly in heart, and you will find rest for your souls. For my yoke is easy and my burden is light" (Matt. 11:29-30).

The church, seeking God's will for its mission, recognizes it in Jesus Christ as a strengthening, enabling will that encourages the participation of the humblest forms of popular organization through which it can make its presence felt throughout the fabric of society. At this point an enormous polemic opens up. It is difficult to discern which of these forms correspond to the kingdom and which are aimed at the acquisition of power for power's sake. But we cannot escape this critical task; we have an obligation always to defend the cause of the marginalized, accepting that they must be the agents of their own destiny. Perhaps the scandal that has always surrounded the WCC's Programme to Combat Racism can be traced to this reading of God's will. Of course we are called to condemn the sin of racism and to fight against it in our own consciences, in the structures of our churches and through our social and political militancy. But, above all, we are called to stand alongside those who suffer from racial discrimination so that they can be the architects of their own destiny and can participate in the building of that tomorrow of greater justice when God's will for fellowship in Jesus Christ will be manifested in all its fullness. Only solidarity with the poor, even as they suffer from the errors they commit, can give credibility to the gospel of a God who took upon himself the lot of the outcast, even to his death on the cross. It is worth noting that the ideas of justice and justification are to be found in the biblical message. The basis on which redress is made in the Jubilee Year is not "right" but the concern to restore, to re-establish and open up history. The justification by faith that we find in Paul follows the same movement: forgiveness of sins, new creation, new beginning, opening to a new tomorrow.

Because we speak the name of Jesus, we dare in baptism for the remission of sins to work in company with the marginalized for the humanizing of the world, calling all human creatures to enter into the dynamic of the kingdom. Here a small "excursus" is needed to link my previous point to this. While our service is meant to be service that enables, and is respectful of the decisions and initiatives that the marginalized of today may take, it is not neutral or aseptic. It is service done in the name of Jesus of Nazareth, service that points towards the one in whom we have received the vision of liberation. We should be doing a disservice to the poor of today if we were to deprive them of the knowledge of him who for love of them and of us himself became poor even to the point of death on the cross and thus gave us fullness of life and a new opportunity in history and for all eternity.

Last, I would like to draw your attention to the fact that in the Lord's Prayer the phrase "Your will be done" is set between two very different and specific perspectives: "Your kingdom come" and "Give us this day our daily bread." We have to make our prayer in the midst of history, in the constant tension between the hope of the kingdom that is to come — the revolutionary demand of a new heaven and a new earth — and the concrete reality of the daily bread needed by our neighbour here and now.

The phrase "Your will be done" has been understood in many Christian circles as a call to resignation, to acceptance of the inevitable in history. When an accident happens, or when there is a death we say, "it is God's will". We have protested against that quietistic interpretation, but we should not forget the hidden truth it contains. In the last analysis, because our hope is in the kingdom that is to come, because we have the assurance since the resurrection morning that God is working for the restoration of all things in Christ, we can place the fruits of our labour — whether successes or failures, moments of joy or extreme frustration — on the altar of a higher wisdom, the altar of a purpose that is able to weave even our failures into the altars of the kingdom that is to come. Painful though it may be, even our conflicts over the interpretation of God's will for a given time can be worked through in hope within the community of faith.

"Your kingdom come, your will be done." Our dream, our hope is for the transformation of all things and we cannot accept that any aspect of life in history should remain outside this all-embracing vision. It is this vision that gives meaning to the life of an old person whose strength is ebbing away and who can do nothing but pray, but in doing so he or she accompanies the struggle of the whole of humanity on the way to the kingdom. It is this vision that enables us to look at the passing generations in the supreme confidence that nothing of that which has been sown in love, even with tears, is lost in the divine economy.

But this all-embracing, global vision of the kingdom to come could lead us astray in two directions: one, falsely eschatological, inviting passiveness while we await the triumphant return of Jesus Christ; and the other, falsely activist, inciting radicalism in which our own ideological convictions are sacralized and all too easily substituted for the kingdom to come. It is our real neighbour and the historic challenge of the times — the daily bread — that will give us the necessary orientation to ensure that the kingdom is inspiration and not alienation, integration and not marginalization; that the kingdom gives us a certainty in hope capable of overcoming all the frustrations of history. The daily bread is essential as a reminder of the neighbour who is actually there and whom we are there to serve. Love for humanity that is not expressed in love for our neighbour is not God's will. So that together we can build the justice of tomorrow, the survival of the oppressed of today is of fundamental importance. The diakonia to which the church is called is a liberating diakonia pointing to the kingdom of God but taking the neighbour seriously and with outstretched hand announcing God's liberating will, telling of the restoring power it offers and the possibility he or she has of participating actively in the dynamic of God's kingdom.

Mission in Christ's way is mission on bended knee, in acknowledgment of God's presence, in grateful contemplation of the life, death and resurrection of our Lord, Jesus Christ, in affirmation of a restoring liberty offered to all creatures, devoting our lives to the cause of the poor in whom we see the cause of the kingdom that is to come. In accordance with Christ's will, the church's mission is to proclaim the ultimate in the midst of the penultimate, to announce the coming kingdom while holding out a glass of water to our neighbour — to proclaim the mystery of God present in history.

Above: Opening worship
Left: Worship in the chapel of the university campus: partici-
pants bringing earth from their country to symbolize that the
earth is our life

Right: Solidarity
walk "walking the way
of the cross"

All photos:
WCC/Peter Williams

Below: Closing worship

Above: Rev. Dr Fred Wilson
Right: Bishop Anastasios
of Androussa

Rev. Dr Eugene L. Stockwell   *Rev. Dr Christopher Duraisingh*   *Rev. Dr Emilio Castro*

Rt Rev. Lesslie Newbigin   *Dr Sylvia Talbot*

Delegates in plenary

Rev. Dr Arie Brouwer　　　*Rev. Dr Allan Boesak*

The youth presentation

Above: Solidarity walk "walking the way of the cross"
Below: Bible study
Below right: A quiet moment for an interview

WCC staff responsible for documentation and electronic communications with the
WCC language service in Geneva

San Antonio and Some Continuing Concerns of the CWME

Christopher Duraisingh

Our prayer these days has been "Your will be done". We have sought to identify the contours of our mission in Christ's way. But has there been a unifying focus and a critical principle for all that we seek to be and do in mission in Christ's way? How can we make sense and bring together the diverse and even disparate concerns, voices and Acts in Faithfulness that we have been led to affirm these days? In our search to speak about God's will in mission has there been something that comes with a compelling power? Is there a particular way of understanding God's will today that can provide a dynamic unity in the task of world mission and move us forward with conviction and passion?

I believe that there is one. It is the eschatological *vision of God gathering up all things in Christ*. Even in the first address of this conference on the theme we heard Bishop Anastasios indicate that the vision of all things being gathered up in Christ has a "close correspondence" with the phrase of the Lord's prayer, "Your will be done". Time and again throughout this conference, whether in worship or in plenary deliberations, we were drawn to envision the will of God that we seek in mission as that which purposes to reconcile and renew all things in Christ. The report of section I begins with an affirmation of God's unconditional concern for unity and fellowship with and among all human beings. Section IV reiterates the same point, saying: "We reaffirm that it is God's firm purpose to unite all human beings in a single community."

● Christopher Duraisingh, director-designate of the Commission on World Mission and Evangelism at the time of the conference, presented this paper during the final plenary session. This is his "impromptu" response to the conference in the light of his perception of the role of CWME in world mission; initial comments of a more personal nature have been omitted.

Section III widens our horizon to discern God's will, and consequently our mission in Christ's way has to do with the renewal of the whole of creation. Section II points out in no uncertain terms the powers that destroy community and the power of God's pain-love and solidarity in Christ through which alone renewed communities in justice and peace are possible. The conference Message that we adopted repeatedly speaks of "weaving a new world community", "solidarity in the quest for a new human community", etc. Therefore I am convinced that in San Antonio this Pauline understanding of God's will for the reuniting of all things in Christ comes to us with a compelling force and can become for us today a central metaphor. I am convinced too that it provides the dynamic unity of all the work that we have done in the four sections. We can gather up our rather diverse deliberations throughout the conference around that vision and move forward in the mission of the church in Christ's way.

Such a vision is made credible by the nature and composition of the delegation in San Antonio. How often we have been reminded these days that this has been one of the most inclusive and ecumenical mission conferences. The conference Message itself refers to "the spirit of universality of the gathering". The Orthodox participation has been fuller and larger. The Evangelicals were inspired to issue a letter to Lausanne II. There has been a higher percentage of women participants, though we have fallen short of the target and more ought to be done to ensure greater balance in the future.

Voices of those who represent grassroots action groups have been heard often and in no uncertain terms; a delegation from China was able to be present after several decades. For the first time in a world mission conference, representatives of communities of other faiths have not only been present but also felt free to express themselves several times. Thematically too, the wholeness of the earth along with the just sharing of it by all has become a major missiological issue. Obviously, all these aspects of San Antonio lead us to understand the will of God that we seek in mission today as that eschatological purpose to gather all things in heaven and earth in Christ. Certainly it is only one way of finding a focus of unity in the conference. Nevertheless, it is a dynamic one with a compelling force.

Such a vision is also *rooted in our "common memory"* within the ecumenical movement and its mission history. From Edinburgh to this day, this eschatological vision has guided its mission thinking and practice. Surveying the forty years of the ecumenical experience within the World Council of Churches, Emilio Castro said to the Central

Committee in Hanover in 1988: "The eschatological vision of the reuniting of all things in Christ is the inspirational model, the object of our efforts and God's promise for the ecumenical task." It is closely related to the ongoing Faith and Order study on the unity of the church and the renewal of human community. The emphasis upon "Koinonia: Sharing Life in a World Community" in El Escorial too resonates the same vision. In this sense, San Antonio continues and furthers that coherent and vital thread which runs through the ecumenical movement. It places Christian witness within its only legitimate locus, God's will to reconcile and renew all things in Christ.

But San Antonio has also forcefully reminded us that such a vision does not arise in a vacuum. It is not an empty dream devoid of a context. The vision is located *within the crucible of suffering and pain* within a world rent asunder by all forms of divisive powers. The voices of the oppressed that we heard, the anguish of the marginalized that we experienced and the anger of the indigenous people that we shared as their identity and lands continue to be plundered point to a bleeding human community and a creation in groaning. The conference Message recalls for us in a powerful way these voices that haunted us in every section and in plenary sessions, reminding us of the world missiological situation today. It is within that context of anguish and pain of a broken creation and humanity that our response to God's will for the reconciliation and renewal of all things will take shape. Time and again as I sat in the plenary or heard reports of voiced struggles or voiceless suffering, the Pauline description of the groaning creation in Romans chapter eight became so grippingly real. Don't you agree that each of us has, here in San Antonio, concrete instances of how the whole creation writhes in pain, like the pain of childbirth, to share in the glorious freedom of the children of God? One of the most moving instances was the plenary session in which we heard women testifying to their experiences of hurt and pain. Yes, it is only from within that context that we are called to affirm that God in Jesus Christ unconditionally wills the renewal of all things. Mission in Christ's way then for us is set within this doubly determined framework, namely the possibility that the Ephesian vision becomes our own but within the concrete context of the whole of creation anguishing and struggling for redemption.

The San Antonio experience included a third significant element too in this missiological context and perspective. It comes from the shared signs of hope and renewal. We heard of the vitality of people's struggles in the face of oppression, of renewal movements among the poor, and emergence of ecclesial communities with liberational potentials in different parts of the world. In fact, one of the sub-themes of section IV specifically studies the mission potential of movements among the poor and within the basic Christian communities. Here then is a third element of the missiological ground perspective that San Antonio so powerfully places before us. It is the present experience and celebration of *the church as the sign and foretaste of God's eschatological purpose* to liberate and renew all things in Christ. Experiences of base communities and action groups in mission point to the church as being the first fruits of God's final summing up of all things in Christ in the power of the Spirit. Here then in San Antonio three inseparably related missiological insights are highlighted — God's unconditional will to gather and renew all things in Christ, the present pain and struggle of human beings and creation as a whole, and the movements of the Spirit of renewal among the poor, which assures us that the vision is a present possibility in Christ even in the midst of our brokenness. These three together constitute for us then a missiological framework, an inspirational model, a dynamic unity of all that we have experienced here in San Antonio with a compelling force. Such an inspirational vision for our mission thinking and practice is rooted in the very life of the Triune God. It needs to be nurtured through prayer and rereading of the Bible.

Before I move on to identify a few specific programmatic implications of the conference for the Commission on World Mission and Evangelism, let me touch upon two wider implications of this conference. The first is missiological; the second is methodological.

First, the experience in San Antonio of listening to the voices of hurt and pain and witnessing the signs of hope and renewal tells us to reaffirm another dimension of our missionary calling. Christ not only sends out even as the Father sent him; he also awaits us to meet him in the poor and the oppressed. We are used to affirming the first but seldom are we aware of the second dimension of our calling. San Antonio is a powerful reminder of the latter. It is Christ who sends his church, but he also awaits his church to be met, acknowledged and served. This double responsibility cannot be forgotten. Hence, mission in Christ's way is not only to awaken faith afresh but also to acknowledge faith where it is found, even as Christ not only mediated God's liberating love but also, with surprise and joy, acknowledged faith even among the "outsiders" to the community of Israel.

The second implication is methodological. The most significant aspect of the conference is the sharing of experiences of the context and practice of mission at the grassroots level by the participants. Stories of missiological involvements dominated the conference. This is in line with the recent theological method that is experienced within the ecumenical movement in general, that it is out of missiological involvement that we discern and reaffirm theological insights. Seldom is it the other way. But it implies that there is a fair amount of work on missiological reflection that needs to be done *after* the conference, reflection that will be true to the experiences voiced and shared. Therefore, the conference mandates the necessary follow-up of reflection and articulation upon all concerned, particularly the members of the Commission on World Mission and Evangelism. The structural and programmatic implications of such a process that begins and builds upon grassroots mission experience in the conference for the WCC may be many and need to be carefully examined.

Careful exploration of the implication of San Antonio will be undertaken at forthcoming meetings of the CWME. But several Acts in Faithfulness relate directly to various concerns and ongoing programmes of many other sub-units of the WCC; therefore CWME needs to listen to and explore together with those sub-units. Even in relation to CWME, San Antonio has either reiterated or highlighted the need to continue programme thrusts that have already been mandated by the Central Committee since Vancouver.

Dialogue with the Evangelicals: Since Vancouver this concern has been important for CWME, and the WCC as a whole. Through consultations and formal and informal conversations arranged by the sub-unit and through the work of a Council-wide task force, I understand that already this concern is being carried out. I am aware of the "forum" character of the sub-unit that necessarily involves the widest possible dialogue. Therefore, dialogue with the Evangelicals needs to be a continued programmatic emphasis of CWME within the overall effort that the WCC as a whole takes in this regard. The role played by the Evangelicals in San Antonio is significant and we need to welcome every opportunity for furthering the dialogue. But the sub-unit will have to bring into the dialogue the mission thinking and practice developed over decades of ecumenical mission history. We need to testify to God's unconditional concern for the coming into being of a common human community, and to the fact that it is this vision that shapes and critiques our missionary practice. In the process, together we shall discover the wholeness of the gospel that testifies to the inclusive and universal love of God for the whole creation.

Awakening of personal faith and discipleship to Christ: On more than one occasion, and more pointedly in section I, we are reminded of the urgent need for renewed confidence in the gospel. We are called to greater commitment to the proclamation of God's love in Christ to all in order that personal faith and discipleship may be awakened in many. The CWME is entrusted with a clear mandate to place this challenge before the member churches of the World Council of Churches. San Antonio has highlighted the urgency of the task, and the commission, through its desk on evangelism, will continue to seek to be faithful to this vocation.

Witness and dialogue: Section I has also highlighted the need to continue to explore the relationship between witness and dialogue. It recognizes that both witness and dialogue presuppose a two-way relationship and that each has its own integrity. The same section report acknowledges too that in our witnessing task we affirm "what God has done and is doing among people of other faiths". We need to rejoice that San Antonio has led us much further in our understanding of the relationship between witness and dialogue. But we are called to continue our exploration further in cooperation with the Sub-unit on Dialogue.

San Antonio has provided a dynamic perspective in the light of which we can better understand our relationship with people of other faiths. It is the perspective that at the very centre of the being of God, and revealed in Jesus Christ, is the vulnerable, self-giving and inclusive pain-love. Our corporate walking the way of the cross as part of our worship and the presentation by women were two instances in which we had glimpses of that love. It is that vulnerable love of the Triune God, made manifest in Jesus Christ, which gives us the ground, pattern and power for our witness and dialogue. We witness to the fact that this all-embracing love of God reconciles and renews all that is alienated from and in conflict with God through Christ. God's love has no boundary. Are we not called to recognize that the pain-love of God in Jesus Christ can have no "out-side"? Therefore, it is the cross of Christ that opens us for dialogue and the affirmation of God's saving presence among persons of other faiths. But exploration of the nature of God's presence and work needs to continue. The Commission on World Mission and Evangelism will be committed to further exploration both at the level of the Council and member bodies.

We are called to witness to the decisiveness of God's love in Christ unequivocally. But our call is to witness, not to judge. Bishop Newbigin somewhere points to the tendency among Christians to quickly move from the witness box to the bench of the judge. How often our concepts of both mission and dialogue are shaped by our eagerness to play the role of judges rather than remaining faithful witnesses to the vulnerable, self-offering pain-love of God in Jesus Christ that embraces the whole human community!

Education in mission: From the very early days, the primacy of the local congregation in mission has been emphasized. New Delhi reiterated this emphasis in the pregnant phrase, "all in each place seeking together to fulfill" the missionary calling. In the early 1960s, the newly constituted Division on World Mission and Evangelism pioneered a study of the "structures for missionary congregations". Sections I and IV in San Antonio have drawn our attention to the urgent need for systematic programmes that will equip local congregations for mission. I take it that San Antonio urges us all, and the CWME in particular, to take seriously the necessity incumbent upon every church to equip people at the grassroots for mission. Through the desk for education for mission, I very much hope CWME will continue to challenge, prod and assist all its member churches to initiate mission education programmes at the grass-roots. Many of you may be aware of the plans for institutes on evangelism already proposed by the evangelism desk. Of course, such a concern cannot be carried out without being in relation to the WCC's Unit III on Education and Renewal. There is another concern very closely related to the equipping of local congregations in mission. It has to do with the training of persons as ministers of the church, essentially as the enablers of God's people for their mission. This needs to be yet another focus if the concern for promoting "missionary consciousness" in member churches is to be actualized. But the role of formation for mission in theological colleges at present is appalling. It is not enough to add a few courses in missiology, though even that would take us a long way from where we are now. The missionary calling of the church must become the underlying perspective and organizing principle of all that goes on in ministerial formation. Such a rethinking and restructuring of theological curricula and method in the light of the perspective of the missionary nature of the church will then lead us to a new understanding of the ministry itself. The urgency of this programmatic thrust in cooperation with Unit III cannot be over-emphasized.

Solidarity with people at the periphery: Melbourne called us in no uncertain terms to stand in solidarity with the poor. That call remains as valid and urgent as ever. Section II in San Antonio has called us to renewed solidarity with those who struggle. But in San Antonio something new has happened; a new dimension is added. Our attention has been called to the fact that between Melbourne and San Antonio, the movements of renewal and struggles for liberation among the poor have become a significant force around the world. Urban rural mission networks and other linkings of action groups testify to that reality. Moreover, here in San Antonio, for the first time in the history of mission thinking, the renewal potential of popular movements and struggles among the peripheral people have become a central missiological theme. What are their missiological implications? What are the implications for our ecclesiology? Some of these questions will be addressed by all of us in the days ahead. But one thing is certain in San Antonio. In their movement from periphery to the centre in Jesus Christ and their experience of power in and through their powerlessness, the poor become the bearers of God's love and power. Hence, *solidarity with the poor becomes the constitutive of the mission of the church*. This would imply that the wholeness of the sub-unit on mission within the World Council of Churches cannot be thought of apart from a clear programmatic expression of the church's solidarity with the people at the periphery. Section II identifies for us the new kind of power of the powerless, the cruciform power. For in the crucified and risen peripheral man, Jesus, it pleased God to manifest the new kind of power, the invulnerability of vulnerable love. As section II identifies, exploration of resistance as a form of witness to this kind of power of God will be another continuing concern of the sub-unit.

The earth is the Lord's

We are all aware that for the first time in ecumenical mission history the affirmation "the earth is the Lord's" has become a vital focus and part of our missionary agenda. As section III developed the theme, we are called not merely to a commitment to the integrity of creation but also to support struggles for the "just sharing" of land and sea. We are also called to commit ourselves for the dismantling of those cultural symbol systems and structures that divide the human community and for the coming into being of an inclusive community of women and men. The WCC as a whole has been concerned with the relation between the gospel and culture for some time now. Further programmatic implications of all these cannot be explored without the cooperation of other sub-units, such as Church and Society, as well as other agencies outside the Council. I am certain that as far as the Commission on World Mission and Evangelism is concerned, it will seek to be faithful to the promptings of the Spirit in San Antonio and to explore new dimensions of the missionary calling of the church in the days ahead.

International relationships in mission: We have heard these days in San Antonio a "renewed call for commitment and action" for the radical restructuring of international relations between churches in mission. The report from section IV expresses a sense of frustration that even though the quest for authentic models of partnerhip in mission has been on the agenda of the WCC "for more than a quarter of a century", not much has happened. Therefore, we are urged to "pledge ourselves to encourage our churches and agencies... setting up common decision-making structures and ensuring reciprocal sharing in mission". The CWME will continue to place this challenge before the member churches as a matter of urgency in the days ahead. With my personal involvement in one such restructured community of churches in mission for the past four years, I commit myself to this concern as a matter of priority. I want to call upon the churches in the south to greater share in initiating new experiments in south-south sharing. There is an immediate need to interpret the nature and shape of partnership in mission from the perspectives of the churches in the periphery — the "perspective of the absentees" in discussions on mission structures until recently.

But in all these, contributions from two recent world consultations need to find a place, namely the Larnaca consultation on diakonia and the El Escorial one on ecumenical resource sharing. Therefore, the quest for structures for authentic "joint action in mission" cannot but be in cooperation with the Commission on Inter-church Aid, Refugee and World Service and the desk on the Ecumenical Sharing of Resources. I consider that it will be very significant if CWME can jointly explore with other related sub-units of the WCC the possibility of making a substantial contribution to this concern at Canberra and beyond.

The church's search for authentic international models of partnership in mission is only its response to and part of God's mission in bringing into being a common human community renewed in justice and peace. All our experiments are only provisional signs of God's intention for all human beings to share life in its fullness towards that one oikoumene. This is our eschatological hope, rooted in the reconciling love of God manifested in the cross of Christ.

San Antonio has been a significant nodal point, a milestone in the ecumenical missionary movement. We have been caught by a vision, the eschatological vision of the will of God already unfolding in Jesus Christ, renewing humanity and creation. We have heard and to some extent shared the anguish and pain of our people. In worship and fellowship, we have seen glimpses of what it is to be a witnessing community, a sign and foretaste of God's will in Christ's way. We go back with a commitment to act in faithfulness. The vision needs to be transferred throughout the world church. The missionary calling of every Christian needs to become contagious. I am aware that one of the tasks committed to the CWME is to assist member churches in their permanent renewal in mission. As I prepare myself to undertake a part in that task in the light of the experience in San Antonio, I want to impress upon you how much I need your prayers and support.

Together may we continue to pray: Your will be done.

Together may we continue to commit ourselves to God's mission in Christ's way.

Together may we enable God's people at the grassroots for their participation in God's mission.

Then we will be prepared to pray together with the world church again in Canberra: "Come, Holy Spirit — Renew the Whole Creation." Amen.

Constitution

of the Conference on World Mission and Evangelism
and the Sub-unit and Commission
on World Mission and Evangelism

Nairobi Assembly 1975, amended
by the Central Committee 1980 and 1989

*1. There shall be a conference on world mission and evangelism of the
World Council of Churches.*

2. Aim
   Its aim is to assist the Christian community in the proclamation of the
gospel of Jesus Christ, by word and deed, to the whole world to the end
that all may believe in him and be saved.

3. Governing principles
   a) The main task of the conference is to provide opportunities for
churches, mission agencies, groups, and national and regional councils,
concerned with Christian mission, to meet together for reflection and
consultation leading to common witness.
   b) The conference shall normally meet once between Assemblies of the
World Council of Churches. It shall be convened at the call of the
Commission on World Mission and Evangelism with the approval of the
Central Committee.
   c) The results of the conference's work shall be communicated to its
constituency by the Commission on World Mission and Evangelism, and
shall also be brought to the attention of the Assembly and Central
Committee of the World Council of Churches through that channel.
   d) Administrative and executive responsibilities of the conference shall
be carried out by the Sub-unit and Commission on World Mission and
Evangelism with the approval of the Central Committee.

4. Membership and affiliation

a) Subject to the approval of Central Committee the Commission shall determine the size, membership and programme of the world conference, with due attention to regional, confessional, sex and age diversity within the overall norms set by the WCC. Due care shall be taken to provide for substantial representation of WCC member churches and CWME affiliated bodies from names submitted by them, along with a substantial number of persons involved daily at the frontiers of Christian mission.

b) Members of the conference shall seek to promote in their councils and churches the aims and findings of the conference, and the work of the Sub-unit on World Mission and Evangelism. They shall draw to the attention of the Commission matters with which they feel it should be concerned. They shall seek to promote support for the work of the Sub-unit.

c) The Commission shall take care to maintain an ongoing communication with member churches and members of the conference following the conference itself, in order that this body of people may assist in following-up conference decisions and may serve as interpreters of developments related to conference follow-up.

d) Consultants and observers may be invited to meetings of the conference by the Commission and the Unit Committee.

e) All councils affiliated to the CWME under the previous constitution shall be regarded as affiliated to the conference under this Constitution, unless they notify to the contrary.

f) Other national councils or regional conferences which accept the aim of the conference may become affiliated to the conference. Churches in countries where there is no affiliated national council may apply for affiliation to the conference. A group of churches organized for joint action for mission in a country where there is an affiliated national council, or such an international or intercontinental group of churches, may also apply for affiliation. Applications for affiliation shall be considered by the Commission. If the application is supported by a two-thirds majority of the members of the Commisssion present and voting, this action shall be communicated to the affiliated members of the conference, and unless objection is received from more than one-third of them within six months, the applicant shall be declared affiliated. There shall be consultation with the member churches of the WCC in the area concerned, except in the case of councils already in association with the WCC.

5. *Consultative relations*

National and regional Christian councils which do not desire to become affiliated with the conference, and churches and other groupings, may, if they accept the aim of the conference, request a consultative relation with the conference. Action on such requests shall be taken by the Commission. Councils and other groupings in consultative relation may send consultants to meetings of the conference, who shall be entitled to speak but not to vote.

6. *Officers*

a) The moderator and vice-moderator of the Commission on World Mission and Evangelism shall be the moderator and vice-moderator of the conference.

b) The conference, at each meeting, may appoint a steering group to meet with the moderator and vice-moderator for the conduct of that meeting of the conference.

7. *Quorum*

One-third of the members of the conference shall constitute a quorum at any given session, provided that those present at the session come from at least three continents and represent at least one-third of the affiliated councils.

8. *Amendment of the constitution*

The constitution of the conference may be amended, subject to the approval of the Central Committee, by a two-thirds majority of the members of the conference, provided the proposed amendment shall have been reviewed by the Commission and notice of it sent to the affiliated councils not less than six months before the vote is taken. The Commission as well as the affiliated councils shall have the right to propose amendments.

Excerpts from the Evening Addresses

Mission in the USA

Arie R. Brouwer

The forms of our mission are many. On the rocky shores of New England, with its stern covenantal Puritan theology, there arose an establishmentarianism of exclusion, and the consequent Baptist and Quaker protest against it. In the middle colonies of New York and New Jersey, with their pragmatic political capitalism, there arose an establishmentarianism of preference. In Virginia, with its worldly enlightenment rationalism, there arose an establishmentarianism of privilege. And in Pennsylvania, no establishmentarianism at all.

And then, out of the wilderness and the byways, there arose a great mighty rushing wind speaking through tongues of Jonathan Edwards, Theodore Frelinghuysen and the Wesleys. Eventually that great wind swept away all forms of establishmentarianism. It helped to move the founders of this nation to write into our constitutional bill of rights the guarantee for all Americans of their first liberty — the freedom of religion — in these words: "Congress shall make no law respecting an establishment of religion or prohibiting the free exercise thereof."

Thus, unfettered and free, the winds of the great awakening and its successor awakenings carried its messengers over the Appalachians. They pressed the frontier across the Mississippi and beyond the Rockies to the golden hills and strands of the west.

● Arie R. Brouwer was general secretary of the National Council of the Churches of Christ in the USA until June 1989.

Farther to the north and west another wind was blowing, eastward across the Bering Sea, carrying hunters and adventurers, and in 1794, the first priests of the Russian Orthodox Church. Settling on the island of Kodiak, they preached the gospel, worshipped God, served the people and built churches in the vast whiteness of the wilderness many decades before Alaska became a part of the United States. Eventually one of those priests who served in Alaska returned to Moscow as Patriarch Innocent. And many years later, after the Russian Revolution, an archbishop in New York returned to Moscow as Patriarch Tikhon.

Most of the American churches, however, remained impervious to the songs and hymns of the Orthodox until we sang them together in the World Council of Churches. That is a parable of ecumenical learning and sharing, demonstrating that we can speak our own tongues and hear our neighbours' tongues best in a community of many tongues.

But that was many years later. The winds that swept across America in the eighteenth and nineteenth centuries carried many spirits. Some of them were harsh, very harsh. Already in their first stirrings in New England and in the middle colonies, those harsh winds had devastated the native American population. Now and then there was a gentle refreshing and renewing breeze of grace and love, but mostly the winds were rapacious. The church, to its credit, built a few shelters against those harsh winds, but to its discredit, not much more. When the winds died away there was heard in the tents and tepees and wigwams of the original peoples of this land, the mournful songs and the weeping and wailing of whole tribes and mighty nations that had been swept away — their lands, their goods, their culture and their religion — gone, gone. We had sown the wind; they had reaped the whirlwind. We are reaping it still...

Now, a few more words about religion in America and particularly about its free exercise. For nearly two centuries now that first liberty has been guarded by our constitutional Bill of Rights. But for most of that time — indeed all of that time — some have been more free than others. The legal establishments of the colonial period disappeared, but cultural establishment did not. Indeed, it grew stronger as an increasingly acculturated mainline Protestantism became the normative religion of the nation. Catholics and Jews and the non-mainline Protestants and all others were neglected — sometimes benignly, sometimes malignantly, as the case might be. National power and foreign mission were fitted together hand in glove, much as they are still today in an even more pernicious fashion in the foreign mission enterprises of many conservative evangelical communities.

In those days, acculturation was the American way. The winds of social change in other parts of the world swept great multitudes of immigrants to these shores and into the American "melting pot". Others came as captives, plucked from their native lands by the cold winds of trade in human beings, clamped in chains, beaten, starved and sold as slaves. The churches were there in works of charity, providing food, housing, health care, education and many other forms of social service — sheltering people from the whirlwinds.

But some among us have not been content merely to build those shelters. They have wanted to wrestle with the whirlwind, to challenge the culture, to cast out the demons.

Amidst the social storms, they have cried out for justice. In the 1930s, following the great depression, the voices of the churches were heard above the whirlwind, crying out against child labour, in support of labour unions, and for health care and public education. In substantial measure, their voices prevailed, and the whirlwind lost its power.

In the 1960s and the 1970s, it again rose and fell as people of colour overcame the most blatant forms of prejudice against them; we all won a few battles in the war on poverty and this nation finally lost the war in Vietnam.

Now it is the 1980s. And the whirlwind is upon the land again. We do not see it and we do not hear it as we did in the '30s and the '60s. The whirlwind has learned how to pass silently over the land. It has even learned how to unfurl our flag in order to hide its terrible work as it sweeps away the family farm, drives tens of thousands from their homes, spreads the plague of drugs and poverty, erodes the foundations of our communities and of our culture, and divides our churches.

Our churches have long been divided over our mission. We all, or nearly all, agree that the hungry should be fed, the naked clothed, the homeless sheltered. We disagree over who should feed them and clothe them and shelter them and we disagree over how they should be fed and clothed and sheltered. Some argue that it is a question of self-reliance; others of charity; and others of the common welfare. We who are your hosts hold these truths to be self-evident, that all human beings are created in the image of God. These are therefore matters of love and of justice.

... At the heart of the American experiment is the free exercise of religion. This is true because, as de Tocqueville noted long ago, religion provides the energy for the American experiment and freedom is its essence.

America is pre-eminently the land where you can find clearly revealed the "dangerous possibilities of human freedom". Those words are from a lecture by Reinhold Niebuhr, a distinguished American ecumenist and no stranger to the World Council of Churches. But, in a parable of ecumenical learning and sharing, I found those words in the last, the very, very last, writings of Allan Paton, who recalled them in this way:

> Niebuhr felt that this rather difficult argument needed some kind of elaboration, and he proceeded to drop his script for the moment, and to dwell on the dangerous possibilities of freedom in the United States itself, the fact that the American ideal of freedom meant the liberty to choose good and to choose evil, so that high endeavour lived alongside vice and corruption and decadence. He did this with a kind of sombre gravity that certainly subdued his audience, and then inflicted on them a heavy blow by saying fiercely of American society, "It's a mess." We were all silent, feeling that the world was beyond redemption, when — after a pause — he suddenly said to us with equal emphasis, "But I like it." It brought down the house, and we felt that there was hope for the world after all.

Yes, there is hope for the world after all.

* * *

According to our laws, all of us who live here have equal right to this land and its wealth. But it is not only those of us who live here. You who visit us may claim it as your own as well. This is true not only in the general human sense that this land, too, is a part of God's creation and therefore should be equally available to all God's children. And this is true not only in the ecumenical sense that we are all one in Christ and are therefore called to share our resources.

It is also true in the economic sense. For many of you, much that you find here has been siphoned, stolen, even robbed from your homelands. You, therefore, have a right to claim — even to reclaim — that wealth as your own — and to do so, not only here, but over all the world until Mary's Magnificat becomes the governing principle of the human community.

Indeed, in the larger global perspective, we who inhabit the powerful nations are always guests. We are often uninvited guests, living at the expense of others even in our own homelands.

* * *

Martin Luther King, Jr, had a haunting way of saying: "I read somewhere. I read somewhere." He would then go on to quote the familiar words and the stirring cadences of our Declaration of Independence or some other text sacred to our national tradition, all the while weaving a lustrous tapestry of biblical teaching. I know of no other American in this century who has equalled him in that capacity, and that is surely a major reason why he, more than any other American in this century, changed the face of this nation by freeing people of colour to hold their heads up high.

... Fifty years before him, Susan B. Anthony and Elizabeth Cady Stanton followed a similar strategy, using those same sacred texts, to set free the women of this male-dominated republic. They, too, changed the face of America by freeing women to hold their heads up high.

... We Christians have always sung the gospel. We Christians in America have sung the gospel in camp meetings, revival services, Sunday schools, student conferences, mission conferences and a thousand other places. We ask you to sing the gospel with us — to sing the Lord's song in a strange land — to sing the gospel for this land, for your land, for all lands.

A Call to Prophetic Faithfulness

Allan Boesak

On the theme of this conference I would like to say a few things from the perspective of one who comes from South Africa. And as I speak to you, the church in South Africa lives and witnesses and suffers under a state of emergency. For many who do not know what that means, it means unfettered wholesale powers. For the minister for law and the police and the army, it means continuing detention without charge or trial. It means torture and legalized murder with impunity. It means no press freedom and the propaganda of the government day after day. It means also the banning of organizations and restrictions on people at this moment, almost five hundred of them, who have to live with restriction orders. It means unprecedented, merciless and brutal war on the population but especially on the children. We know this is so because we really face a government that is driven by fear and desperation.

● Allan Boesak is president of the World Alliance of Reformed Churches.

This is the situation under which we come to meditate with you and to think with you on the theme of this conference "Your will be done". I think this prayer "Your will be done" is first of all a call to battle. It is a call on the church to seek to establish signs of God's kingdom in this world, it is a call on the church to try and find ways and means in which the will of God can be seen, and be seen to be done and understood by the church and by the world. It is a call on the church to join with God in God's struggle to make God's will clear to the people of his heart, so that what we do and how we live would be in accordance with what God wants us to do.

For many of us in the church it is a time of great temptation to give in to our fear, the temptation to be bought, the temptation to be silent, the temptation to withdraw from the world, the temptation to lose our spirituality of combat. But we, as Christians, know, my brothers and sisters, that Jesus Christ is Lord. We also know that we are therefore called by this Jesus to proclaim his Lordship in the world in every single area of life. We also know that there is not one single inch of life that does not fall under the Lordship of Christ. We also know that Christians, therefore, have a responsibility in and for the world. Our faith is at stake here.

We know that in South Africa, because apartheid is presented as a Christian policy. We know that in South Africa, because the government claims to be a Christian government. We know that our faith is at stake because the constitution of that country begins with the words: "In humble submission to almighty God..." Everything else that follows in the constitution and everything else that follows in the terms of the deeds of the South African government stands under this word: "In humble submission to almighty God..." We therefore know that in our country the credibility of the gospel is at stake. And when churches like the Dutch Reformed Church even today cannot unequivocally say that apartheid in all its forms is a sin, is contrary to the gospel, then we have to deny the system in order to be faithful to Jesus Christ who is the Lord of the church.

When that happens we know that the gospel, the name of Jesus Christ is still at stake in that country. And there is no way that we can withdraw from this world. In this world this name is being denied not by those who do not know Jesus Christ as Lord but by those who confess Jesus Christ as Lord. Finally and ultimately there at the heart of the conflict between the church and the state in South Africa today is the question of the Lordship of Jesus Christ.

Who will have the last word? Is it the ideology of apartheid or is it the demands of the gospel? Who will have our ultimate loyalty? Is it the forces and the powers of evil that rule that land or is it Jesus Christ who is the Lord of the church? Who in the end will get our ultimate obedience? Is it the state president and his police force and the army, or is it Jesus Christ who is our Lord and Saviour?

So we have learned that in the struggle against this system we are involved in the political battles of our country, not in spite of our faith but because of our faith. Not in spite of our discipleship but because of our discipleship. You cannot be a Christian in South Africa and support apartheid. You cannot be a Christian in South Africa and not fight against apartheid. And that is why the prayer "Your will be done" is a call to prophetic faithfulness of a church.

The church is not prophetic when we make our decisions in assembly or in the synod or wherever. The church is only prophetic when we have somehow found the courage to live that confession in the world and to live out God's will in the world.

God's will means that the order of this world ought to be inverted, so that the first shall be last and the last shall be first. But how many of us in the church want to understand that? Do we understand that the prayer "Your will be done" is a call to conversion and repentance meant for us in the first place? Do we understand that the prayer "Your will be done" is for us a submission to what God wants for us in this world, even should it include pain and sacrifice? The prayer "Your will be done" Jesus prays in Gethsemane. Do we understand here the cost of discipleship? How to pay the price of faith? How to share the pain of those who are in pain?

I often think about this, my brothers and sisters, as the debate on violence and non-violence runs on in South Africa and elsewhere in the world. We have learned, much to our sorrow, how difficult it is to walk the road of non-violent resistance in a country where all forms of non-violent resistance have been declared criminal not only by the state but most recently also by a court of law. We have learned the pain of what it means to try to impress upon people with non-violent means our desire simply to be free. To make clear to them that we are serious when we say the words of the freedom charter, words that we have made our own: "South Africa belongs to all of its children, black and white." We have tried to knock at that door and to make them understand this is what we want for all of the people of this land. What Chief Luthuli said so long ago is still true: "We have knocked and knocked at a closed and locked door."

I can certainly call to mind holding in my arms the body of a nine year old boy who had on a little T-shirt with the words: "Please take care of this little bear." He had bullet wounds in his body and he died while I stood with his mother. You call to mind all of this, as the young people ask you the question: "Give us a good argument why we should still persist with this," I must honestly say to you that I do not know many arguments any more. What makes it even more difficult, my brothers and sisters, is the apalling hypocrisy of the West and so many of us in the church when it comes to this issue.

We have pleaded and pleaded and pleaded with these countries who constantly ask of us to remain non-violent, not to become violent and to try peaceful means, we have pleaded with them to impose sanctions on the South African government as a peaceful non-violent means to bring that government to its senses. They have refused that. But they are the people who keep on saying, you must employ non-violent means. And when the South African government turns around and kills our children, they still do not find any good reasons to act.

I know that if the situation in my country should deteriorate to the extent where civil war could no longer be stopped, if the moment will come, as one young person said to me, that we will only learn reconciliation and a new South Africa and understanding after we have waded through rivers of blood, if that moment comes the responsibility would not be primarily on the shoulders of those in South Africa who, after centuries of oppression, have decided to take up the gun. The responsibility will lie with those who could have helped in these days and who refused to, who closed their ears to our pleas when we asked them to apply non-violent means of pressure. And we understand that when that moment comes, these will be the very people who will turn around and who will say: "See, we told you so. Black people in South Africa have always been violent."

We understand all of that. It is with this difficulty in mind that I ask: what does it mean to pray "Your will be done" when this issue is discussed? To still know in spite of all the arguments, to still know in spite of the hypocrisy, to still know in spite of the difficulty to remain faithful, to still know, is this not the way of the gospel? To know that your soul shall be destroyed as certainly as the soul of those who govern us has been destroyed by the violence they have employed to subdue us? To struggle on, holding on to what is good and still to say "Your will be done?" To be able to accept the suffering without necessarily waiting for that moment of vengeance when you can say: Now I will pay back to you what you have done to me.

I do not say that black South Africans are not tempted by this. I do not say for one moment that I am not tempted by this. I only say to you that more than ever before in my life I know what it means to struggle with these very, very basic issues. And if it is that we achieve something without too much bloodshed in that country, it will only be for the grace of God and for the mercy and love God somehow still must have for that country. And maybe also because we have learned to pray "Your will be done" and also we have learned to take the cup and drink it.

"Your will be done" is a call to battle, a challenge to the church, a call to conversion, a call for repentance, a call for discipleship, but it is also that prayer which spells out so clearly that certainty of the church which is the heartbeat of our faith. Namely that whatever happens in this world, "Your will shall be done. Your will shall be done." Ultimately we know that in spite of the military power, in spite of the violence, in spite of the oppression, in spite of our fear sometimes, it is not the will of those who wish apartheid to continue that will prevail. It is not the will of those who allow our children to die that will prevail. It is not those who force us into those concentration camps called "homelands" that will prevail. Your will shall be done, on earth as it is in heaven. Because we know that, we can actually walk through life with a certainty that many people find hard to understand and a certainty that certainly scares most white South Africans to death.

My son is now 10 years old. When he was seven we had a candlelight campaign. We asked everybody on a Wednesday night to put out the electricity and to put a candle in their windows, as many windows as they wanted. And it went marvellously well. The campaign grew and just about everybody would have that candle.

We made certain that everybody understood that the candle was the symbol of our faith. That in spite of the darkness of oppression and apartheid Jesus Christ is the light of the world. That light has come into this world and the darkness will not overcome it. It was a sign of hope. It was also a sign of our commitment that this light shall prevail, even in that country. And so Allan and his little friend David walked down the street to go and remind the neighbours: "Today is Wednesday. You must have your candles in the window." To make sure that everybody under-stood, he actually took a candle with him. On their way back there was a police vehicle, right there in our street. The policeman saw them walking with the candle. I should say of course that by that time when the campaign was going so well the South African government had already said that nobody should have these candles in their homes. Candles had become a threat to state security, a sign of subversion and of revolution. "No candles," they were saying. And I know that the police would actually come in, break down people's doors and go into the house to blow out the candles. It was only funny if it was not your house.

So this policeman jumped out of the car, saw the candle, grabbed Allan and David, shook them and said: "Now if I see you walking the street again with this candle, you'll see what will happen to you." And the kids came home shaken up and scared. We talked about this, but in the end Allan asked me a most profound question. I haven't heard such a profound theological question in any synod that I have attended. He said: "Daddy, why is the government afraid of a candle?"

I think that says more about the South African government than they will ever know. It means, yes, indeed they are afraid of this candle. It also means that as that candlelight leaks out they will be gone. And little Allan knows that now, because his daddy told him so.

It is a wonderful thing to be able to say to your children: "I am in this battle now, but you don't have to worry. But you don't have to fight, because your fight is with other things you see." My son will one day speak to this gathering, but he will not come and tell you about children dying, or about children in detention, or about P.W. Botha or whatever their names may be as the years go by. He will not tell you about these things. He will speak to you of other things. Of love and justice and compassion and mercy that our country in the end learned to understand.

And so the prayer "Your will be done" is a prayer for the church to become God's will in the world, to be freedom in the midst of slavery, to be unity in the midst of dissension and strife, to be hope in the midst of hopelessness and despair, to be love in the midst of hatred, to be strength in the midst of powerlessness. "Your will be done," God, in my life. "Your will be done" in this conference. "Your will be done" in this church. "Your will be done" on earth as it is in heaven.

As surely as God's sun will rise tomorrow for the people of my tortured land, apartheid will disappear, oppression will have no place any more. My children will walk the streets without fear. Mothers will not needlessly cry over children who have gone into exile and do not know how to return home. Our fathers will not wake up wondering what will happen today to their children as schools open. Our churches will no longer be tear-gassed as we pray for those in detention. Dogs will no longer be let loose in our school yards. Because God's will will have been done. God's will will surely be done.

A Mission to Modern Western Culture

Lesslie Newbigin

It is a great joy to be at this meeting to see that the integration of mission and church for which I was so deeply concerned thirty years ago now is a reality. As I look back on my own participation in this as the last general secretary of the old International Missionary Council and the first director of the WCC's Division on World Mission and Evangelism, I feel very much that I failed to fulfill all the hopes that we had when that integration took place. Therefore, it is a great joy to see how, under the leadership of those who have followed me as director, the vision has been more and more fully realized. We can today speak truly of a body that represents mission in six continents, for six continents, from six continents.

It is a very special joy that my old friend Christopher Duraisingh is to be the one who carries us forward into the next period. He and I have been friends for a very long time, which means that we have also had lots of theological arguments. It is that itself which is a token of our friendship and trust. I remember that Henrik Kraemer of beloved memory often used to say that what we most need is someone with a theological head and a missionary heart. I think that Christopher Duraisingh is a man with a theological head and a missionary heart.

It was about thirty years ago that another very dear friend, John Coventry Smith, then director of the Commission on Ecumenical Mission and Relations of the United Presbyterian Church, coined the phrase "mission in six continents". I remember him coming up to me during the New Delhi assembly and saying: "Isn't that a phrase that would describe what we are looking for: mission in six continents?" And now, I feel that this conference itself represents that reality in a way that certainly the missionary conferences of earlier years had not fully realized. I believe with all my heart that this is the way that God is calling us.

I was led to remember a little incident at the Bangkok conference, one of the predecessors to this conference which took place in 1971, something which does not appear in the conference reports but is the thing that

---

● Lesslie Newbigin was the first director of the Commission on World Mission and Evangelism.

I remember most. It was during one of the early plenary sessions and we were having a discussion about the global situation of Christian world mission. The man sitting beside me was General Simatupang of Indonesia. He made an intervention in the debate. I don't remember what he said but I do remember that as he came back and sat down beside me I heard him say under his breath: "Of course, the number one question is: can the West be converted?"

That became for me an existential question... While I was struggling with that question I happened to be visiting a famous library and was going along the shelves, looking at the titles of the books. I chanced upon the title of a French book, *La crise de la conscience européenne* by Paul Hazare, "the crisis of Europe's consciousness". I thought that might be helpful. I read it and began to reflect about that crucial point when Europe took a turn in a new direction. That point, which those who passed through it called "the Enlightenment", was roughly the middle decades of the eighteenth century.

That word enlightenment is a very significant word because it is a conversion word. It is the word used of the Buddha for his conversion. At that point as you look back you can see that at least the educated elite of Europe, the intellectuals of Europe took a decisive turn from one creed to another, from one way of understanding the world based upon a thousand years of biblical tradition and the authority of the Bible.

If one asks what were the essential elements in that conversion, at the risk of being very naive one could say that in the first instance it was the dawning of a belief that there could be available to us a kind of knowledge which is undoubtable, which is clear and distinct so that there are no fuzzy edges, no mysteries but clear, distinct unquestionable knowledge; that the human reason, unfettered by traditions or authority, by its own sheer rational power would be able to arrive at indubitable knowledge which does not require a personal commitment, which does not involve a personal risk but which is simply fact. Fact which no one can doubt, which is simply so. That anything in the nature of mystery, of imagination, of intuition, of vision that cannot be stated in these exact indubitable terms belongs to a second level of knowledge. It is the level at which you don't say "I know", but you say "I believe".

The classic picture which has operated as the background of the European mind for at least 200 or 300 years was the picture provided by Newton's astronomy and physics in which the world is understood not in terms of the purpose for which it exists, but in terms of the causes which make it work. That was the decisive turning point which created a dichotomy within the whole of Western thinking, between a public world of facts which you know and a private world of beliefs and values which are the matter of your personal choice.

Can you realistically find in the Bible, in the Christian tradition, a stand-point from which you can radically call into question the whole set of assumptions which govern a culture?

The relation of the Christian gospel to the reigning world-view in the modern Western world is not to show that the gospel is plausible. It is to show that that plausibility structure itself is breaking down and that there is an alternative way of understanding the world which is radically different from the one that reigns here.

One of the Latin American liberation theologians has written words which I find very significant. He said: "The point is to understand the world through the text." The Bible ought to function not as the object of my study. The Bible should be the whole background of my thinking because, in all my thinking, all my acting, all my deciding, there is a background of assumptions which I do not question except when some special event occurs that causes me to question. It is in the light of all those assumptions about what the story is about and about who I am that I make my decisions from moment to moment. The Bible functions properly, not as the object of our examinations but as the context within which we seek to understand the world. I find that an enormously important insight.

During my years in Birmingham I have been impressed by the vitality of the black-led churches. They are among the few churches that show real signs of vitality in our kind of urban culture. The vitality of these churches arises from the fact the Bible is not so much something that they study as it is their own story. We crossed the Red Sea and Pharaoh's army was drowned. We were fed with manna in the wilderness. That's who we are. We were led by the fiery cloudy pillar through the desert. That's who we are. We were there when they crucified the Lord. We were there when God raised him from the tomb. That's who we are. That's our story. And it is in the light of that story, living in that story, that we cope with the world.

Now if that is true, it raises in my mind two issues which are very relevant to the questions that we are discussing in this conference. The first is this: on what bases are we conducting the interfaith dialogue about which we are rightly concerned in this conference? There cannot be any mission to the world without dialogue, without listening as well as speaking. If the dialogue is based upon the contemporary world-view which I have been seeking to describe (because nearly all of this dialogue is conducted in European languages which are shaped by this modern culture) then, of course, we are in this world of values and not in the world of facts.

We are sharing experiences and value judgments which are in any case a matter of personal choice and, therefore, pluralism naturally operates. We are not in the world of facts where pluralism is something that we are seeking to overcome because we want to know what is actually the truth, the real human story, the story that makes sense of human life. Is it the story which is told in the Bible, the story in which there is only one hero, namely the awesome merciful mighty Lord whose crucial action in history is there in the ministry and death and resurrection of Jesus?

Or is that simply part of a private world called religion, whereas the real world is governed by a different vision of the story? If we accept that basis then I do not believe the dialogue really leads us into the truth.

The real dialogue, and I think the most important dialogue for us now, is the dialogue between the biblical understanding of the human story and that understanding of the human story which is dominating Western culture and increasingly the culture of the world. And so, I am seeing it as the crucial missionary task that we challenge and claim the high intellectual ground of our Western culture. I know when I say this I am accused of being elitist. Of course elite just means elect and you cannot remove the doctrinal election from the Bible. (And when I get to the age of 90 I am going to start a society for the protection of elites.) But you cannot avoid the question of challenging the intellectual high ground, claiming the ground that rules our public life.

At the same time you have got to work at every other level, including the level of the simplest local congregation. Every one of these is vital and you cannot say yes to this and no to that. We need both.

But the second reason why this issue is relevant to the work of our conference here is that the question raised by Simatupang is one that will not go away. Simatupang was looking at Western culture from the standpoint of a more ancient culture, the standpoint that could look from the outside and see the witnesses of Western culture in a way that I did not and could not. Because, as I said earlier, this Western culture is something which is penetrating into every part of the world, particularly the urbanized sections of the world. Missionaries themselves have been among the great agents of secularization. As I look back on my own life as a missionary in India, I realize now in a way that I never did at that time that I was not only carrying the gospel but that I was also a carrier of this so-called modern world-view which I now see to be breaking down because it is false. As I look back on my own judgments I realize that over and over again I was judging situations, thinking that I was making a Christian judgment. But that judgment I was making was shaped more by my training as an Englishman, a product of an English school and university education, than the judgment that arises from living in the world of the Bible.

I know how slowly it was that I came to see that. I believe that it must be part of our agenda as a Commission for World Mission that we address ourselves to that issue. If we are really serious when we speak about mission in six continents, then one of our toughest tasks, I think, is precisely the one that I try to outline: to challenge the high intellectual ground of our culture. I said earlier on that if I look at the life of the church in my own country I think that, as compared with previous centuries, the ministers and the people are more devoted, more committed to the gospel than was normally the case a hundred years ago. They are much more involved in the political and social implications of the gospel than they were a hundred years ago. I think that one cannot fault them at that point.

One asks: why is it then that the church tends to be so defensive, and even so timid in the faith, of the claims of what we call modern culture? The answer is that we have allowed ourselves, we have allowed the gospel to be co-opted into a subordinate position in this world of values where it cannot challenge what is called the world of facts. We must recover the courage to recognize that it is this world of so-called facts that we have to challenge, that we have to claim the high ground. We have to do as St Paul says in his letter to the Corinthians, "to bring every thought in captivity to Christ". That must be one of the central tasks of a commission that takes all six continents for its agenda.

"Risking Obedience"
Youth Pre-conference Report

The youth conference: a process begun

Approximately one hundred young people met for two and a half days (18-21 May 1989) in San Antonio, Texas, under the theme "Risking Obedience".

We came to tell stories. We came to listen to stories. Why story-telling? Because our stories are real and concrete — they are not abstract. We tell our stories because we are affected differently by the issues we face and respond to them in different ways. Yet our stories are interconnected, as we are inter-related.

We shared our stories of risking obedience in our own situations. From out of these stories we felt pain, fear, confusion, helplessness, depression, constraint and voicelessness. It was important to grapple with them, but we also felt the strength of prayer, of hope, joy, affirmation, creativity and empowerment. We listened to stories of individuals who challenged an extravagant consumerist life-style; who marched in the streets; who organized; who raised people's awareness of the problems of those who live in war-torn lands; who were jailed, beaten and tortured. We were challenged by the stories of young martyrs who took the ultimate risk of obedience.

We have learned that there is no one way of risking obedience. Our understanding of the Bible and God's will for us must be constantly in dialogue with the context in which we find ourselves.

We have different and diverse stories, yet they are inter-related and intertwined. Our stories reminded us that we all belong to God's world. We are a community of believers that produced a very big story — a story that affirmed that what affects one affects the other.

We felt the presence of God at work in those stories and made the affirmation that this big story is God's story written and acted out by people who have taken the risk of obedience.

We grouped ourselves by region to confront issues we felt had affected us the most: social injustice, need for empowerment of people, biased media, misuse of faith, violence, human rights violations, development debate, minority discrimination/oppression, sexism, fundamentalism, brain drain, graft and corruption, foreign intervention, militarization, proclamation of the word, personal obedience and evangelism, the growing divide between rich and poor, homelessness, individualism, consumerism, environmental/ecology concerns, the church and its relation to state structures, the relationship between Eastern and Western Europe, alienation and the need to reaffirm the strength of community.

North-South relationships

After the regional reports, we entered a spirited but often painful discussion, wrestling with North-South relationships. This was vividly illustrated by the observation that a baby born in the South today is born into debt to a baby born in the North. This grossly unjust relationship led us to reflect on patterns of relationship that have poisoned and that continue to poison human history. The affluence of the rich is inextricably linked to the exploitation of the poor.

The abundance that God intended to be shared in justice has been hoarded and is enjoyed by a few who continue to demand more. Is it not ironic that the South, which has been the source of affluence, is accused of indebtedness?

The countries in the North have systematically kept the countries of the South in deprivation and other dependences. The South becomes a cheap source of raw materials and labour, and an open market for the North's goods. Unequal trade treaties and protectionist policies prevent the South from economic recovery.

Within both North and South, the socio-economic division also exists. There is a minority in each who have wealth and power and a majority that are poor and powerless. The wealthy in the South also hold political power and are in collaboration with the wealthy in the North in maintaining unjust systems. We commit ourselves to work for the transformation of this relationship so that God's will be done.

Mission in solidarity

Mission, as it has been practised in the past, is bound up with North-South relationships. Churches, by their silence, have supported this relationship. In some cases, churches have actively sided with the oppressors.

We felt and expressed anger, guilt, hopelessness and helplessness as we engaged in the discussion. We did not always have the answers. The cry rang out: What are we to do? What can we do now? What will we do?

Hearing these cries yet finding hope in Christ, we commit ourselves to search ways of building relationships and structures of mutual solidarity. The centre of mission is Jesus Christ who calls us to solidarity; a solidarity that seeks the vision and goal of children born equal, not only in God's eyes but in ours as well; a solidarity that acknowledges the sins of our ancestors and our perpetuating of those sins through unjust systems of development that lead to indebtedness and injustice; a solidarity which acknowledges that the physical wounds resulting from torture, the psychological wounds of people without hope, the polluted wounds of our planet are all interconnected — a solidarity that strives for just economic relationships throughout the whole inhabited world.

To the youth of the North, this can be expressed in the following concrete manner:

1) begin to create awareness about the poor, the marginalized and the suffering minorities in their own societies;

2) extend awareness-building to issues in the international community, stressing that often the suffering of the South stems from socio-economic moves by the governments of the North and big business interests;

3) mobilize opinion towards the suffering of the international community because of the oppressive economic order propped up by biased information networks;

4) begin a process (from the local church, community or school) whereby representations and lobby can be made to government officials protesting the harsh conditions and policies imposed on the South by their own governments, the International Monetary Fund and the World Bank.

While agreeing that the North continues to exploit the South by siphoning off the latter's wealth and resources, and while agreeing that too often the North has exploited areas of conflict in the South to justify the sale of lethal arms and other related products, the youth of the South admit that people of the South do contribute to the worsening of their situation. The youth of the South can:

1) call attention to some cultural practices that continue to divide people in the South; tribalism, ethnic chauvinism, religious triumphalism, point to our failure to live with our diversities;

2) resist and overthrow dictators who have muzzled the freedom of people and who resort to militarization and heavy military expenditure to maintain their unpopular regimes;

3) resist and reject corrupt leaders who enrich themselves at the expense of their countries, serving as "commission agents" of the transnational companies;

4) challenge the socio-economic policies of their national governments that lead to high infant mortality rates, illiteracy and food shortage;

5) commit themselves to establish self-reliance and self-determination.

Mission as network-building

We have affirmed our inter-relatedness while we act and struggle in our own particular context; we realize that our struggles are inextricably linked with the struggles of others.

One cannot create conditions of self-determination and self-empowerment for oneself unless one also advocates the same conditions for everybody else.

Thus it is very necessary to build a network of people committed to take risks of obedience so that God's will will be done on earth.

Concretely, we have committed ourselves to:

1) taking stock of the existing ecumenical networks and finding creative ways to use these structures for networking and solidarity purposes;

2) covenanting with each other to be in contact for mutual sharing of stories and concerns, and for mutual edification and encouragement;

3) pledging to go back to our own particular communities to raise awareness of issues: mobilize and organize our people, as well as *relate* them with other groups having similar goals and objectives; we can do a lot more to learn from networks outside our own structures and to join hands with them, extending the horizons of our issues — taking other people's issues as part of our own, and sharing each other's particular struggle; providing opportunities for interaction among committed movements and persons to take place.

Mission as proclamation

In our discussions it was also recognized that apathy, indifference and selfishness have blinded many rich people to the needs of the poor and oppressed. It is through a total transformation brought about by turning to the living God that such negative individualism will be overcome. For this to come about we are called to engage in proclaiming in words and deeds the good news of Jesus Christ to all persons. In his own proclamation about the kingdom of God, the heart of Jesus' message does not ultimately lie in what he said, but more in who he was and what he did. The ultimate proclamation is his cross and resurrection. In this, Christ proclaims salvation, which is liberation from everything that oppresses human beings. This proclamation validates and gives life and power to his word. Our motivation to be concerned for justice, peace and the integrity of creation comes from our confession of Jesus Christ as Lord. This compels us to seek the radical transformation of unjust structures. As God's people we invite others, North and South, to share in our community of faith. Together with all who share our common concerns we seek to serve whole persons in the totality of their need.

A message to the churches

We also come with a message to the churches. This message is not meant to disassociate ourselves from the churches for we, too, are part of the one body of Christ. As we address this message to you, we are at the same time addressing it to ourselves.

> In the last days, God says, I will pour out my Spirit on all people. Your sons and daughters will prophesy, your young men will see visions, your old men will dream dreams. Even on my servants both men and women, I will call out my spirit in those days, and they will prophesy (Acts 2:17-18).

The church we are part of today has forgotten that the church is called to be a community. There is a gap between the leadership of the churches and the people they lead. Our community is made up of young and old, rich and poor, men and women, laity and clergy. All of us make up this community and all are a significant part thereof. All of us are co-workers with God.

Mission is God's and he calls us to participate in it. Therefore, God's will and not ours should be the agenda.

Let us proclaim God's will. Let our proclamation be a prophetic one. Let us challenge the structure of oppression as Isaiah did (Isa. 10:1-2).

Let us question our rites and outward religiosity as Amos did (Amos 51:21-24).

Let us shake the foundations of the power base of the Pharisees and scribes as the Lord himself challenged the bases of the religious structures of his times (Matt. 23:13-36, Luke 11:37-54).

Let us risk obedience!

We came together. We wrestled with issues and problems. We did not always arrive at a consensus. We left some questions hanging in the air. We did not produce a great treatise on mission, but we have identified some issues that the churches need to address.

We came together as strangers. We are still strangers in many ways but the seed of solidarity has been sown and is starting to sprout.

God of justice and peace, may your will be done and may you give us the power, the grace and the courage to risk obedience in the way of Christ. Amen.

In Solidarity
with Women in Struggle

During one of the plenaries the conference heard a call for commitment for solidarity with women. Women delegates felt strongly that many issues of vital importance for the wholeness of women everywhere in the world were not sufficiently considered. It is only with restored dignity that women made in God's image will become credible agents of God's mission at home and to the world. Through the testimonies of women from various regions and contexts they called on the conference for action.

When we reflect on the theme "Your will be done on earth as it is in heaven", we realize that there are specific issues that have not been fully dealt with. We wish to address this conference with the following specific concerns and ask for your personal commitment in action.

We, women of *Africa*, are deeply concerned over the 14 people who have just been sentenced to death in Christian South Africa; over the continued detention and harassment of children in the whole of Africa; over growing poverty in Africa and the suffocating debt crisis which especially affects women.

We hereby resolve:
— to pledge our solidarity with those victims sentenced to death;
— to call for the immediate release of innocent children in detention —
  we are weeping for our children;
— to campaign for economic justice in Africa and for the total eradica-
  tion of the apartheid system.

We call on all women at the conference to pledge their solidarity in action.

* * *

We the *Asian* women delegates wanted to bring to this assembly the issues of prostitution, sex abuse and the flesh trade, which are reinforced by male domination.

Prostitution, sex abuse and male domination are felt and have been suffered by women in almost all Asian countries. This has become a cancer of our society. In some cases the flesh trade and prostitution have become part of the country's tourism. In the Philippines this is reinforced by the presence of the US military bases. It is lamentable that the groups which take advantage of this situation are tourists from Europe, the United States and Japan. This reduces women to mere commodities.

We women delegates appeal to this assembly to support us in our determination to stop this exploitation by:

— making these issues a primary concern of your churches so that they may undertake information and education campaigns on the situation and dignity of women in the reign of God;

— encouraging the churches to denounce the systems which perpetuate and reinforce exploitation of women in any form in church and society.

* * *

When we, women of the *Caribbean*, think of the theme "Your will be done", and the contradicting influence of drugs, especially cocaine, upon our nations, our youth and the danger of their influence upon our nations' children, we are appalled. Because of unemployment, even women are slipping into this trade by selling small quantities in their communities. They are usually being used by someone who pays well for the risks.

Young people who become pushers and tourists are often found bringing in cocaine or trying to take gango out with them. Controlling the trade costs the nations millions of dollars per year. This could be spent in different ways. Our churches pray for deliverance from these evils, that God's will may be done.

About six weeks ago, 3000 lbs of gango was found on an aeroplane and a fine of half a million dollars was charged. An agreement was reached that if this should happen again, then Jamaican planes would no longer come to American airports. That would be hard on our tourist trade and on employment, and we are working hard to prevent it.

We ask the CWME to help in lessening the demand. We also ask help in finding markets for the arts and crafts done by women in our churches.

* * *

We, women of *Europe*, call your attention to poor women in many of our European cities and villages who are exploited as cheap labour. Women in Europe work in their own small houses and small unhealthy workshops to sell clothes, peel shrimp and to assemble small industrial items. They are poor women, single women, and migrant women. These women work for low wages, with no job security, health or other insurance, and in very bad conditions.

We need to support and work with these women who struggle to survive in our communities.

We especially mention the women of Cyprus where many people suffer because of the split families. They struggle to keep families together, and they need our support.

* * *

Due to racism in the *United States of America*, people of colour experience poverty. The fastest growing group of women in poverty is made up of children, and 40 percent of them live in households headed by women. They also experience prisons, suicide, drugs, unemployment, teen-age pregnancies, hate groups and neo-Nazi para-military organizations.

We ask for your prayers and, where possible, your commitment to help eradicate racism. Through all of this, people of faith still have the dream that some day....

Oh! freedom, oh! freedom, over all of us.

* * *

We, women of *Canada*, draw attention to the feminization of poverty in Canada. Most of the poor people in Canada are women and the children they support. This is because in Canada, most single-parent households are headed by women who alone bear the responsibility of supporting their children. At the same time, child-care facilities for working women are inadequate and expensive, and in addition, women are paid lower wages and salaries than men. We ask you to support women everywhere who struggle against discriminatory poverty.

* * *

We, women of *Latin America*, want the end of colonialism especially in regard to the case of Puerto Rico. We long for respect of the right to self-determination of all of our people. But above all, we want peace for Central America. No more bloodshed in Central America. No more killing of our youth — our sons, women, husbands and fathers. No more orphans and widows of war.

This means no more United States intervention in the region:
— no more financial military aid that prolongs the war in El Salvador and makes genocide possible in Guatemala;
— no more mobilization of US troops and intimidation as in the case of Panama; no more direct or indirect support to the contras in Nicaragua which attack the rural communities and kill the peasantry;
— no more military enclaves as in the case of Puerto Rico and more recently of Honduras, which force us to become accomplices of aggression, destruction and death against our brothers and sisters not only in the rest of the region but also in Asia and Africa.

We affirm respect for the right of people's self-determination and to live in peace.

* * *

We, women of the *Middle East* adhere to this testimony:

"I am a Lebanese woman coming from Beirut after a stay of two months in the shelter. My family is still there, in bombing and shelling; our only airport is closed. We have one or two hours of electricity and water daily. Most serious for me as a woman is that the educational system is paralyzed as schools and universities are closed. Our country is like a patient, a very sick one, in an intensive care unit. Please do not let us die.

"I beg you to keep in mind that our war is not a religious one. We are not fighting each other. We are living a horrible nightmare because of other people's wars.

"I am an Orthodox. I live in West Beirut (referred to in the news as Muslim). I am the principal of an Orthodox high school, 85 percent of my students are Muslim. I love them all. I worry about them all. I have 927 of them in the shelter and the only help I can give them is to speak to you on their behalf. Their identity is linked with terrorism and they abhor it. They would like to live in peace like all other children in the world. Coming from Lebanon I also want to stress my wholehearted support for an independent sovereign Palestinian state on Palestinian soil.

"Sudan is suffering and struggling and Cyprus is carrying the cross of division. We have a lot of suffering and struggle in the Middle East.

"Finally, please don't let your children ask you one day, when you read the Bible to them, what you have done to the cedars of the land, the cedars of Lebanon. Thank you."

* * *

We, women of the *Pacific Islands*, would like to share three points with you:

1. Nuclear-free Pacific: We ask you to support us in our work to clear the Pacific air, sea and land from nuclear tests and from polluted nuclear wastes. We claim to have a free Pacific, free in the sense of individual freedom, freedom within the families and free countries. Therefore we seek your support...

2. An independent Pacific: We ask for an independent Pacific. As we really know in our hearts, an independent Pacific has its rights based in the kingdom of God through Jesus Christ.

3. Equality between men and women: They have to share in everything: physical life and spiritual life too. We need to share in the family, share in the church, and in the total life of the Pacific islands as the theme of this conference says: God's will be done!

Best wishes for all women, may God bless our mission in Christ's way.

Reflections on Encuentro

The scope and style of the encounter

ENCUENTRO! An encounter — with God, with the risen Christ, with one another, with our world in its beauty and pain!

We are five hundred Christians, women and men, who spent five days participating in a world mission conference organized by the World Council of Churches that brought people from nearly one hundred nations to San Antonio. We came from 44 states, 20 denominations; 119 of us are students at 32 theological seminaries. We are Asian Americans, Hispanics, African Americans, Native Americans and Caucasians — a rich mixture of colours and cultures. In our encounters with each other, we came to believe that no church, race or nation has a monopoly on mission and evangelism. Mission demands unity. Never again can we be content in our separateness. Our strength for mission in Christ's way — the conference theme — comes as we seek to witness together. But simply rejoicing in our community is not enough. Our love for the world must be demonstrated by costly service. We reject false divisions between local and universal, mission and evangelism. We have experienced wholeness and want to share it.

In this ecumenical context we encountered a new integrity for evangelism. Sharing the good news of God in Jesus Christ changes both the bearer of that message and the one who receives it. God is the evangelist! Again and again God claims and changes those whose lives are turned towards God. Evangelism cannot be confined to individual conversion alone. Our practice of mission and evangelism must judge and guide our cultural, political and economic life.

Although many despaired of the Russian and Chinese churches, we received the good news that hundreds of churches are being opened in the USSR and five thousand Protestant churches have come to life in China in the last decade. For the first time in more than three decades, a delegation of Christians from China attended such a world mission conference. We experienced afresh, through the new life of these churches, God's resurrecting power.

From around the world we heard stories of suffering, struggle and hope. Witnesses testified to the power of the gospel to equip them for mission. Their perseverance is a source of hope and life. In obedience to the will of God, we seek to participate with all who struggle for dignity and justice. Through the testimony of Allan Boesak of South Africa, we received the good news that God's Holy Spirit sustains and empowers those who dare to do mission in Christ's way.

A biblical concern for the stewardship of the earth reminded us that our responsibility is not only to evangelize the people of six inhabited continents, but to preserve the ecological integrity of the ocean depths, the atmosphere, and all the islands of the sea. As Christians we see the "world as sacrament", as God's gift to be used, offered in thanksgiving, and replenished for future generations.

A new missionary style lies ahead for our churches, shaped by the very good news it is committed to share. North American churches have failed to honour the cultures into which missionaries have been sent. We affirm the style of seeking to understand and receive the grace of God already present in other cultures. We recognize a certain Western instinct to dominate that must end. Authentic mission will require new partnerships free of dependency. Spiritual resources will take precedence over financial resources. Wrestling with cultural forces as they both distort and disclose the gospel becomes an urgent mission mandate. Our society is increasingly pluralistic, multi-faith and multi-ethnic.

To foster the creative interdependency that makes community possible, we must develop authentic dialogue, taking seriously our own faith as well as other faiths. Our vision requires the inclusion of people of all ethnic identities.

Commitment to mission in Christ's way leads us to contend with the secular structures of human life. It insists on our allowing our own lives as Christians to be shaped by the gospel. Too often we have reduced the gospel to words alone — too much, we have allowed our measure of faithfulness to become little more than growth in numbers. We have been too ready to deal in power relationships rather than to risk the vulnerability that is the way of the cross. Those with wisdom and courage from lands beyond our own are teaching us new vitalities of faith.

In Bible study, singing, worship, prayer, conversation with our global partners we have found a new confidence in God's word, a new optimism for the future. We have tasted in a living, global fellowship nothing less than a new life in Christ! What has been ours in these days, we pray for all Christians and for all the world.

A letter to North American churches

In the conclusion of the letter to North American churches, the five hundred Christians, women and men, attending the Encuentro in San Antonio, Texas, wrote:

> In Bible study, singing, worship, prayer and conversation with our global partners we have found a new confidence in God's word, a new optimism for the future. We have tasted in a living, global fellowship nothing less than a new life in Christ! What has been ours in these days, we pray for all Christians and for all the world.

To reflect on the experience one calls forth the mind-stretching encounters with the speakers, the emotional momentum towards action that almost overwhelmed the participants as the South African reality was expressed by Allan Boesak, the influential interaction with the Commission on World Mission and Evangelism delegates, the inspiring worship services and Bible study, and the list could go on and on.

One cannot minimize the importance of meeting with the world mission leaders of the universal church. It was exciting, and challenging, to greet and hear major addresses by Emilio Castro, Eugene Stockwell, Allan Boesak, Raymond Fung, Michael Oleksa — all speaking to the mission issues facing the churches of the world and, more particularly, the role of the North American churches and Christians in relating to the same. "Your will be done" became a special prayer for us as we resonated to the call to mission made upon Christians in risk places around the world and recognized our mandate to respond in similar ways. The debate initiated by Stockwell around dialogue and relationships with persons of other faiths and ideologies became more relevant as we listened to the participants from these faiths, invited to the conference, speaking to the question, "Is Jesus the only way?" For those of us in the Encuentro sessions the issue was not resolved but it did cause deep searching and individual but tentative conclusions.

Closely linked to that discussion came the challenge from Fung towards a new understanding of evangelism, using the sixty-fifth chapter of Isaiah as an agenda or model: the church in partnership with the world in justice, peace and integrity of creation; an invitation to discipleship, taking up the cross and following Jesus; an invitation to a renewal of worship in the church, beginning with prayer. That may sound familiar, but as we heard it articulated again we became aware of how often we reject the agenda!

The Bible studies, led by Dr Forbes, brought new and fresh insights to well-known passages: the Magnificat, the Song of Hannah, the Good Samaritan — all took on relevant meanings in light of God's mission in Jesus' way.

Interaction with international persons from the conference through the seminars and conversations probably was the most influential towards a new understanding.... People were sharing what they had heard from the Chinese, who were there as the first delegates from that country to such a World Council of Churches' conference for over three decades, or the life story of the Bolivian woman trapped in the factory providing illegal drugs to the United States, or the risks taken by Christian witnesses in situations of oppression. Stories of a hostage in Lebanon, a caregiver of abandoned children in South Africa, a clergyman in the struggle in the Philippines, bring to mind the necessity of solidarity with our brothers and sisters who suffer, and our responsibility to work in the United States of America for just international policies and practices.

... Central to the theme, "Your will be done — Mission in Christ's way," were the several worship services. Of special significance was the opening experience of the conference in which the Encuentro group participated. Imagine worshipping in a Southern Baptist church, led by a variety of international leaders, including an Orthodox bishop, where the word is presented by a Roman Catholic archbishop from San Antonio using a Mariachi band and children dancing up the aisles with flowers, and all of us responding musically to the prayers, concluding with the great amen from Africa to the beat of drums!

... In the closing worship we were forcefully reminded by Christopher Duraisingh, director-elect of the Commission on World Mission and Evangelism, of the new tasks of mission and evangelism we must assume. We prayed in commitment:

...open our eyes to your vision of the world;
send us forth as faithful witnesses
to the love of God in Jesus Christ.
In all that we do
may we be obedient to your will.

Lois Miller, USA

San Antonio in May of '89 was hot. That's putting it mildly; new heat records were set, with each day surpassing the previous one. Merely walking from one Trinity University campus building to the next was a wilting experience.

That might serve as a metaphor for Encuentro. Certainly there was cause for concern in the months leading up to the event. Would the presence of some five hundred North Americans intermingling with the CWME delegates for five days — sitting in on their plenaries, eating meals with them, inviting them to Encuentro seminars and workshops — become a distraction? Would it be viewed by church representatives from around the globe as yet one more instance of USA presumption and arrogance and an attempt to dominate? Would we Americans try to impose our own mission and evangelism agendas on the gathered delegates?

Or would we listen? Would we try, really try, to reconsider our own agendas in respect to voices interpreting the call of God out of diverse situations and contexts?

... I am convinced that, to a truly astonishing extent, Encuentro succeeded in achieving its intended goals. Genuine and rewarding encounters abounded. Helpful and hopeful new insights emerged in session after session. Strangers became acquaintances, acquaintances became friends. The exchanges at times became heated, certainly; but no one wilted. The fires ignited at Encuentro were searing, not withering, fires. The value of such a crucible for forging new alliances and new understandings was gratefully affirmed by Christopher Duraisingh at the closing worship when he observed that, henceforth, all CWME events would do well to follow the San Antonio model in providing an "encounter" between conference delegates and the churchfolk of whatever setting in which they found themselves meeting.

Encuentro. It's a Spanish word, reminding North Americans that the San Antonio site is a sort of boundary city between peoples of two different languages and cultures. I came expecting an encuentro with Christian people of experiences and contexts and understandings very different from mine, and challenging mine. That I found, and so much more.

We encountered one another in enlivening ways. Allan Boesak jolted us with the reality of the risks involved in daring to proclaim God's judgment on all that opposes God's will, and called for us to "accept our freedom in God's name". We were moved by his narrative that, to a repressive regime, even so minimal an act as lighting a candle may appear as a revolutionary action. Emilio Castro stirred us in the opening worship with his challenge to "mainline" churches in the USA that finding ourselves moved to the "sidelines" may become an occasion for renewed vitality as we look for the presence of God in the world, not so much in centres of power but among the marginalized, the disempowered, the struggling poor with whom God identifies.

... We encountered a rich variety of worship forms and traditions in deeply moving ways. It became transparently clear that vitality in worship is never a problem where the certainty of purpose of the worshipping body is at the forefront. Two experiences stand out, for me. One is the splendid cacophany of sound that arises when hundreds of worshippers are simultaneously repeating aloud the Lord's Prayer in whichever language we first learned to pray it. The second is the experiencing of the "African great amen" with which was concluded the opening worship at Trinity Baptist Church, and which lingered on long into the night as we were unwilling to let go of this rhythmic, pulsating expression of united faithfulness for which we yearn.

... Somehow the encounter went beyond exposure to new partners-in-mission and fresh insights, to encounter with an empowering presence at the very core of those relationships and visions of possibility. The expanding of horizons of awareness was at the same time a penetration into the depths of the divine Spirit who moves among us with life-expanding gifts.

Finally, I would dare to suggest that in San Antonio we encountered the future. I have in mind particularly the exciting fact that fully 119 of the 497 Encuentro registrants, nearly a fourth in all, were seminarians. This is a new dimension for WCC functions and an extremely promising step. That North American seminary students took this conference with such seriousness bode well for the development of globally informed leadership in the churches of the United States. My domain in the US is theological education. We work all too often with a very limited focus on our responsibilities, unleavened by exposure to realities beyond our immediate cultural contexts. The encounter of so many and so diverse a body of seminarians with persons and issues and perspectives involving very different experiences can only broaden in a vital way the process of formation for ministry.

David P. Polk, USA

... As a Latin American I see with ever greater interest the dialogue with churches of the developed world. I believe faith provides the departure point to state and restate on North-South relationships, so damaged by international political action in our continent. Of course, this dialogue cannot and must not be limited to assemblies nor to Christians who take part in them. It must be translated into concrete and urgent actions so that Latin America may recover its freedom and self-determination, its right to abundant life, peace and justice, and human rights, which are the inalienable rights of every human being, of every child of God.

Aracely E. de Rocchetti, Uruguay

An Orthodox Response

to the WCC conference
on mission and evangelism

Dear Brothers and Sisters,

We, the Orthodox participants in this conference, men and women from Orthodox churches throughout the world, unanimously express to you the joy and happiness we have experienced during our participation in this gathering, which allowed us all the opportunity to deepen our understanding of evangelism and mission in Christ's way.

We wholeheartedly thank all those who have laboured to make this conference a significant ecumenical event.

We wish, however, to draw your attention to some major concerns:

a) We have noticed that in some conference documents and in worship services there has been a distortion of the constitutional basis of the World Council of Churches and of some fundamental tenets of our common faith.

b) Faith in the Triune God constitutes *the basis* of the World Council of Churches. The confession of the holy name of the Father, the divinity of the Son and the existence of the Holy Spirit as an hypostasis (person) and their unity in the divine essence of God is the fundamental presupposition of the participation of the Orthodox churches in the World Council of Churches.

c) We unequivocally affirm that Jesus Christ is our God and Saviour. "He is the way, the truth and the life" (John 14:6). He is the one who saves us and leads us to unity.

d) We cannot accept any tampering with the language of the Bible or any attempts to rewrite it, or make it conform to the beliefs or ideology of any particular culture, denomination or movement.

e) While the issue of the fuller participation of women in the life of the church should be a subject of study in the World Council of Churches, their ordination to priesthood is not, for us, subject to debate, since it is contrary to the Christology, ecclesiology, Tradition and practice of the early church.

We submit this for consideration in a spirit of love, for the sake of the integrity of our Christian fellowship and of our unhindered ecumenical involvement in the World Council of Churches.

San Antonio, 31 May 1989   The Orthodox participants

* * *

This presentation was followed by two statements which should be recorded here:

In the first line of Section I, we expressed "joy for the growing unity among Christians". I wish to speak to this in the context of the statement made by the Orthodox churches.

I ask the Orthodox churches to accept that the other denominations also consider themselves to be true to the witness of the Bible, of the church and the Triune God. If we are to relate to each other we need to accept each other in our differences and as equals. As a woman, an ordained woman and a part of the Reformed tradition of the church, I was deeply hurt by their statement. How may I express joy for the growing unity when I experience such rejection and hurt?

Rev. Elisabeth Jane Nash (Reformed, UK)

I hope that we have not been misunderstood. I would like to underline that what we have said has been said in love. We have simply tried to express our faith. Therefore, we are very upset if anyone has been hurt by this expression of our faith. I would suggest that the document presented by the Orthodox participants should be circulated so that everybody can read it, reflect on it and see that there is nothing of a bad feeling in it against anybody, ordained or not.

Secondly, I wish to clarify that any woman who is ordained in her own church has all our respect. If the church accepts this practice, we respect it. It does not mean that we reject it or do not agree with it. Churches have been following certain practices since the first century.

We made the presentation in love and humility, hoping that you will listen to us as Christian brothers and sisters.

Bishop Antonios Marcos (Coptic Orthodox, Kenya)

A Letter from the Africa Regional Group

Dear sisters and brothers in Christ,

We write to you as fellow members of the body of Christ from the continent of Africa. We have been attending the World Council of Churches' world conference on mission and evangelism, San Antonio, Texas, 22 May to 1 June 1989. We came here as delegates from member churches of the WCC, national councils of churches, commissioners of CWME, observers, consultants and accredited representatives from action groups on the cutting edge of the churches' mission and witness for justice.

We address you in the renowned tradition of the primitive church, by a letter of love and inspiration and in the pastoral, prophetic and missionary tradition of our faith. Like John, we hear the word of God and the testimony of the Spirit saying to us today: Write what you see in a book and send it to the seven churches... (Rev. 1:11). We write not only what we see and hear but also what we experience and believe.

We came to San Anotnio overjoyed and burdened. Overjoyed because God called us and continues to call many in our continent to acts in faithfulness. We are here to express the joy of our common faith; to dance to the beat of the drum and to sing songs of inspiration in the tradition of the exiles in a foreign land. We came in faithfulness to the proclamation "Your will be done". During our time here we were enriched by the fellowship of many Christians from other lands and our eyes were opened to the richness and diversity of cultures in the service of the gospel. More particularly, our hearts are filled with joy with the people of Namibia as they anticipate the fruits of many years of painful struggle as that last remaining colony in Africa moves towards statehood.

We are, however, burdened too. We came here with our hearts heavy with the pain of our land and its peoples. We want to share with you fully our concern about the violation of human rights in ever-increasing spirals in too many of our countries. We heard the young people among us calling us to risk obedience for the sake of the justice of God. We heard of a bishop threatened with murder and treated in a demeaning manner because he preached against corruption, abuse of power and violation of human rights.

We have consistently called for the dismantling of apartheid and the restoration of human dignity, peace and justice for all in that sad country, South Africa. We renew with urgency the universal call for the implementation of mandatory and comprehensive economic sanctions against the apartheid regime. We are alarmed at the escalation of violence in South Africa. Judicial executions have increased especially in those cases where the political motive is not considered an extenuating circumstance. There has developed an easy resort to the principle of "common purpose" to get convictions as yet another form of state repression. As we write, some 14 persons have been sentenced to death, among them a 60-year old woman. We ask you to pray for them and to campaign for an end to this barbaric system.

Elsewhere in the continent, we have been experiencing the resurgence of tribalism and nationalism. Wars and low-intensity conflicts are being waged through the length and breadth of the continent: from Morocco to Mauritania; the Horn of Africa down to Mozambique; the Sudan, Chad, Angola and South Africa. There are coups d'état and floods of refugees are fleeing to neighbouring states and further afield. Many are dying of starvation. Our land is bleeding and our people are crying out for peace. As a result of this instability, national priorities are distorted: huge amounts are being spent on war and armaments which enrich the armaments industry of the West and the East. Militarism is a luxury Africa can ill afford.

Africa has become the dumping ground of nuclear and toxic waste, which pollutes our shores and seas, our rivers and atmosphere. Africa's ecological system and her wealth have been extravagantly exploited. As we write, many countries in Africa are reeling under the debt burden imposed on their economies by the rich nations of the world. Many of our economies are on the brink of collapse; our dependency has become proverbial; we can no longer even feed our own people. Enter the International Monetary Fund and the World Bank. Economic policies have been imposed which not only increase the levels of poverty and take away our right to self-determination and sovereignty but also undermine Africa's cultural and spiritual values. Subsidies have had to be removed from essential commodities and the currency has been substantially devalued, further increasing poverty. Such a state of affairs contributes to national instability, greed and individualism. Africa's communal values, traditional ways of life and our "humanness" *(ubuntu)* are devalued.

You will understand the depth of our sorrow as we write this letter. We do it because we know that the Bible teaches that when one part of the body suffers then all suffer. A burden shared is a load lightened. Our fortunes are inextricably intertwined. What your nations and churches do or fail to do, somehow affects our lives. So we plead for your understanding and for our common affirmation of kingdom values in our common world.

With everyone else in this conference, we have been challenged to acts in faithfulness. We, collectively and individually, pledge to uphold these acts agreed upon here. We hold firmly to the faith so forcefully proclaimed here and we challenge our societies to live in faithfulness and obedience to "mission in Christ's way".

> Strive for peace with all people, and for holiness without which no one will see the Lord (Heb. 12:14).

We have pledged to call a follow-up conference on mission and evangelism in Africa with the help of the All Africa Conference of Churches. We shall put ourselves to account, within three years, for our stewardship of the resources entrusted to us by San Antonio. We shall test and review our faithfulness and we shall challenge those in authority in new and authentic ways.

How can your church and government respond to this call from Africa? Please take this challenge with you and remember Africa constantly in your prayers.

> As they went out, they came upon a man of Cyrene, Simon by name; this man was compelled to carry his cross (Matt. 27:32).

Today, Africa is still being compelled to carry that cross for the world. That is both our privilege and our burden.

Yours in his service
The Africa Regional Group

A Letter from those with Evangelical Concerns to the Lausanne II Conference

Among the participants at the San Antonio conference were those with a deep commitment to evangelical concerns. The following are excerpts from a letter addressed by them to the Lausanne II Manila conference, July 1989. For reasons of space, this document has been excerpted. The full text is available upon request from the Commission on World Mission and Evangelism of the World Council of Churches.

Our sisters and brothers in Christ.

We bring greetings with this letter from all your sisters and brothers in Christ gathered at this World Council of Churches conference on "Your will be done — Mission in Christ's way".

We have taken part in this conference in the spirit of the aim of the Commission on World Mission and Evangelism which we affirm: "to assist the Christian community in the proclamation of the gospel of Jesus Christ by word and deed to the whole world to the end that all may believe in him and be saved" (from the constitution of the CWME)....

I. We wish to share with you many of the good things we have learned and been enriched by at this conference.

We have appreciated the rich diversity of the make-up of the conference. The World Council has sought to reflect the worldwide people of God. Forty-three percent of the delegates are women, seventy percent are from the two-thirds world and fifteen percent are youth. It has also sought a balance of lay and ordained people, and to involve the gifts of women equally with those of men, and we commend this to the Lausanne movement.

We have been enriched by the worship and the Bible study. The worship has drawn on the word of God; it has made use of verbal and nonverbal activities and has drawn on prayers and devotions from many cultures and different languages to express our devotion to God. An early morning walk with meditation on the passion, death and resurrection of Jesus was particularly powerful. Our six Bible studies on the Gospel of Luke have been a means of sharing, and of building relationships of fellowship, learning and trust with those from whom we are divided by denomination or race, and of building community around the word of God. We have had a chance to hear and learn from other Christian traditions as equally committed as we are to following Christ.

We have welcomed the importance given to the cross of Jesus in this conference. The cost of suffering as we share the good news of Jesus has been stressed. The cross is to be at the heart of all authentic Christian witness, both in our words and in our life.

We have appreciated the openness of the conference process. Through its group work the conference has given space for all views to be heard and represented. This openness has given ample opportunity for evangelical concerns to be voiced and to find expression in conference documents. Since we recognize that the worldwide evangelical family has a rich diversity of views held in submission to the authority of scripture, we would welcome a similar process in evangelical conferences....

We have valued the concern at this conference for justice for all peoples of the earth and a proper concern for the stewardship of earth's resources. It is a particular privilege, and a commendation of the witness of the church, that many people from suffering and oppressed groups feel that they can find in the company of Jesus' disciples a listening ear to and indeed a platform for their cries. The fact that World Council of Churches conferences are places where they can voice their concerns should be seen as a very positive affirmation of how the poor see the church.

On the other hand, in many cases the mission that the poor undertake includes a strong evangelistic outreach in proclaiming Jesus. If and when this dimension of their mission is filtered out, this creates a further oppression of the poor.

We feel that the expression of concern for the rights of the poor must not be misunderstood as showing that the World Council of Churches has relinquished the central concern of devotion and faithful witness to Jesus. For he is the very basis for the compassion and justice that requires that the voice of the poor be heard. But care is needed lest this emphasis be misused to redefine the central Christian affirmations in terms of the most strident cries against oppression. Jesus was indeed a prophet and exercised a prophetic ministry. But unless Jesus is also acknowledged as the

Saviour crucified for the sin of the world and the Lord risen as the victor over all evil, we are without hope and without God in the world.

We have been encouraged by the way in which Christians from many traditions have joined here in confessing Jesus Christ as Lord and Saviour of the world and in affirming that they cannot point to any other way of salvation but Jesus Christ. We ask that you join us in refusing to identify the WCC declarations about the cries of the oppressed for justice as a retreat from an affirmation of the centrality and finality of Jesus Christ.

II. We wish to encourage you to pursue a number of concerns which you bear as a gift and a trust for the worldwide body of Christ.

In worship, we evangelicals have a strong tradition of expounding the word of God with relevance to the lives of the hearers. In addition to being a lived faith, our faith is a *preached faith* which uplifts and inspires. We would have welcomed more of this in our worship times here and believe this is an area where the Lausanne movement can contribute.

We have appreciated the contributions of Africans at San Antonio, but we have missed the full range of the experience of the *black-led churches and denominations* in the West. They have often not been able to find their way into the mainline churches or their associations. We have learned much from these black-led churches and from immigrant churches in the West. We missed an expression of their strong sense of mission and evangelism, and their powerful combination of preaching and worship. We commend their contribution to the gatherings of the Lausanne movement.

A whole tradition in Christian mission draws particularly on Jesus' ministries of *healing and deliverance* from demonic possession. We have missed serious reflection and consideration of this in this conference and believe that there are those within the Lausanne movement who can contribute this to the mission of the wider church....

Evangelism and *socio-political involvement* are both part of our Christian duty, as the Lausanne Covenant of 1974 reaffirmed. Many thousands of evangelicals have found innovative ways to issue the invitation to follow Jesus Christ in the context of engaging in social action. Encouraged by what we have seen God do through these, we give thanks to God and urge you to pursue a stronger relationship between proclaiming and demonstrating the good news in relation to the social and political dimensions of life....

For too long, the World Council of Churches has been perceived as being involved with justice without relation to justification of sinner; and the Lausanne movement has been perceived as being concerned for personal justification without reference to the personal and corporate sin at the root of injustice. Without an affirmation of the invitation of Jesus to repentance, faith and discipleship, mission among the poor for justice can become indistinguishable from the economic developmental notion of eradicating poverty without respect to the many cultural and human values of poor communities.

The Lausanne movement takes seriously *the exclusive claims made in the Bible for Jesus Christ* as the final revelation of God, and the only saviour for all humankind. *Mission and Evangelism — an Ecumenical Affirmation* of CWME states that "Christians owe the message of God's salvation in Jesus to every person and to every people" (para. 41). "The proclamation of the gospel includes an invitation to recognize and accept in a personal decision the saving Lordship of Christ. It is the announcement of a personal encounter, mediated by the Holy Spirit, with the living Christ, receiving his forgiveness and making a personal acceptance of the call to discipleship and a life of service" (para. 10)....

We feel that it is important that the Lausanne movement share ways in which many have come to faith in Jesus Christ from other religious traditions, and how the gospel has been shared with integrity with those of other faiths. This would be an important contribution to the life of the World Council and of the worldwide church.

There is a special need for the Lausanne movement to relate authentic evangelism in the context of social concern and witness in relation to people of other faiths. First, many of those who have never heard of Jesus are both poor and are adherents of other faiths. Our commitment to evangelism requires that we take their settings seriously. Secondly, there is an ambivalent Christology in some expressions of Christian witness. Some assert that Christ's spirit is present salvifically in all religions and thus sever Christ from Jesus of Nazareth. Others affirm that Jesus is the prophet and sufferer who takes the side of the poor to the exclusion of his role as transcendent Lord, Saviour and King. While denying that Jesus is the only way of salvation, some assert that justice for the poor is the only way of mission. We, like you, do not accept this.

III. We venture to suggest a number of areas in which new and creative initiatives could be undertaken.

This WCC conference at San Antonio had about three hundred delegates and four hundred other participants. There was an overlap for the first four days with Encuentro, a North American conference held by the WCC on the same theme. Our conferences shared the same campus, met at meal times and in worship, and had a number of joint sessions where the North American conference sat in on our plenary session. The model has much to commend it.

We are aware of the pressure on Christian resources and personnel and of the image portrayed to the world through holding two separate world conferences on mission at San Antonio and Manila in one year.

We are also aware that one of the goals of the Lausanne movement is to be a catalyst in fostering efforts for evangelization and providing networks to that end. So we ask that you seriously consider the possibility that the next world conference of the Lausanne movement be planned to take place with the next World Council conference on mission and evangelism on a similar model to the Encuentro conference and the World Council conference here — that is, that they be held simultaneously, on the same site and share a number of sessions....

Participants

Participants

Abraham, Rev Kanjarathara Uthup
Accredited Visitor, USA
Mar Thoma Syrian Church of Malabar

Abugan, Rev Corazon C
Delegate MC, Philippines
United Church of Christ
in the Philippines

Ada, Rev Kokou Samuel
Consultant, France
Evangelical Church of Togo

Adhikari, Mr Sudhir
Delegate CWME, Bangladesh
Eangladesh Baptist Sangha

Adjali, Ms Mia
Host country observer, USA
United Methodist Church

Adly Shohdy, Ms Nancy
Resource, Egypt
Coptic Orthodox Church

Agullhas, Rev Richard
Delegate CWME, South Africa
Evangelical Lutheran Church
in South Africa

Ahrens, Prof Dr Theodor
Delegate CWME, FRG
Evangelical Church in Germany

Ahrens, Sister Luise
Host country observer, USA
Roman Catholic Church

Akhura, Rev Okang'a Levi
Delegate MC, Kenya
African Church of the Holy Spirit

Akrofi, Very Rev Dr Justice O
Delegate CWME, Ghana
Church of the Province of West Africa

Al-Zehlaoui, Rev Fr Joseph
Delegate MC, Cyprus
Greek Orthodox Patriarchate
of Antioch and all East

Alwis, Rev Arthur Stanley
Delegate CWME, Sri Lanka
Sri Lanka Baptist Sangamaya (Union)

Amjad-Ali, Rev Dr Charles
Leader, Pakistan
Church of Pakistan

Anastasios of Androussa, Bishop
Delegate Commission, Greece
Church of Greece

Anderson, Rev Canon James Raffan
Consultant, UK ·
Church of England

Anderson, Ms Devon Elizabeth
Delegate MCC-USA
Episcopal Church, USA

Anderson, Rev Robert Scott
Leader, UK
Church of Scotland

Anderson, Rev Dr Lesley
Consultant, UK
The Methodist Church

Anderson, Rev Dr Henry
Host country observer, USA
Presbyterian Church (USA)

Anthony, Mr Alvin Rodney
Resource, South Africa
Church of the Province
of Southern Africa

Antonie of Transsylvania, Metropolitan
Delegate MC, Romania
Romanian Orthodox Church

Ao, Ms Theresa,
Delegate CWME, India
Eaptist Church, India

Ao, Mr Puna
Resource, India
Eaptist Church, India

Apac, Ms Maria Aurora
Leader, USA
Roman Catholic Church

Appies, Mr Leonardo
Leader, South Africa
Church of the Province
of Southern Africa

Araneta, Lt Maria Luisa
Delegate CWME, Philippines
Salvation Army

Arcand, Ms Monique Yvette
Accredited Visitor, Canada,
United Pentecostal

Argenti, Rev Fr Cyrille
Delegate Commission, France,
Ecumenical Patriarcate
of Constantinople

Arnason, Rev Vigfus Thor
Delegate MC, USA
Evangelical Lutheran Church
of Iceland

Arnold, Dr Walter
CC member, FRG
Evangelical Church in Germany

Asaabea Awuku, Rev Dr Juliana
Delegate CWME, Ghana
Methodist Church, Ghana

Asaad, Sister Agapie
Resource, Egypt
Coptic Orthodox Church

Assakura, Ms Maria Regina
Delegate CWME, Brazil
Episcopal Church of Brazil

Audi, Metropolitan Elias
Delegate MC, Lebanon
Greek Orthodox Patriarchate
of Antioch and all East

Austin, Ms Johanna
Accredited Visitor, Guinea
Anglican Diocese of Guinea

Avramides, Rev Fr Stephen
Delegate MC, Greece
Church of Greece

Ayete Labi, Rev Fr Kwame Joseph
Leader, Ghana
Greek Orthodox Patriarchate
of Alexandria

Aykazian, Rev Fr Vicken
Resource, Switzerland
Armenian Apostolic Church

Azariah, Rev Masilamani
Resource, India
Church of South India

Bacerra, Rev Laura Luz A
Delegate CWME, USA
Christian Church (Disciples of Christ)

Bakke, Dr Raymond J
Consultant, USA
American Baptist Churches USA

Banki, Dr Judith
Consultant, USA
Jewish Consultant

Barolin, Ms Adriana Silvina
Delegate CWME, Argentina
Evangelical Church of the River Plate

Barsamian, Very Rev Fr Khajag
Delegate MCC, USA
Armenian Apostolic Church

Basmajian, Ms Nancy
Delegate MCC, USA
Armenian Apostolic Church

Becker, Rev Henje Rudolf Adolf
Delegate CWME, FRG
Evangelical Church in Germany

Becker, Ms Friedgard
Delegate CWME, DDR
Federation of the Evangelical Churches
in the GDR

Bell, Rev John Lamberton
Leader, UK
Church of Scotland

Bello Contredras, Rev Monica
Delegate CWME, Chile
Methodist Church of Chile

Bena-Silu, Mr
Delegate MC, Zaire
Kimbanguist Church

Beni, Mr Phillip
Delegate MC, Cook Islands
Cook Islands Christian Church

Berends, Mr Kornelis
Delegate CWME, Netherlands
Reformed Churches in the Netherlands

Bisnauth, Rev Dr Dale
Consultant, Barbados
Presbyterian Church Guyana

Blommaert, Ms Isabelle
Delegate MC, Belgium
United Protestant Church of Belgium

Bohl, Superintendent Siegfried
Delegate CWME, DDR
Federation of the Evangelical Churches
in the GDR

Bolt, Rev Cawley St Clair
Delegate CWME, Jamaica
Jamaica Baptist Union

Boonstra, Rev John
Consultant, Switzerland
United Church of Christ, USA

Boots, Ms Nora
Delegate CWME, USA
United Methodist Church

Bootsma, Dr Hans
Consultant, Netherlands
Netherlands Reformed Church

Bosakov, Metropolitan Joseph
Delegate MCC, USA
Bulgarian Orthodox Church

Bosch, Prof David
Leader, South Africa
Dutch Reformed Church

Botha, Dr Johan George
Delegate CWME, South Africa
Dutch Reformed Mission Church
of South Africa

Botha, Rev Nico Adam
Accredited Visitor, Netherlands
Dutch Reformed Mission Church

Bozabalian, Archbishop Nerses
Delegate MCC, USSR
Armenian Apostolic Church

Brampton, Rev Fiona
Delegate CWME, England
Church of England

Brankin, Rev Joseph
Delegate CWME, UK
Roman Catholic Church

Breeze, Ms Lynne Kathryn
Resource, UK
United Reformed Church
in the United Kingdom

Bridges, Rev Flora
Delegate MCC, USA
National Baptist Convention
of America

Brookes, Rev Graham Frederick
Delegate CWME, Australia
Uniting Church in Australia

Brouwer, Rev Dr Arie
Delegate CWME, USA
Reformed Church in America

Brown, Rev Julia Marie
Delegate MCC,UUSA
Christian Church (Disciples of Christ)

Brown, Rev John P
Delegate Commission, Australia
Uniting Church in Australia

Browne, Ms Doris Iyamide
Delegate CWME, Sierra Leone
United Methodist Church

Bula, Ms Omega
Resource, Kenya
United Church of Zambia

Burkard, SAC, Sister M Clementia
Consultant, Italy
Roman Catholic Church

Buser, Ms Dorothee
Delegate CWME, Switzerland
United Methodist Church

Cabrera, Ms Escolastica
Resource, Mariannas Islands
Kristo Rai Church-Garapan

Cabrera, Ms Gloria T
Accredited Visitor, Mariannas Islands
Kristo Rai Church

Calderon, Rev Rene
Host country observer, USA
Church of the Brethren

Canales, Sister Delia
Consultant, Mexico
Roman Catholic Church

Canelos de Salazar, Ms Haydée
Delegate CWME, Ecuador

Carmen, Ms Andrea
Leader, USA
American Indian religion

Cave, Rev Robin
Delegate CWME, New Zealand
Church of the Province of New Zealand

Chen, Rev Prof Zemin
Guest, China
China Christian Council

Chkadua, Metropolitan David
Delegate MC, Georgia USSR
Georgian Orthodox Church

Cho, Dr David J
Consultant, Korea
Presbyterian Church of Korea

Christopolos, Ms Nancy
Delegate MC, USA
Ecumenical Patriarchate
of Constantinople

Chrysostomos of Peristerion,
Metropolitan
Delegate MC, Greece
Church of Greece

Chun Chae Ok, Dr
Resource, UK
Korean Methodist Church

Ciobotea, Rev Dr Daniel DJ
Delegate MC, Romania
Romanian Orthodox Church

Clark, Mr John Mullin
Delegate CWME, United Kingdom
Church of England

Clark, Colonel William
Consultant, UK
The Salvation Army

Clark, Mrs Jean Barbara
Accredited Visitor, UK
The Salvation Army

Claydon, Rev David
Consultant, Australia
Anglican Church of Australia

Clement, Ms Marilyn
Leader, USA
United Methodist Church

Constable, Rev Margaret S
Delegate CWME, South Africa
United Congreg Church
of Southern Africa

Contreras Hernandez, Ms Susana
Delegate MC, Mexico
Methodist Church of Mexico

Cooney SMSM, Sister Emerentiana
Accredited Visitor, Italy
Roman Catholic Church

Couchell, Rev Fr Dimitrios
Delegate MC, USA
Ecumenical Patriarchate
of Constantinople

Creevey, Rev William
Host country observer, USA
Presbyterian Church (USA)

Crow, Dr Paul
Resource, USA
Christian Church (Disciples of Christ)

Cunville, Rev Rieweh Robert
Accredited Visitor, India
Khasi Jaintia Presbyterian Synod India

Damian, Rev Evaristo
Consultant, Uruguay
Evangelical Methodist Church
in Uruguay

Davis, Rev Edmund
Delegate Commission, Jamaica
Church of the Province
of the West Indies

Davis, Sister Julia Zita Augustina
Delegate CWME, Jamaica WI
Methodist

Dayton, Dr Donald
Consultant, USA
Wesleyan Church of America

de Paris, Mr Jorge Alberto
Delegate CWME, Argentina
Evangelical Methodist Church
of Argentina

de Souza, Presbitera Leizete Miranda
Delegate CWME, Brazil
United Presbyterian Church of Brazil

Deenabandhu, Rev Manchala
Delegate CWME, India
United Evangelical Lutheran
Church in India

Delaney, MM, Sister Joan
Consultant, Switzerland
Roman Catholic Church

den Hollander, Ms Jet
Delegate CWME, UK
Reformed Churches in the Netherlands

Devasundaram, Mr Alexander
Leader, India
Church of South India

Dietz, Rev Frank
Host country observer, USA
United Church of Christ

Dimitrov, Prof Ivan
Resource, Bulgaria
Bulgarian Orthodox Church

Dores, Ms Maria Das
Delegate MC, Angola
Evangelical Pentecostal Church
of Angola

Drooby, Ms Nabila
Consultant, USA
Muslim Consultant

Dupuis, SJ, Rev Father Jacques
Consultant, Italy
Roman Catholic Church

Duraisingh, Rev Dr DJ Christopher
Leader, UK
Church of South India

Durrah, Ms Bettie J
Host country observer, USA
Presbyterian Church (USA)

Ebenezer, Ms Dorothy Dayasheela
Delegate MC, India
Church of South India

Eck, Ms Diana L
Consultant, USA
United Methodist Church

Eklou, Ms Akuwavi Keli
Delegate MC, Togo
Evangelical Church of Togo

Elliott, Rev Donald
Consultant, UK
United Reformed Church in the UK

Elouti, Rev Emmanuel
Delegate Commission, Cameroun
Eglise Evangelique du Cameroun

Epting, Dr Karl-Christoph
Resource, FRG
Evangelical Church in Germany

Escamilla, Dr Roberto
Accredited Visitor, USA
United Methodist Church

Eteuati, Rev Vaiao Ala'Ilima
Delegate MC, Western Samoa
Methodist Church in Samoa

Faulk, Dr I Carlton
Delegate CWME, USA
Christian Methodist Episcopal

Ferreira, Rev Namir Griebler
Delegate CWME, Brazil
Methodist Church in Brazil

Ferreira Colombino, Rev Hortensia
Delegate CWME, Paraguay
Disciples of Christ

Ferrou Osta, Ms Maria Cristina
Delegate MC, Uruguay
Evangelical Methodist Church
in Uruguay

Findley, Ms Alice M
Consultant, USA
American Baptist Churches, USA

Flores, Most Rev Patrick F
Consultant, USA
Roman Catholic Church

Flores Ponce, Mr Roberto Pablo
Accredited Visitor, Peru
Methodist Church of Peru

Foley, Ms Penelope Norah
Delegate CWME, Australia
Uniting Church in Australia

Formilleza, Ms Prima
Delegate CWME, Philippines
Convention of Baptist Churches
in the Philippines

Fox, Dr H Eddie
Consultant, USA
United Methodist Church

French, Ms Birgitte Thaarup
Delegate CWME, Zaire
United Methodist Church

Fubara-Manuel, Rev Benebo Fubara
Delegate MC, Nigeria
Presbyterian Church of Nigeria

Fuchs, Rev Werner
Leader, Brazil
Evangelical Church of Lutheran
Confession in Brazil

Fuentes, Mr Eduardo
Accredited Visitor, USA

Gaffaro de Valera, Ms Loida M
Delegate CWME, Venezuela
Presbyterian Church of Venezuela

Gagua, Mr Boris
Delegate MC, Georgia USSR
Georgian Orthodox Church

Gaitân Cornejo, Rev Jorge Eliecer
Delegate CWME, Costa Rica
Baptist Church

Ganaba, Ms Olga
Accredited Visitor, USSR
Russian Orthodox Church

Garkusha, Ms Valentina
Delegate MC, USSR
All-Union Council
of Evangelical Christians-Baptists

Garrard, Ms Jennifer
Delegate CWME, Great Britain
The Presbyterian Church of Wales

Gasser, Ms Elaine M
Delegate CWME, USA
United Methodist Church

Gillespie, Ms Judith M
Delegate CWME, USA
Episcopal Church

Gitari, Rt Rev Dr David Mukuba
Delegate Commission, Kenya
Church of the Province of Kenya

Golda, Rev Mag Manfred
Delegate CWME, Austria
Evangelical Church,

Goltz, Rev Prof Dr Hermann
Consultant, Switzerland
Federation of Evangelical Churches
in the GDR

Gonnet, Rev Hugo
Delegate CWME, Uruguay
Iglesia Evngelica Valdense
del Rio de la Plata

Gonzalez-Garaboa, Mr Dominick
Accredited Visitor, Greece
Greek Orthodox Archdiocese
of North & South America

Gorski MM, Rev Father John
Consultant, Bolivia
Roman Catholic Church

Grant, Dr Jacquelyn
Delegate Commission, USA
African Methodist Epicopal Church

Gray, The Venerable John
Delegate CWME, New Zealand
Church of the Province of New Zealand

Gray, Ms Anne Frances
Accredited Visitor, Australia
Uniting Aboriginal & Islander
Christian Congress

Gregson, Ms Kendra
Delegate MC, Canada
Anglican Church of Canada

Grillo, Dr Eunice
Delegate CWME, Cuba
Evangelical Convention
"Los Pinos Nuevos"

Guest, Mr Kenneth
Host country observer, USA
United Methodist Church

Habib, Rev Dr Samuel
Delegate MC, Egypt
Synod of the Nile Evangelical Church

Hahn, Rev Horst Emil
Delegate CWME, FRG
Evangelical Church in Germany

Hahn, Ms Anna Martha
Accredited Visitor, FRG
Evangelical Church in Germany

Hakonen, Ms Anja Anneli
Delegate CWME, Finland
Orthodox Church of Finland

Hall, Ms Marjorie
Delegate CWME, Australia
Anglican Church of Australia

Hall, Mr William
Accredited Visitor
Australia, Anglican Church of Australia

Harakas, Rev Dr Stanley
Leader, USA
Ecumenical Patriarchate
of Constantinople

Harling, Rev Per
Delegate Commission, Sweden
Church of Sweden

Harman, Rev Robert J
Accredited Visitor, USA
United Methodist Church

Harmon, Rev E Taylor
Host country observer, USA
Evangelical Lutheran Church
in America

Harmon, Rev Robert
Delegate CWME, USA
United Methodist Church

Harms, Ms Dorothea
Delegate CWME, FRG
Evangelical Church in Germany

Harne, Rev Pekka Antero
Consultant, Finland
Evangelical Lutheran Church
of Finland

Harrison, Mr David
Accredited Visitor, USA
Native American

Harvey, Rev Dorothy Margaret
Leader, New Zealand
Presbyterian Church of New Zealand

Hauser, Rev Albrecht
Consultant, FRG
Evangelical Church in Germany

Haverluck, Ms Gerry
Accredited Visitor, Canada
United Church of Canada

Haynes, Dr Michael E
Consultant, USA
Baptist

Heideman, Mr Eugene P
Consultant, USA
Reformed Church in America

Held, Dr Heinz Joachim
Delegate CWME, FRG
Evangelical Church-FRG

Helgemo, Rev Marlene
Delegate CWME, USA
Evangelical Lutheran Church
in America

Henderson, Mr Harold Ross
Consultant, Switzerland
Uniting Church of Australia

Hendrick, Rev John R
Host country observer, USA
Presbyterian Church (USA)

Heng-ching Shih, Professor
Consultant, Taiwan, ROC
Buddhist Consultant

Herbst, Ms Ursula
Delegate Commission, GDR
Federation of the Evangelical Churches
in the GDR

Hermansson, Mr Mats
Delegate CWME, Sweden
Church of Sweden

Herzog, Rev Hermann Emil
Resource, Switzerland
Swiss Protestant Church Federation

Hewitt, Rev Roderick R
Consultant, UK
United Church of Jamaica
and Grand Cayman

Hial, Mr Subas Chandra
Delegate CWME, India
United Evangelical Lutheran Church

Hickel, Rev Giselher
Resource, GDR
Federation of the Evangelical Churches
in the GDR

Hlengwa, Rev Thulani
Delegate CWME, South Africa

Ho, Rev David
Consultant, Jamaica
Christian Brethren Assemblies-Jamaica

Hoesl, Dr Marcella
Accredited Visitor, UK
Roman Catholic Church

Hoffman, Dr Gerhard
Leader, FRG
Evangelical Church in Germany

Hoffman, Ms Barbel
Accredited Visitor, FRG
Evangelical Church in Germany

Horak, Dr Cyril
Consultant, Czechoslovakia
Evangelical Church of Czech Brethren

Hotchkin, Rev Fr John
Consultant, USA
Roman Catholic Church

Humbert, Dr John O
Host country observer, USA
Christian Church (Disciples of Christ)

Hunzicker, Rev Atilio Juan
Delegate CWME, Argentina
Evangelical Church of the River Plate

Iannuarij, Rev Fr
Delegate MC, USSR
Russian Orthodox Church

Ibrahim, Metropolitan G Yohanna
Delegate MC, Syria
Syrian Orthodox Patriarchate
of Antioch-All the East

Imathiu, Bishop Lawi,
Delegate MC, Kenya
Methodist Church in Kenya

Irinarh, Rev Fr Igumen
Delegate MC, USSR
Russian Orthodox Church

Isaacs, Deacon Theodore
Delegate MC, USA
Armenian Apostolic Church

Jakovljevic, Rev Dr Radivoj
Delegate MC, Czechoslovakia
Orthodox Church of Czechoslovakia

Jarjour, Ms Rosangela
Delegate Commission, Cyprus
National Evangelical Synod
of Syria & Lebanon

John, Ms Tabitha Dak
Delegate CWME, Sudan
Evangelical Presbyterian
Church Khartoum

Johnson, Dr Emmett
Delegate CWME, USA
American Baptist Churches USA

Johnson, Ms Eleanor
Delegate CWME, Canada
Anglican Church of Canada

Johnson, Ms Thelma L
Host country observer, USA
United Methodist Church

Johnson, Mr Leroy
Resource, USA
Progressive Baptist Church

Jones, Ms Glynis Lorraine
Delegate CWME, Trinidad
Church of the Province
of the West Indies

Jones, Dr Tracey K
Guest, USA, United Methodist Church

Jones, Ms Junia M,
Guest, USA,
United Methodist Church

Jong Wha Park, Rev
Resource, Korea
Presbyterian Church
in the Republic of Korea

Jorge Oropesa, Dr Isaac Manuel
Delegate CWME, Cuba
Presbyterian Reformed Church in Cuba

Jorgensen, Rev Tor Berger
Delegate MC, Japan
The Church of Norway

Joseph, Mr Peter
Delegate CWME, Burma
Burma Baptist Convention

Juda, Ms Lebohang
Delegate CWME, South Africa
Methodist Church of South Africa

Kafity, Rt Rev Samir
Delegate MC, Jerusalem
Episcopal Church in Jerusalem
& the Middle East

Kagoro, Ms Major Syria
Delegate CWME, Zambia
Salvation Army

Kalil, Ms Eudora Mary
Delegate CWME, El Salvador
El Salvador Baptist Association

Kamau, Ms Grace Njoki
Delegate MC, Kenya
African Christian Church and Schools

Kamau, Ms Alice Mugure
Delegate MC, Kenya
Church of the Province of Kenya

Kamp, Ms Jane
Accredited Visitor, USA
Evangelical Lutheran Church
in America

Kanda, Rev Kenji
Delegate CWME, Japan
United Church of Christ in Japan

Kane, Rev Fr Thomas A
Leader, USA
Roman Catholic Church

Kapinga, Patriarch Kayuwa
Delegate MC, Zaire
Church of Christ in Zaire
(Community of Light)

Kappauf, Ms Carolyn Barbara
Delegate CWME, FRG
Evangelical Methodist Church

Karamaga, Rev Dr Andre
Resource, Rwanda
Presbyterian Church of Rwanda

Karlsson, Rev Birgit
Delegate CWME, Sweden
Swedish Baptist Union

Karotemprel, SDB, Rev Fr Sebastian
Consultant, India
Roman Catholic Church

Karsay, Rev Eszter
Delegate MC, Hungary
Reformed Church in Hungary

Ke Myung Chu, Rev
Delegate CWME, Korea
Presbyterian Church of Korea

Khodr Haidar, Ms Milia
Leader, Lebanon
Greek Orthodox Patriarchate
of Antioch and all East

Khumalo, Dr Ben
Resource, FRG
Evangelical Church in Germany

Kim, Rev Dr Choon-Young
Accredited Visitor, Korea
Korean Methodist Church

Kim Hyun-Soon, Dr
Delegate CWME, Korea
Presbyterian Church of Korea

Kim So-Young, Rev Dr
Accredited Visitor, Korea
Presbyterian Church of Korea

Kimba, Rev Mutombo Ilunga
Resource, Zaire
United Methodist Church

Kimhachandra, Rev Dr Sint
Delegate CWME, Thailand
Church of Christ in Thailand

Kirkpatrick, Rev Clifton
Delegate Commission, USA
Presbyterian Church (USA)

Kishkovsky, Rev Fr Leonid
Delegate CWME, USA
Orthodox Church in America

Klasson-Wennlund, Ms Margareta Elisabet
Delegate CWME, Sweden
Church of Sweden

Klein, Prof Dr Christoph
Delegate Commission, Romania
Evangelical Church
of the Augsburg Confession

Klutz, Rev Fr Qasha Charles
Delegate MC, USA
Holy Apostolic Catholic
Assyrian Church of the East

Knoch, Rev Dr Michael Walter
Resource, Portugal
Evangelical Presbyterian Church
of Portugal

Kodic, Bishop Mitrofan
Delegate MC, USA
Serbian Orthodox Church

Koech, Mr Geoffrey
Delegate MC, USA
Greek Orthodox Patriarchate
of Alexandria

Kofe, Rev Laumua
Delegate MC, Tuvalu
Church of Tuvalu

Kontoyorghi, Ms Argyro
Resource, Kenya
Church of Greece

Koukoura, Dr Dimitra
Resource, Greece
Church of Greece

Kownacki, Rev Fr Robert
Host country observer, USA
Roman Catholic Church

Kozlowski, Mr Mikolaj
Delegate MC, Poland
Autocephalic Orthodox Church in Poland

Krause, Rev Bernd
Accredited Visitor, DDR
Federation of the Evangelical Churches
in the GDR

Kuchera, Mr Murombedzi Mhlanga
Leader, Zimbabwe
United Church of Christ

Kuze, Ms Reiko
Resource, Japan
United Church of Christ in Japan

Kwon Ho-Kyung, Rev
Accredited Visitor, Korea
Presbyterian Church
in the Republic of Korea

Laiser, Bishop Thomas
Accredited Visitor,Tanzania
Evangelical Lutheran Church in Tanzania

Lall, Dr Sarla
Host country observer, USA
United Methodist Church

Lang, MM, Rev Fr Joseph R,
Consultant, USA
Roman Catholic Church

Langerak, Ms Ana
Leader, Costa Rica
Evangelical Lutheran Church
of Costa Rica

Laursen, Rev Thorkild Schousboe
Delegate CWME, Denmark
The Evangelical Lutheran Church
of Denmark

Lee Hyun Sook, Ms
Delegate CWME, Korea
Presbyterian

Lee Oo Chung, Ms
Delegate Commission, Korea
The Presbyterian Church
in the Republic of Korea

Lehmann-Habeck, Rev Dr Martin R
Resource, Zimbabwe
Evangelical Lutheran Church
of Zimbabwe

Lenssen M Afr., Rev Fr Jan
Consultant, Italy
Roman Catholic Church

Libbey, Rev Scott S
Consultant, USA
United Church of Christ

Lin Kuang-Jung, Rev
Delegate MC, Taiwan
Presbyterian Church in Taiwan

Lin Mei-Jung, Ms Yvonne
Resource, Taiwan
Presbyterian Church in Taiwan

Livernois, Rev Thomas
Host country observer, USA
Evangelical Lutheran Church
in America

Lockmann, Bishop Paulo T de Oliveira
Delegate CWME, Brazil
Methodist Church in Brazil

Losche, Ms Elfi Christine
Delegate MC, DDR
Federation of the Evangelical Churches
in the GDR

Lowry, Rev Boyd
Host country observer, USA
Presbyterian Church (USA)

Lumbama, Rev Elija Katema
Delegate CWME, Zambia
United Church of Zambia

Lumbantobing, Rev Bonar Hasudungan
Delegate CWME, Indonesia
Lutheran Church

Mabuza, Rev Wesley Madonda
Delegate CWME
South Africa
Methodist Church of Southern Africa

Madrid de Bueso, Ms Haydee
Delegate CWME, Honduras
Reformed Church

Magagula, Rev Jeremiah Bheki
Leader, Swaziland
Evangelical Lutheran Church

Makarij Ivanow-Frankovsk, Archbishop
Delegate MC, USSR
Russian Orthodox Church

Malaba, Ms Theodora Thoko
Delegate CWME, Zimbabwe
Methodist Church in Zimbabwe

Malik, Ms Nudrat Christina
Delegate CWME, Pakistan
Church of Pakistan

Malik, Eishop Alexander John
Delegate Commission, Pakistan
Church of Pakistan

Manning, Rev Basil
Leader, Botswana
United Congregational Church
of Southern Africa

Mar Eusebius, Bishop Philipos
Delegate MC, India
Malankara Orthodox Syrian Church

Marak, Ms Monita
Delegate MC, Bangladesh
Church of Bangladesh

Marchant, Rev Dr Colin
Delegate CWME, UK
Baptist Union of Great Britain

Marigza, Rev Reuel Norman
Leader, Philippines
United Church of Christ

Markos, Bishop Antonius
Delegate MC, Kenya
Coptic Orthodox Church

Marple, Dr Dorothy J
Leader, USA
Evangelical Lutheran Church in America

Martinez, Dr Salvador T
Consultant, Thailand
United Church of Christ
in the Philippines

Masemola, Rev Sipho
Delegate CWME, South Africa
Church of the Province
of Southern Africa

Matsikenyiri, Mr Patrick
Leader, Zimbabwe
United Methodist Church

Matsuoka, Dr Fumitaka
Host country observer, USA
Church of the Brethren

Matthey, Rev Jacques Edouard
Delegate CWME, Switzerland
Swiss Protestant Church Federation

Mausia, Ms Mele Malingakivaha
Delegate MC, Tonga
Free Wesleyan Church of Tonga

May, Mr Jeffrey
Delegate CWME, Australia
Churches of Christ in Australia

Mazive-Ngomae, Ms Maria Marcos
Delegate CWME, Mozambique
Presbyterian Church of Mozambique

Mbama, Rev Alphonse
Accredited Visitor, Congo
Evangelical Church of the Congo

McAleese, Sister Mary
Accredited Visitor, UK
Roman Catholic Church

McCoy, Rev Michael John
Accredited Visitor, South Africa
Church of the Province
of Southern Africa

McKay, Mr David William
Delegate CWME, Canada
Religious Society of Friends

Meade, Ms Alfreda
Delegate MC, Montserrat
Church in the Province
of the West Indies

Meissner, Rev Herbert
Consultant, FRG
Evangelical Church in Germany

Mella Daza, Rev Ricardo
Delegate CWME, Chile
Pentecostal Church of Chile

Mendez, Rev Alberto Moises
Delegate CWME, Mexico
Baptist Convention

Merahi, Rev Kefyalew
Delegate MC, Ethiopia
Ethiopian Orthodox Church

Mesilaudia, Ms Pele Helen
Delegate MC, Papua New Guinea
United Church in Papua New Guinea
& Solomon Islands

Mghwira, Ms Elisha Anna
Delegate MC, Tanzania
Evangelical Lutheran Church
in Tanzania

Mihaith, Bishop Nifon, Delegate MC
Romania
Romanian Orthodox Church

Millenaar, Ms Cristina
Consultant, Argentina
Reformed Church of Argentina

Mitri, Dr Tarek
Resource, Cyprus
Greek Orthodox Patriarchate
of Antioch and all East

Mizuno, Rev Jiro
Host country observer, USA
United Methodist Church

Mkwakwami, Rev Dr Watson M
Delegate CWME, Zimbabwe
United Church of Christ

Momblanch, Rev Raul Pedro
Delegate CWME, Argentina
United Evangelical Lutheran Church

Montgomery, Mr David John
Delegate CWME, Ireland
Presbyterian Church in Ireland

Moodley, Mr Ronnie
Resource, England
Church of England

Morrison, Rev Mary Brown
Delegate CWME, Scotland
Church of Scotland

Mota Dias, Rev Dr Zwinglio
Delegate Commission, Brazil
United Presbyterian Church of Brazil

Mothibe, CA, Sister Monica
Consultant, South Africa
Roman Catholic Church

Motte, FMM, Sister Mary
Consultant, USA
Roman Catholic Church

Moyer, The Rev John C
Resource, USA
Presbyterian Church (USA)

Mueller, SVD, Rev Karl
Consultant, FRG
Roman Catholic Church

Muller-Stover, Dr Irmela
Delegate CWME, FRG
Evangelical Church in Germany

Mundey, Rev Paul
Consultant, USA
Church of the Brethren

Murray, Rev Deborah Lynn
Delegate CWME, Canada
United Church of Canada

Mutiso-Mbinda, Rev Fr John
Consultant, Italy
Roman Catholic Church

Mxadana, Mr Gobingca George
Leader, South Africa
Church of the Province
of Southern Africa

Myint, Ms Sann Sann
Delegate Commission, UK
Burma Baptist Convention

Naaman, Rev G M
Delegate MC, Pakistan
Church of Pakistan

Najarian, Fr Haigazoun
Delegate MC, USA
Armenian Apostolic Church

Najm, Rev Dr Michel
Delegate Commission, USA
Greek Orthodox Patriarchate
of Antioch and all East

Namises, Ms Rosalinda
Delegate CWME, Namibia
Roman Catholic Church

Nash, Rev Elizabeth Jane
Delegate CWME, UK
United Reformed Church
in the United Kingdom

Nazarkin, Protodiakon Vladimir
Delegate MC, USSR
Russian Orthodox Church

Necula, Rev Prof Nicolae
Delegate MC, Romania
Romanian Orthodox Church

Nehme, Dr Layla
Delegate MC, Cyprus
Greek Orthodox Patriarchate
of Antioch and all East

Nelson, Rev Julius Sarwolo
Consultant, Liberia
United Methodist Church of Liberia

Nevskaja, Ms Olga
Accredited Visitor, USSR
Russian Orthodox Church

Newbigin, Bishop James Edward Lesslie
Guest, UK
United Reformed Church
in the United Kingdom

Ngoy, Ms wa-Banze
Delegate MC, Zaire
Church of Christ in Zaire
(Episcopal Baptist)

Ngwa, Ms Befu Catharine
Delegate MC, Cameroon
Presbyterian Church in Cameroon

Nita, Mother Moniale Nazaria
Delegate MC, Romania
Romanian Orthodox Church

Nkwe, Ms Maggie Malethola
Delegate Commission, South Africa
Church of the Province of Southern Africa

Nobanda, Ms Nomathemba Lilly
Delegate CWME, South Africa
Roman Catholic Church

Nordhaug, Rev Halvor
Consultant, Norway
Church of Norway

Nottingham, Dr William J
Delegate CWME, USA
Christian Church (Disciples of Christ)

O'Brien, Ms Denise
Delegate CWME, USA
United Methodist Church

Ochos-Krueger, Ms Ninfa
Resource, USA
Roman Catholic Church

Okada, Ms Noriko
Delegate CWME, USA
United Church of Christ in Japan

Oleksa, Rev Michael
Leader, USA
Orthodox Church in America

Oliveira, Rev Orlando Santos de
Delegate CWME, Brazil
Episcopal Church of Brazil

Oliver, Dr Alfred Jetti
Delegate CWME, India
Church of South India

Oodathil, Rev Thomas
Delegate MC, India
Malankara Orthodox Syrian Church

Osunsanmi-Wood, Rev Bertrice Y
Delegate CWME, USA
United Church of Christ

Ovsyannikov, Mr Vjatcheslav
Delegate MC, USSR
Russian Orthodox Church

Padillo Olesen, Ms Elisabeth
Leader, Nepal
United Church of Christ in Philippines

Pagura, Bishop Frederico J
Delegate Commission, Argentina
Evangelical Methodist Church
of Argentina

Palma, Ms Maria
Delegate MC, Chile
Pentecostal Mission Church

Pannell, Dr William
Consultant, USA
United Methodist Church

Panossian, Rev Dirayr
Delegate MC, Cyprus
Armenian Apostolic Church

Panteleimon of Zakynthos,
Metropolitan
Delegate MC, Greece
Church of Greece

Park, Dr Jong Wha
Resource, Korea
Presbyterian Church
in the Republic of Korea

Park Pong Bae, Rev Dr
Delegate CWME, Korea
Korean Methodist Church

Parker, Mr Garry O
Host country observer, USA
United Methodist Church

Pasco, Bishop Tito
Delegate CWME, Philippines
Philippine Independent Church

Passa, Rev D Sailali
Delegate MC, New Caledonia
Evangelical Church
in New Caledonia-Loyalty Isles

Patelos, Prof Constantin
Leader, Greece
Greek Orthodox Patriarchate
of Alexandria & all Africa

Paulo, Rev Mena
Delegate CWME, Angola
Baptist Evangelical Church in Angola

Peiris, Rev Lionel James Harold
Leader, Sri Lanka
Church of Ceylon

Pennybacker, Rev Albert M
Host country observer, USA
Christian Church (Disciples of Christ)

Pereira, Mr Henrique
Accredited Visitor, Brazil
Roman Catholic Church

Perlman, Ms Susan
Consultant, USA
Conservative Baptist Association

Perrochet, Ms Martine
Delegate MC, Switzerland
Swiss Protestant Church Federation

Pik-Wan Wong, Ms Helena
Delegate CWME, Hong Kong
Hong Kong Chinese Church of Christ

Piwang, Mr George
Delegate MC, Uganda
Church of Uganda

Platon, Rev Fr
Delegate MC, USSR
Russian Orthodox Church

Plummer, Rev Steven
Host country observer, USA
Episcopal Church

Pohl, Ms Garland Debner
Host country observer, USA
Roman Catholic Church

Popescu, Rev Prof Dumitru
Delegate MC, Romania
Romanian Orthodox Church

Porter, Mr David William
Delegate CWME, Northern Ireland
Baptist Union of Great Britain

Powell, Rev Rosalind Y
Host country observer, USA
Presbyterian Church (USA)

Powers, Rev Patricia
Accredited Visitor, Brazil
Episcopal Church of Brazil

Quismundo, Rev Jorge R
Consultant, Philippines
United Church of Christ
in the Philippines

Radano, Msgr John A
Consultant, Italy
Roman Catholic Church

Rae, Rev Keith Darwin
Host country observer, USA
United Methodist Church USA

Rajashekar, Dr J Paul
Consultant, Switzerland
United Evangelical Church in India

Rakotoson, Rev Charles
Delegate CWME, Madagascar
Malagasy Lutheran Church

Ramage, Jr, Dr David
Host country observer, USA
Presbyterian Church (USA)

Rao, Mr K L Seshagiri
Consultant, USA
Hindu Consultant

Raprap, Rev Luther Zwingli
Delegate CWME, Indonesia
Protestant Church in the Moluccas

Rasoanirina, Ms Perline
Delegate CWME, Madagascar
Church of Jesus Christ in Madagascar

Reiss, Ms Dorothea
Delegate CWME, FRG
Evangelical Church in Germany

Rey, Mr Alain Charles
Delegate CWME, France
Reformed Church of France

Rhee, Dr Syngman
Delegate CWME, USA
Presbyterian Church (USA)

Rigos, Rev Dr Cirilo A
Consultant, UK
United Church of Christ
in the Philippines

Riojas, Ms Rosanne
Consultant, USA
Roman Catholic

Roach, Ms Pat
Host country observer, USA
Presbyterian Church (USA)

Robinson, Sandra Lynn
Host country observer, USA
Universal Fellowship
of Metropolitan Community Ch's

Romero, Rev Daniel
Delegate MC, USA
United Church of Christ

Sahiouny, Rev Dr Salim
Consultant, Lebanon
National Evangelical Synod
of Syria and Lebanon

Salikin Antang-Baboe, Rev Yappie
Delegate CWME, Indonesia
The Kalimantan Evangelical Church

Salvador, Rev José da Silveira
Delegate MC, Portugal
Evangelical Presbyterian Church
of Portugal

Samuel, Rev Dr B Vinay Kumar
Consultant, India
Church of South India

Sanchez Llada, Mr Daniel
Delegate MC, Spain
Spanish Reformed Episcopal Church

Sandner, Rev Peter
Delegate Commission, FRG
Evangelical Church in Germany

Santana de Velez, Ms Ruda Eunice
Leader, Puerto Rico
Disciples of Christ

Sauca, Decon Ioan
Delegate MC, Romania
Romanian Orthodox Church

Schlegel, Rev Joachim
Delegate CWME, DDR
Federation of the Evangelical Churches
in the GDR

Schmidt, Ms Ursula Elisabeth
Leader, DDR
Federation of the Evangelical Churches
in the GDR

Schwab, Rev Wayne
Consultant, USA
Episcopal Church

Schwantes, Dr Milton
Leader, Brazil
Evangelical Church
of Lutheran Confession in Brazil

Scouteris, Prof Dr Constantine
Delegate MC, Greece
Church of Greece

Sen, Rev Noel Sushil
Delegate MC, India
Church of North India

Sepulveda, Rev Juan
Leader, Chile
Iglesia Pentecostal

Serapion, Bishop
Delegate MC, Egypt
Coptic Orthodox Church

Sergei of Solnechnogorsk, Archbishop
Delegate MC, Switzerland
Russian Orthodox Church

Shah, Dr Natubhai
Consultant, UK
Jain Consultant

Shamy, Rev Eileen Lyley
Delegate MC, New Zealand
Methodist Church
of Aotearoa/New Zealand

Shaw, Ms Linda
Delegate CWME, Canada
Presbyterian Church in Canada

Shirieda SDB, Rev Fr Masayuki
Consultant, Italy
Roman Catholic Church

Sieunarine, Rt Rev Everson
Delegate MC, Trinidad
Presbyterian Church
in Trinidad & Tobago

Silman, Rev Ms Janet
Delegate Commission, Canada
United Church of Canada

Silva Leite, Ms Otilia
Resource, Brazil
United Presbyterian Church in Brazil

Singh, Dr Godwin Rajinder
Consultant, Thailand
Methodist Church in India

Singha, Ms Promila Kamani
Delegate MC, Pakistan
Church of Pakistan

Siwu, Rev Richard A D
Accredited Visitor, Indonesia
Christian Evangelical Church
of Minahasa, Indonesia

Smedjebacka, Rev Dr Lars Henrik Evald
Delegate MC, Finland
Evangelical-Lutheran Church of Finland

Smetana, Rev Pavel
Delegate MC, Czechoslovakia
Evangelical Church of Czech Brethren

Smit SDB, Rev Fr Anthony
Consultant, Holland
Roman Catholic Church

Smith, Rev Io Mavornie
Delegate CWME, UK
New Testament Assembly

Sobottka, Mr Emil Albert
Delegate CWME, Brazil
Evangelical Church
of Lutheran Confession in Brazil

Sodladla, Ms Nonzame
Accredited Visitor, South Africa
Church of the Province
of Southern Africa

Sosa, Pastor Pablo
Leader, Argentina
Evangelical Methodist Church
of Argentina

Sowemimo, Ms Abiola Ibidunni
Delegate MC, Nigeria
Church of the Province of Nigeria

Speck, Rev Dixon Modupeh
Delegate CWME, Sierra Leone
West African Methodist Church

Stavenga-van der Waals, Rev Huiberdina
Delegate CWME, The Netherlands
Netherlands Reformed Church

Steib, SVD, Bishop James Terry
Consultant, USA
Roman Catholic Church

Steinbach, Ms Janice Mae
Delegate MC, Canada
Moravian Church in America

Stenstrom, Dr Gosta
Consultant, Sweden
The Mission Covenant Church of Sweden

Stephenson, Rev John Henry
Delegate CWME, Australia
Anglican Church of Australia

Steuernagel, Dr Valdin R
Consultant, Brazil
Evangelical Church
of Lutheran Confession in Brazil

Stockwell, Mrs Margaret S
Accredited Visitor
Switzerland, United Methodist Church

Stockwell, Ms Martha E
Accredited Visitor, USA
United Methodist Church

Stowers, SMSM, Sister Patricia
Consultant, Italy
Roman Catholic Church

Stransky, CSP, Rev Fr Thomas
Consultant, Israel
Roman Catholic Church

Stuart, Rev Canon Peter Alan
Consultant, USA
Church of the Province of New Zealand

Suggs, Rev J Dale
Host country observer, USA
Christian Church (Disciples of Christ)

Sundquist, Dr John A
Accredited Visitor, USA
American Baptist Churches USA

Sy, Mr Abdoul Hamidou
Resource, Senegal
Muslim

Szabo, Rev Marianna
Delegate MC, Hungary
Evangelical Lutheran Church
in Hungary

Szarek, Rev Jan Jerzy
Delegate MC, Poland
Evangelical Church
of the Augsburg Confession

Tadeo, Mr Jaime
Resource, Philippines
Philippine Independent Church

Talbot, Dr Sylvia
CC member, USA
African Methodist Episcopal Church

Talbot, Bishop Frederick
Accredited Visitor, USA
African Methodist Episcopal Church

Tananone, Mr Baw
Delegate CWME, Thailand
Church of Christ in Thailand

Tarasar, Ms Constance J
Resource, USA
Orthodox Church in America

Tarazi, Ms Rima
Leader, Jerusalem
Episcopal Church
in Jerusalem and the Middle East

Taufa, Rev Lopeti
Delegate Commission, Tonga
Free Wesleyan Church of Tonga

Taylor, Rev Canon Humphrey Vincent
Delegate CWME, England
Church of England

Tchiflianov, Rev Fr Blagoy
Delegate MC, Canada
Bulgarian Orthodox Church

Telleria Juarez, Ms Norma de
Delegate CWME, Bolivia
Evangelical Methodist Church
in Bolivia

Temme, Rev Jon
Delegate CWME, Canada
Evangelical Lutheran Church
in Canada

Teo Sew Eng, Ms Doreen
Leader, Malaysia
Methodist Church in Malaysia

Theophilus, Bishop Zacharias Mar
Delegate MC, India
Mar Thoma Syrian Church of Malabar

Thiagarajah, Ms Thayalini
Delegate CWME, Sri Lanka
Church of South India

Thomas, Ms Mary
Delegate CWME, India
Malankara Orthodox Syrian Church

Thomas, Mr Gideon
Delegate MC, Namibia
Evangelical Lutheran Church
in Namibia

Thompson, Ms Susan
Delegate CWME, Wales
Methodist

Thomsen, Dr Mark W
Delegate MC, USA
Evangelical Lutheran Church
in America

Thurber, Rev Dr Newton
Consultant, USA
Presbyterian Church (USA)

Tilghman, Ms Doreen
Leader, USA
United Methodist Church

Tolen, Dr Aaron
CC member, Cameroon
Presbyterian Church of Cameroon

Toma, Ms Taumuafa
Delegate MC, Western Samoa
Congregational Christian Church
in Samoa

Tranholm Mikkelsen, Rev Inge
Delegate Commission, Denmark
Evangelical Lutheran Church
of Denmark

Triebel, Dr Johannes
Delegate CWME, FRG
Evangelical Church in Germany

Truex, Ms Sandra
Delegate MC, USA
Greek Orthodox Patriarchate
of Antioch and all East

Tsetsis, Rev Dr George
Delegate MC, Switzerland
Ecumenical Patriarchate
of Constantinople

Tumakaka, Ms Jangdikasih Sukmawati
Delegate CWME, Indonesia
Protestant Church in W Indonesia

Turner, Rev Gordon B
Leader, Canada
United Church of Canada

Vaccaro, Rev Jorge Julio
Delegate CWME, Argentina
Church of God (Argentina)

Valerio, Rev Ilda
Delegate MC, Angola
Evangelical Congregational Church
in Angola

Valesquez, Mr Wilfrido
Accredited Visitor, USA

van Butselaar, Dr G Jan
Consultant, Netherlands
Reformed Churches in the Netherlands

van der Werf-Stelling, Ms Margreet
Delegate CWME, Netherlands
General Mennonite Society

van Houten, Dr Richard L
Accredited Visitor, USA
Christian Reformed Church
of North America

van Luyn, Mr Ole
Consultant, UK
Reformed Churches in the Netherlands

van Oosterzee, Rev Nicolaas
Leader, Netherlands
Netherlands Reformed Church

Varughese, Mr George
Resource, England
Church of England

Vassiliadis, Prof Dr Petros
Leader, Greece
Church of Greece

Vernon, Ms Sadie Geraldine
Delegate MC, Belize
Religious Society of Friends

Veronis, Ms Pearl
Delegate MC, USA
Ecumenical Patriarchate
of Constantinople

Veronis, Rev Fr Alexander
Host country observer, USA
Ecumenical Patriarchate
of Constantinople

Vesin, Rev Milos
Leader, Yugoslavia
Serbian Orthodox Church

Villena Villegas, Rev Lic Rolando
Leader, Bolivia
Evangelical Methodist Church
in Bolivia

von Allmen, Rev Dr Daniel Hermann
Delegate Commission, Switzerland
Swiss Protestant Church Federation

Walker, Mrs Gail P
Delegate MC, USA
Moravian Church in America

Wang Shen-Yin, Bishop
Guest, China
China Christian Council

Wang Shen-Yin, Ms
Guest, China
China Christian Council

Wasinga, Ms Batiyeoki Yosiya
Delegate MC, Zaire
Church of Christ in Zaire
(Community of Disciples)

Wehmeier, Ms Ulrike Gertrud Gefa
Delegate CWME, Brazil
Evangelical Church
of Lutheran Confession in Brazil

Wennlund, Dr Karl Anders
Accredited Visitor, Sweden
Church of Sweden

Wesley, Ms Suzan
Resource, Sudan
Presbyterian Church in the Sudan

Wietzke, Dr Joachim
Consultant, FRG
Evangelical Church in Germany

Wigglesworth, Rev Dr John Christopher
Consultant, Scotland UK
Church of Scotland

Wild, Rev Thomas
Delegate CWME, France
Evangelical Lutheran Church of France

Wilson, Very Rev. Dr Lois M
CC member, Canada
United Church of Canada

Wilson, Sir Ronald
Accredited Visitor, Australia
The Uniting Church of Australia

Wilson, Ms Elizabeth S
Accredited Visitor, Switzerland
Reformed Church in America

Wise, Ms Leah
Leader, USA

Workman, Mr John Allington
Resource, Barbados
Methodist Church
in the Caribbean & Americas

Wu, Rev Ai-En
Guest, China
China Christian Council

Yabaki, Rev Akuila D
Resource, Fiji
Methodist Church in Fiji

Yager, Mrs Lorele
Delegate CWME, USA
Church of the Brethren

Ying, Ms Gao
Guest, USA
China Christian Council

Zhang, Xiang-Yong (Richard)
Guest, USA
China Christian Council

Zheng, Rev Yu Gui
Guest, China
China Christian Council

Zheng, Ms Jing-an
Accredited Visitor, China
China Christian Council

WCC Staff and Co-opted Staff

Alt, Ms Catherine
Swiss Protestant Church Federation

Appiah, Ms Evelyn
Methodist Church, Ghana

Ariarajah, Rev Dr Wesley
Methodist Church, Sri Lanka

Behs, Mr Edelberto
Evangelical Lutheran Church of Brazil

Binder, Mr Ulrich Thomas

Buss, Rev Theo
Swiss Protestant Church Federation

Campbell, Rev Joan
Christian Church (Disciples of Christ)

Cano, Ms Andrea
United Church of Christ

Castro Pombo, Rev Dr Emilio Enrique
Evangelical Methodist Church in Uruguay

Chan Seong Foong, Ms
Methodist Church in Malaysia

Chaperon, Ms Danielle
Roman Catholic

Coates, Rev Tony
United Reformed Church
in the United Kingdom

Coleman, Ms Elisabeth-Donata,
Church of England

Conway, Mr David Martin
Church of England

Cudre-Mauroux, Mr Gilbert
Roman Catholic Church

Cullot, Ms Martine
Roman Catholic Church

Cunanan, Rev Jose P M
The United Methodist Church,
Philippines

David, Rev Canon Kenith A
Church of the Province
of Southern Africa

De Rycke, Mrs Désirée
Roman Catholic Church

Delaraye, Ms Pilar
Roman Catholic Church

Delmonte, Ms Elisabeth
Waldensian Church
of the River Plate Area

Demont, Ms Christiane

Dominguez, Mr Michael
Christian Church (Disciples of Christ)

Dominguez, Ms Dorcas
Christian Church (Disciples of Christ)

Dorris, Deacon Tom
Evangelical Lutheran Church in America

Drewes-Siebel, Ms Renate G
Reformed Churches in the Netherlands

Faerber, Mr Robert
Evangelical Church
of the Augsburg Confession

Faerber-Evdokimoff, Ms Tomoko
Ecumenical Patriarchate
of Constantinople

Fanchette, Rev Gerard Jocelyn Philippe
Roman Catholic Church

Ferris, Dr Elizabeth
Religious Society of Friends

Fischer-Duchable, Ms Nicole
Swiss Protestant Church Federation

Freidig, Ms Marlise
Swiss Protestant Church Federation

Fung, Mr Raymond
Hong Kong Baptist Convention

Gay, Ms Yasmina
Muslim

Ginglas-Poulet, Ms Roswitha Helga Lucia
Roman Catholic Church

Granberg-Michaelson, Rev Wesley Scott
Reformed Church in America

Gregory, Ms Yvonne
Church of England

Hahn, Mr Udo
Evangelical Church in Germany

Haller, Ms Erna
Swiss Protestant Church Federation

Hammar, Rev Anna Karin
Evangelical Lutheran Church of Sweden

Jacob, Rev Fr Sydney Michael
Church of the Province
of the West Indies

Janda, Rev Canon Clement
Episcopal Church of Sudan

Kaiser, Ms Helga Anneliese Charlotte
Evangelical Lutheran Church-FRG

Katsuno, Ms Lynda
United Church of Canada

Kelly, Ms Catherine Elizabeth
United Church of Canada

Kemppi-Repo, Ms Eeva
The Evangelical Lutheran
Church of Finland

Kok, Mr Jan H
Reformed Church in the Netherlands

Lamberth, Mr David
Presbyterian Church (USA)

Lambiel, Ms Catherine-Nadia
Roman Catholic Church

Ledger, Ms Christine
Anglican Church of Australia

Lee-Rieben, Ms Silvia

Lemopulo, Mr Yorgo
Ecumenical Patriarchate
of Constantinople

Leslie, Mr David
Presbyterian Church (USA)

Limouris, Rev Prof Dr Gennadios
Ecumenical Patriarchate
of Constantinople

Linn, Rev Gerhard
Evangelical Church-GDR

Lloyd-Sidle, Rev Patricia
Presbyterian Church (USA)

Lucke, Rev Hartmut
Swiss Protestant Church Federation

Marchena, Mr Donald Bruno
Roman Catholic Church

McClellan, Ms Monique
Presbyterian Church (USA)

Opocensky, Mr Tomas
Evangelical Church of Czech Brethren

Ortega, Rev Ofelia
Presbyterian Reformed Church in Cuba

Palma, Ms Marta
Pentecostal Mission Church

Payne, Rev Clifford
Church of God (Anderson, Indiana)

Pinon, Mr Fernando,
Roman Catholic Church

Pityana, Rev N Barney
Church of the Province
of Southern Africa

Richter, Ms Dorothee Madeleine
Swiss Protestant Church Federation

Ross, Ms Dawn Marie
Presbyterian Church in Canada

Roulin, Ms Arlette

Sabev, Prof Dr Todor
Bulgarian Orthodox Church

Sbeghen, Ms Renate Elisabeth
Evangelical Church-FRG

Seater, Rev Robert
United Church of Christ

Smith, Ms Francis
United Church of Christ

Sovik, Ms Ruth
Evangelical Lutheran Church
of America

Stabenbordt, Mr Pierre
Ev. Church-Augsburg Confession
of Alsace & Lorraine

Stockwell, Dr Eugene L
United Methodist Church

Stromberg, Ms Jean
American Baptist Churches USA

Stunt, Ms Heather
Church of England

Tatu, Ms Evelyne
Roman Catholic Church

van Beek, Mr Huibert
Netherlands Reformed Church

van Drimmelen, Mr Robert
Wilhelmus Fredrik
Reformed Church in the Netherlands

Van Elderen, Mr Marlin
Christian Reformed Church
in North America

Velez-Sotomayor, Mr William

Visinand, Mrs Elizabeth
Swiss Protestant Church Federation

Voigt, Ms Helga
Evangelical Church in Germany

Vuagniaux, Ms Gabrielle
Roman Catholic Church

Williams, Mr Peter
Evangelical Lutheran Church
of Denmark

Wilson, Rev Dr Frederick R
Presbyterian Church (USA)

Zierl, Ms Ursula
Evangelical Lutheran Church-FRG

Stewards

Abernethy, Ms Thelma
Northern Ireland, Church of Ireland

Biakokoz, Ms Irena
Poland, Polish Orthodox Church

Bipul Barrel, Mr Benedict
Bangladesh, Bangladesh Baptist Sangha

Brandner, Mr Tobias
Switzerland, Swiss Protestant
Church Federation

Brukner, Mr Robert Gerard
Canada, Roman Catholic Church

Casera, Rev Diosdado
Philippines, United Church of Christ
in the Philippines

Cuambe, Mr Gaspar Jotamo S
Mozambique, Methodist Church
Mozambique

Dean, Ms Ana
USA, Evangelical Lutheran Church
in America

Deeb, Ms Rula
USA, National Evangelical Synod
of Syria & Lebanon

Ephrem, Mr Karim
Syria, Syrian Orthodox Church

Fernandez-Calienes, Mr Raul
USA, Presbyterian Church (USA)

Figueroa de Anzolabehere, Ms Rosana
Uruguay, Open Brethren-Uruguay

Franklin, Rev Rodney
USA, National Baptist Convention

Garcia Morris, Ms Rebeca Elizabeth
Cuba, Presbyterian Reformed Church
in Cuba

Jean Baptiste, Ms Mimaude
Haiti, Evangelical Community of Haiti

Klenk, Mr Juan Pablo
Republica Argentina, United Evangelical
Lutheran Church

Lauridsen, Ms Hanne Karhula
Denmark
Evangelical Lutheran Danish Church

Lima Soares, Ms Rosana
Brazil, Methodist Church in Brazil

Locatin, Mr Daniel
Guadeloupe, Roman Catholic Church

Lovell-Martin, Rev Nigel Leon Michael
Guyana, Moravian Church in Guyana

Marite, Mr Makalo
Lesotho, Lesotho Evangelical Church

Mendis, Ms Priyanka Shiromi
Sri Lanka, Church of Ceylon

Moricz, Julia A
USA, Orthodox Church of America

Muzigo, Ms Rosette Kawaaluko
Uganda, Church of Uganda

Njoh, Mr Hans Ekems
Cameroon, Presbyterian Church
in Cameroon

Nordstrom, Ms Marie
Sweden, Church of Sweden

Nunn, Ms Mavis
Canada, Presbyterian Church in Canada

Pongpanlux, Mr Suchart
Thailand, Church of Christ in Thailand

Rapenda, Mr John Odera
Kenya, Coptic Orthodox Church

Samoladas, Mr Efthimios
Greece, Church of Greece

Schwarz, Ms Beate
DDR, Federation of the Evangelical
Churches in the GDR

Stewart, Mr Wayne Glenfield
Jamaica, WI, Methodist Church
in the Caribbean and the Americas

Swan, Ms Kristina
Australia, Uniting Church in Australia

Tay, Ms Yawa Enyonam Seraphine
Togo, Evangelical Church of Togo

Tkatchouk, Ms Liudmila Georgievna
USSR, Russian Orthodox Church

Vahakangas, Mr Mika Samuel
Finland, Evangelical-Lutheran Church
of Finland